The Contexts of Teaching
In Secondary Schools:
Teachers' Realities

edited by
**MILBREY W. McLAUGHLIN,
JOAN E. TALBERT,
and
NINA BASCIA**

Teachers College, Columbia University
New York and London

Published by Teachers College Press, 1234 Amsterdam Avenue
New York, NY 10027

Library of Congress Cataloging-in-Publication Data

The Contexts of teaching in secondary schools : teachers' realities /
    edited by Milbrey W. McLaughlin, Joan E. Talbert, and Nina Bascia.
      p.   cm.—(Professional development and practice series)
    Based on papers commissioned by Stanford University's Center for
Research on the Context of Secondary School Teachers and Teaching,
presented at a planning meeting in February of 1988.
    Includes bibliographical references (p.   ).
    ISBN 0-8077-3027-0 (alk. paper).—ISBN 0-8077-3026-2 (pbk. :
alk. paper)
    1. High school teaching—United States.   I. McLaughlin, Milbrey
Wallin.   II. Talbert, Joan E.   III. Bascia, Nina.   IV. Stanford
University. Center for Research on the Context of Secondary School
Teachers and Teaching.   V. Series.
LB1737.A3C63   1990   90-30093
373.11'02'0973—dc20   CIP

ISBN 0-8077-3027-0
ISBN 0-8077-3026-2 (pbk.)

Printed on acid-free paper
Manufactured in the United States of America
97 96 95 94 93 92 91 90   8 7 6 5 4 3 2 1

Contents

Foreword

The purpose of the Professional Development and Practice Series is to present research, documentation, cases, stories, and descriptions of cutting-edge work that is being done in education today. The series is meant to highlight bold and innovative thinking in education. The first volume in the series, *Building a Professional Culture in Schools*, was an edited collection that included today's foremost thinkers in education whose work focuses on a new conception of the school. The present volume, like its predecessor, also breaks new ground: It calls for a rethinking of the very meaning of "context" by taking a deep and broad look at the multifaceted influences on teachers. This innovative approach can have a tremendous influence not only on research and policy, but also on the important international reform agenda of schools. I am extremely pleased to have this book become part of the series and take its rightful place as a significant contribution to the literature.

This edited volume makes a major contribution to our understanding of research, policy, and practice in the secondary school. Its overarching theme—that there are multiple, embedded contexts that have effects on teachers' work—has never been better explicated. McLaughlin, Talbert, and Bascia have brought together the major research and policy analysts in the field to build a framework that considers the complexity of the forces influencing the life of a teacher in secondary school—not as a simple set of one-to-one connections, but through several different lenses. Some of the authors discuss the sociocultural context of teaching—the educational value systems and social-class communities that shape a teacher's work life. Another group of authors devote their attention to the organizational context within which teachers work, including the characteristics of individual districts, schools, and departments. A third group analyzes the impact that movements for change in secondary education—professionalization, school improvement, and curriculum reform—have had on teachers' work lives. In all three areas the contributors delineate factors that "enable" and "constrain" teachers in their work with students. The result is a powerful case for a new understanding of both policy and practice that sets forth a new research agenda on a broadened view of what we have come to understand as the "contexts" of the secondary school.

This collection is particularly significant for its overriding "bottom-up" (rather than "outside-in" or "top-down") perspective. The authors build a case for the social construction of teachers' work from the teacher's perspective, a view that, though long absent from the literature, is a necessary component to our full understanding of the secondary school context.

Ann Lieberman
Series Editor

Preface

The chapters in this volume are the result of papers commissioned by Stanford University's Center for Research on the Context of Secondary School Teaching, for presentation at a planning seminar, held in February 1988, that was the center's first step in developing a research agenda for examining the secondary school workplace.

The center was established in the Fall of 1987, through funding from the Office of Educational Research and Improvement (OERI), U.S. Department of Education (Grant No. G0087C0235), with the mission to advance knowledge on contextual factors that affect secondary school teachers and teaching and, in turn, student outcomes. The analyses and conclusions presented in this volume do not necessarily reflect the views or policies of OERI.

The planning seminar that gave birth to this volume was enormously helpful in framing the center's research agenda. It provided rich substance to our notion of the secondary school workplace as a system of embedded contexts. Each scholar provided a different and important way of seeing the proverbial elephant, illuminating a contour of the work environment that significantly affects how teachers think and feel about their work. Taken together, these authors describe a complex set of conditions that operate jointly to define particular workplaces of secondary school teachers and their students—workplaces that are permeated by multiple contexts, rather than being "nested" within them like the center of an onion.

As reflected in this book, the center's workplace seminar brought together educational researchers who work in separate lines of research, many of whom were talking together for the first time. Without exception, participants felt that the new perspectives on the secondary school workplace offered by others' research sharpened their own work and defined more clearly its contribution to our understanding of factors that shape secondary school teaching. Indeed, the chapters that emerged from the seminar working papers reflect considerable advance in many authors' thinking about their niche in the movement to improve conditions of secondary school teaching. We hope the reader will share our sense of achieving new understanding by juxtaposing—and pulling together in one place—distant but complementary strands of research on the secondary school workplace.

1

The Contexts in Question:
The Secondary School Workplace

MILBREY W. McLAUGHLIN and JOAN E. TALBERT

How is it that two teachers with the same educational background and professional aspirations who are teaching in the same objective school context—in schools with similar levels of resources and student and community characteristics, for example—can develop substantively different instructional goals, practices, and student learning outcomes? How is it that two departments in the same high school can establish quite different teaching and learning environments and outcomes? Scholars and educational leaders alike must consider why secondary school teachers, departments, schools, and school systems can achieve dramatically disparate results with comparable resources.

The long-standing conception of the teaching "context" as being comprised of a school's fiscal resources and its students' socioeconomic background is no longer a powerful explanatory construct: Within ostensibly the same context, striking differences in teaching and learning occur. To design settings that will promote excellence for high school teachers and their students, educators require sophisticated understanding of the multiple embedded contexts that define the secondary school workplace and shape teaching and learning within them.

THE ROLE OF CONTEXT IN EFFECTIVE TEACHING

Early research on teacher effectiveness focused primarily on teachers' personal traits (Waples & Tyler, 1930). By the late 1970s, research on teacher effectiveness centered on general methodology (Gage, 1978) and the role of the curriculum (Schwab, 1978). Further research considered teachers' effectiveness in terms of their skills as professional decision makers who use a repertoire of competencies to meet instructional goals and student needs (Brophy & Good, 1986). Finally, the focus on methodology and curriculum was meshed with a consideration of teachers' repertoires of competencies, yielding the understanding that a secondary school teacher's pedagogical skills are subject specific and context particular (Shulman, 1987).

As ideas about the tasks of teaching have changed from the relatively mechanistic notions that spawned an industry of teacher-proof curricula to recognition of teaching as a professional enterprise requiring individual judgment, we have also come to understand that effective teaching depends on more than just teachers' subject-matter knowledge and general pedagogical skills or even pedagogical content knowledge. Effective teaching depends significantly on the contexts within which teachers work—department and school organization and culture, professional associations and networks, community educational values and norms, secondary and higher education policies. The research literature has concentrated on effects of school conditions on teachers and teaching, a focus paralleled by state and local "school improvement" programs designed to improve teaching and learning conditions in the schools.

Vivid descriptions of teachers either thwarted and constrained or stimulated and challenged by the settings in which they operate highlight many ways in which the school context shapes teaching and thus student outcomes (e.g., Lightfoot, 1983; Powell, Farrar, & Cohen, 1985; Sizer, 1984). Factors such as effective school discipline policies, regular teacher supervision, and comprehensive feedback to teachers emerge as most significant in explaining unusually effective inner-city schools (Ashton, Rodman, & Doda, 1983; Lortie, 1975; Rosenholtz, 1985, 1989; Rutter, Maughan, Mortimore, & Ouston, 1979). Likewise, many analysts account for ineffective schools or classrooms in terms of factors such as blocked communication patterns between teachers and administrators, inadequate opportunities for skill development, or the lack of clear schoolwide goals (Boyer, 1983; Bredeson, Furth, & Kasten, 1983; Brookover, Beady, Flood, Schweitzer, & Wisenbaker, 1979; Goodlad, 1984).

Research prompts us, then, to see effective teaching as the product of individual attributes and the settings in which teachers work and learn to teach.

At the most fundamental level, context matters because effective teaching depends on teachers' opportunity to choose materials, objectives, and activities they believe are appropriate for themselves and for their students. Does the curriculum fit the class? Does it fit the interests and background of the teacher? Are the necessary materials available? These factors have a direct impact on what teachers can do. For example, the California English teacher now required by state mandate to teach *Beowulf*, a text he is not familiar with or fond of, may be less effective next year than he was this year with the curriculum he built from his literary favorites. Similarly, the biology teacher making do with six dissecting pans for her laboratory class of 25 students faces a substantively different classroom task than does a colleague in another district with a fully supplied laboratory.

Effective teaching also depends on another, more complicated set of factors, namely, how teachers think and feel about what they do. Teachers, through shared values and beliefs, individually and collectively mediate the influence of context conditions on student outcomes. Researchers have noted that teachers' attitudes, beliefs, and feelings about their work play an important role in supporting or undermining effective practice. Central among these important constructive teacher dispositions are

- *Motivation.* This describes teachers' willingness to expend consistently high effort in their work (Ashton et al., 1983; Lortie, 1975; McLaughlin & Marsh, 1978).
- *Conception of task.* This involves teachers' belief that they are responsible for encouraging individual accomplishment and for responding to a wide range of student needs, as opposed to a view of classroom responsibilities as primarily custodial and disciplinary (Chapman & Lowther, 1982; McLaughlin, Pfeifer, Swanson-Owens, & Yee, 1986).
- *Enthusiasm over subject matter.* This describes teachers' excitement about sharing their subject-area knowledge and discipline with students, in contrast to resigned coverage of course content (Doyle, 1986; Macrorie, 1984; McPherson, 1972). As Dewey warned in the early 1900s, if teaching becomes neither terribly interesting nor exciting to teachers, it is hard to expect teachers to make learning terribly exciting to students.
- *Sense of efficacy.* This reveals teachers' belief that they are making a positive difference in their students' growth and capacity (Ashton et al., 1983; Berman & McLaughlin, 1978; Bredeson et al., 1983; Lortie, 1975; McLaughlin & Marsh, 1978).

These teacher dispositions influence both the nature and the quality of classroom practice. They are neither predetermined traits, like height or eye color, nor mainly a product of teacher training and preparation, like breadth and depth of subject-area expertise and pedagogical understanding. While they can certainly be influenced by effective teacher preparation programs and nurtured through supportive induction programs for new teachers, these important teacher qualities are also shaped and defined by the *contexts* of teaching.

The school—as formal organization and as sociocultural system—is one important context of teaching; in fact, teaching effectiveness and the school workplace are inextricably related. However, the secondary school workplace is more broadly defined by the larger societal and community culture; by the educational policy system and school sector; and by higher education and work organizations, professional associations, and networks. It is more narrowly defined by the subject-area department. Each of these contexts of secondary education can define teachers' work, inhibit or support professional authority over classroom instruction, and affect teachers' thinking and feeling about their work with students. These diverse contexts interact to shape teachers' professional roles and dispositions and, in turn, students' educational experiences. Teaching effectiveness is shaped by the complex interplay of the multiple embedded contexts of the secondary school workplace.

This volume expands the notion of workplace conditions that enable or constrain secondary school teachers' best work and professional growth, to include contexts beyond and within the school site.

TREATMENT OF CONTEXT IN PRIOR RESEARCH

Educational researchers have defined and analyzed context in substantively different ways. In conventional research on teacher effectiveness, for example, where context has rarely been considered at all (see Doyle, 1986), it is discussed almost exclusively in terms of classroom variables such as students, curriculum, and materials. (See Brophy & Good, 1986, for a review of relevant literature.) Research on the social organization of the classroom has expanded this discussion of discrete classroom variables by looking at factors such as teacher/student relations and classroom technology (Boocock, 1978). This line of research examines ways in which teachers establish more and less productive contexts for students' work.

The "effective schools" research has focused primarily on school climate conditions associated with desired student outcomes. Principal leadership, clear instructional goals, and high expectations for student success are prominent aspects of this look at the context of teaching (Brookover et al., 1979; Edmonds & Frederikson, 1979; Rutter et al., 1979). Again, the focus of analysis is site-level context correlates of student success, and, except for the British study by Rutter et al. (1979), comparisons of more and less successful schools have been limited mainly to urban elementary schools. (See Brophy & Good, 1986; Purkey & Smith, 1983, for review and critique of this extensive research literature.)

Antecedent work in the "school effects" tradition examined quantitative site-level factors such as per-pupil expenditure, student/teacher ratio, student socioeconomic status, and time in school (Averch, Carroll, Donaldson, Kiesling & Pincus, 1972; Centra & Potter, 1980; Coleman et al., 1966; Jencks et al., 1972; McPartland, Epstein, Karweit, & Slavin, 1976; Summers & Wolfe, 1975; Wiley, 1976). Recent extensions of this line of work include quantitative measures of school climate conditions highlighted in the effective schools literature, such as goal consensus, student discipline, and academic expectations of the school as predictors of student achievement (Bryk & Driscoll, 1988; Lee & Bryk, 1989). This line of research has drawn heavily upon national surveys of high school students and schools to analyze site-level correlates of student educational outcomes.

An emerging line of research on workplace conditions of schooling moves beyond site-level influences on student outcomes to explore factors that support productive teacher roles and dispositions, such as collegiality, teachers' role in decision making, instructional support, and resources for professional development (Bacharach, Bauer, & Shedd, 1986; Bishop, 1977; Little, 1982; Rosenholtz, 1985, 1989). As in the lines of research on context effects on student outcomes, this research focuses on school organization and climate as the context of teachers' work. However, the new line of research prompts us to take the teacher's perspective in analyzing and evaluating educational contexts.

These different lines of research on the school workplace contribute significantly to researchers' and practitioners' ability to understand how schools can achieve desired outcomes. Still, conceptions of context have limited value for informing policy, because they address only a particular contextual slice of the educational setting in which teachers and students work (the school as an organization) or because they address only a particular condition of effective teaching. For example, Little's (1982) research shows clearly that collegiality is an important source of motivation and satisfaction for teachers. But what kinds of conditions within and outside the school setting foster teachers' collegiality? How does collegiality interact with other workplace conditions to affect teachers' dispositions and work with students? The complexity of teachers' worklife and factors that shape choices and adaptations is funneled through researchers' lenses and problem frameworks and may not represent realities as they are experienced by teachers in their work.

This new stream of research has come a long way toward identifying productive conditions of teaching but not far at all toward understanding how they are established within complex, embedded contexts of teaching or how policy can constrain or enable them.

The recent work of Susan Rosenholtz (1989) represents an important step in this direction. Her study of teachers in a large sample of Tennessee elementary schools examined how desirable teaching conditions—shared school goals, teacher collaboration, teacher learning, teacher certainty, and teacher commitment—were related to one another and to school management and district organizational culture and policies. Rosenholtz observed, for example, that district policies that delegated authority to school administrators and teachers over personnel selection, goal setting, resource allocation, and decisions on instructional needs were associated with higher levels of teacher commitment.

Three features of Rosenholtz's (1989) study represent important contributions to the line of work on the teacher workplace. First, a range of desirable teaching conditions were examined, in concert and in relation to structural conditions of school organization. For example, teacher collaboration was analyzed in relation to teachers' shared goals and certainty in the school setting and in relation to the school's decision structure. Second, the relevant organizational context of the teacher workplace was extended beyond the school boundary to include district conditions. Third, the role of teachers in socially constructing conditions of the workplace was explicitly recognized in the study's attention to the *meaning* of work and workplace to teachers.

In our view, a social constructionist perspective on teachers' work and workplace is critical if we are to understand how context shapes teaching and to craft productive organizational and policy environments in education. What we call here the "bottom-up" perspective on the teaching workplace asks *what* and *how* particular context conditions are significant for teachers' perceptions and experiences of their work environment and their conceptions of teaching goals and tasks.

Further, we need to expand the boundaries for analyzing the teaching workplace beyond school administrative units, to include the critical contexts that constrain and enable productive teaching conditions. This conceptualization is inextricably tied to the bottom-up perspective on workplace, since teachers' experiences of their work environment and the context factors that shape the meaning of teaching are not confined by classroom doors or school fences.

THE SECONDARY SCHOOL WORKPLACE AS MULTIPLE EMBEDDED CONTEXTS

Expanding boundaries for conceptualizing and analyzing the teacher workplace is particularly important for research and policy focused on secondary education. In terms of prior research, conclusions about the primacy of school-level factors in promoting desirable student outcomes have been based largely on evidence from elementary school settings. Unlike secondary schools, these settings are relatively undifferentiated, apart from grade-level divisions. The subject-area department boundaries established within the typical high school represent organizational subunits within which different educational structures and processes, collegial relations, and organizational cultures can be established. As examples, tracking practices can and do differ among departments in the same school, teacher collaboration and support can vary greatly by department in a school, and conceptions of student achievement and expectations for their success can vary according to departmental cultures. (See Scott, 1988, for a review and synthesis of organizational research and theory on the significance of subunits in complex organizations.)

In terms of practice and policy, subject area is a primary nexus of high school teachers' professional training and identity and of their collegial relations inside and outside the school setting, and it is central in framing secondary education reform policies and initiatives. The subject area in which one teaches represents an important conduit for out-of-school influences on conditions of work for secondary school teachers. A state or district policy can constrain the instructional choices of science teachers but have no effect on history teachers, or vice versa. A change in the admissions standards of the state university system or local college can impact one subject area but not another. A local business initiative or a professional network may become a context of teaching in one subject area but not in others within the same district or school.

A bottom-up perspective on the teacher workplace means looking at the important contexts of secondary school teaching through the eyes of teachers. We ask which contexts of the teaching job—of secondary education and of the teaching profession—shape a teacher's work, through setting goal and role priorities, limiting instructional choices, and affecting dispositions.

The bottom-up perspective requires the researcher or policy analyst to conceive of the secondary school workplace as composed of embedded contexts and to describe its contours and substance *as relevant to teachers.* The parameters or configurations of the workplace are not the same for all secondary school teachers, nor is the salience of a given parameter the same for all teachers in similarly configured settings. This is because the embedded contexts of secondary school teaching have different landscapes as one moves between national systems and cultures, across state and local educational systems, across parent communities within the same system, between public and private sectors, or across subject-area departments. Thus, teachers' construction of their workplace and the significance of any particular context for their work will necessarily be conditioned by its relevance and character and by its meaning in the context of other salient workplace conditions.

This volume represents a first step in mapping the multiple embedded contexts of the secondary school workplace. It also illustrates bottom-up, contextualized approaches to understanding and promoting educational improvement through teachers' professional development, school change processes, and reform policies.

Figure 1.1 depicts the scope of this volume's analyses of contextual conditions that define the teacher workplace. A separate chapter is devoted to aspects of each of these five contextual "layers." The schematic ordering of contexts does not imply more and less distant or salient dimensions of the workplace; rather we assume that conditions within each contextual domain permeate the work life of teachers and operate in concert to shape the nature and meaning of teachers' work. Collectively, the chapters of this book begin to describe the diverse embedded contexts of the secondary school workplace.

The book is organized into three parts. The first, on sociocultural contexts, includes analyses of educational value systems and social-class communities. In Chapter 2 Karen Seashore Louis examines how social and community values influence the quality of teachers' work life. Drawing upon research from the United States, Western Europe, and Japan, Louis looks at the ways in which national educational values and patterns of school organization (e.g., expectations for school autonomy and parental choice, conceptions of professionalism) directly or indirectly shape the ways in which teachers' view their task. Both education policy and practice, Louis concludes, must acknowledge the import of social and community values for schools and teachers in designing efforts to improve practice and the quality of the workplace.

Mary Haywood Metz, in Chapter 3, examines social classes as a context for teaching and learning and asks how differences in community culture and social systems affect the teacher workplace. Metz's research shows not only that social class has a significant impact on the social construction of the school workplace, but also *how* it influences what teachers do in their classes. Social class "gets into" schools through community pressures and through students' cultural patterns. Teachers' own social-class background affects their attitudes toward students and their definitions of the teaching job. Metz found, however, that school principals transmit community pressures differently, thereby mediating the salience and effects of social-class culture in the school. This chapter elaborates how these teacher, student, community, and principal influences interact to affect teachers' professional lives significantly.

FIGURE 1.1. The Secondary School Workplace: Embedded Contexts

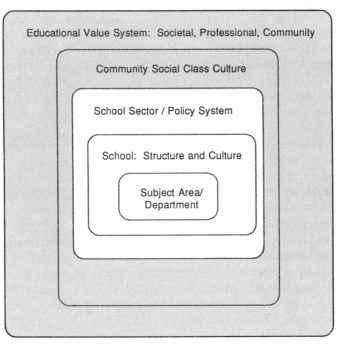

Educational Value System: Societal, Professional, Community

Community Social Class Culture

School Sector / Policy System

School: Structure and Culture

Subject Area/
Department

☐   Sociocultural Context   ☐   Organizational and Policy Context

Part II of this volume includes analyses of school organizational contexts and conditions that matter for teachers' work lives. Chapter 4 highlights salient features of teachers' work life in independent schools. Arthur G. Powell uses three analytical themes to distinguish the independent school workplace from that typically constructed in the public sector, namely, a purposeful educational community, a scale of operations that is small and human, and a preoccupation with respect and dignity for the roles of students and, particularly, teachers. Powell shows how these themes play out in the independent school environment to shape expectations for teachers' work and, in turn, teachers' role conceptions and vocational identity.

In Chapter 5 Thomas B. Corcoran uses findings from recent surveys and case studies of public school teachers and schools to identify factors that shape the teacher workplace and so the outcomes of efforts to reform teaching and schooling. Corcoran provides a framework for critical examination of current workplace reforms. His analysis contrasts teachers' views of the workplace, studies of effective schools, and the assumptions about workplace that drive reform efforts. He finds that the workplace conditions of most teachers do not measure up to the conditions identified as productive by the effective-schools literature or by the 1987 Institute for Educational Leadership study. His analysis shows the interconnectedness of multiple workplace factors and how they operate together to create positive or dysfunctional conditions for teachers' work.

Susan Moore Johnson, in Chapter 6, explores the significance of high school departments for the work life of teachers, a line of questioning neglected in prior research on school workplace conditions. Johnson draws upon her interviews with teachers in a sample of public and private high schools in Massachusetts to describe how departments work and to suggest what departments mean to teachers. Teachers in both the private and public sector say that the subject-area department is their primary professional reference group and that working in different departments, even within the same school, is like working in different organizations. Johnson analyzes how departments function in her research sites, as well as the formal and informal factors that contribute to variation among them as workplaces.

The last part of this book analyzes the means for change, focusing on three levers for improving secondary education—teachers' professional development, school improvement, and curriculum reform policies. The authors of these chapters each provide a bottom-up, contextualized analysis of dimensions and processes of change in the embedded contexts of secondary school teaching.

Judith Warren Little, in Chapter 7, uses diverse literatures to assess the conditions that influence teachers' professional development in secondary schools. Her analysis takes a multilevel view of professional development and considers the full range of aspirations teachers might pursue over a career of 30 or 40 years. Little's conceptions of career extend beyond technical knowledge and skill to embrace teachers' membership in the larger professional community. Using this expanded frame of "career" and "professional development," Little discusses features of the secondary school workplace that shape teachers' formal and informal professional development opportunities and interests.

Chapter 8 takes up what we do and do not know about change processes in secondary schools. Based on an analysis of recent studies of change in secondary schools, Michael G. Fullan derives lessons about the character of the change process and its generalizability to diverse settings. These lessons then are examined in terms of the general literature on effective change processes, with the goal of identifying promising strategies for secondary schools, gaps in knowledge about planned change in secondary schools, and ways in which secondary schools present special problems for change.

In Chapter 9 William H. Clune examines the tensions and interplay between educational reform policies and school context in shaping the secondary school curriculum and teachers' instructional choices. Taking a bottom-up perspective on policy goals and instruments, Clune portrays schools and teachers as more-or-less equal partners with the policy system in constructing the school curriculum, as policy mediators, as policy critics, and as policy constructors. He draws upon his and others' recent research at the Center for Policy Research in Education (CPRE) for evidence supporting each view of the dialogue between curriculum policy and schools, and he traces the lessons they provide for policy makers. Clune's chapter highlights for researchers and policy makers the implications of seeing educational policies from the bottom up, within the embedded contexts of the secondary school workplace. The chapter also points to the policy system and its goals and instruments as among the multiple contexts that shape the teacher workplace.

Together these chapters treat the multiple contexts of secondary school teaching in a way that highlights the dynamic and context-embedded nature of the workplace. They suggest ways in which multiple and often diffuse context conditions interact to shape teachers' conception of their work, expectations for students, motivation and efforts, and sense of accomplishment. The context in question is one in which individuals, institutions, and the broader social and policy community all play a role in the ongoing construction of the secondary school workplace.

REFERENCES

Ashton, P. T., Rodman, B. W., & Doda, N. (1983). *A study of teachers' sense of efficacy: Final report.* Gainesville: University of Florida, Foundations of Education.

Ashton, P. T., & Webb, R. (1986). *Making a difference: Teachers' sense of efficacy and student achievement.* New York: Longman.

Averch, H. A., Carroll, S. J., Donaldson, T. S., Kiesling, H. J., & Pincus, J. (1972). *How effective is schooling? A critical review and synthesis of research findings.* Santa Monica, CA: Rand Corporation.

Bacharach, S. B., Bauer, S. C., & Shedd, J. B. (1986). *The learning workplace: The conditions and resources of teaching.* Ithaca, NY: Organizational Analysis and Practice of Ithaca, New York.

Berman, P., & McLaughlin, M. (1978). *Federal programs supporting educational change* (Vol. 7). Santa Monica, CA: Rand Corporation.

Bishop, J. M. (1977). Organizational influences on the work orientations of elementary teachers. *Sociology of Work and Occupation, 4,* 171–208.

Boocock, S. S. (1978). The social organization of the classroom. In R. H. Turner (Ed.), *Annual review of sociology* (pp. 1–28). Palo Alto, CA: Annual Reviews.

Boyer, E. L. (1983). *High school: A report on secondary education in America.* New York: Harper & Row.

Bredeson, P. V., Furth, M. J., & Kasten, K. L. (1983). Organizational incentives and secondary school teaching. *Journal of Research and Development in Education, 16,* 52–56.

Brookover, W., Beady, C., Flood, P., Schweitzer, J., & Wisenbaker, J. (1979). *School systems and student achievement: Schools can make a difference.* New York: Praeger.

Brophy, J. E., & Evertson, C. (1974). *Process-product correlations in the Texas teacher effectiveness study: Final report.* Austin: University of Texas, R & D Center for Teacher Education.

Brophy, J. E., & Good, T. L. (1986). Teacher behavior and student achievement. In M. C. Wittrock (Ed.), *Handbook of research on teaching* (pp. 328–375). New York: Macmillan.

Bryk, A. S., & Driscoll, M. E. (1988). *The school as community: Theoretical foundations, contextual influences, and consequences for teachers and students.* Madison: University of Wisconsin, National Center on Effective Secondary Schools.

Centra, J. A., & Potter, D. A. (1980). School and teacher effects: An interrelational model. *Review of Educational Research, 50,* 273–291.

Chapman, D. W., & Lowther, M. A. (1982). Teachers' satisfaction with teaching. *Journal of Educational Research, 75,* 240–247.

Coleman, J. S., Campbell, E. Q., Hobson, C. J., McPartland, J., Mood, A. M., Weinfeld, F. D., & York, K. L. (1966). *Equality of educational opportunity.* Washington, DC: U.S. Government Printing Office.

Doyle, W. (1986). Classroom organization and management. In M. C. Wittrock (Ed.), *Handbook of research on teaching* (pp. 392–431). New York: Macmillan.

Edmonds, R. R., & Frederikson, J. R. (1979). *Search for effective schools: The identification and analysis of city schools that are instructionally effective for poor children.* East Lansing: Michigan State University, Institute for Research on Teaching.

Gage, N. (1978). *The scientific basis of the art of teaching.* New York: Teachers College Press.

Goodlad, J. I. (1984). *A place called school.* New York: McGraw-Hill.

Jencks, C., Smith, M., Ackland, H., Bane, M. J., Cohen, D., Gintis, H., Heyns, B., & Michelson, S. (1972). *Inequality: A reassessment of the effects of family and schooling in America.* New York: Harper & Row.

Lee, V. E., & Bryk, A. S. (1989). A multi-level model of the social distribution of high school achievement. *Sociology of Education, 62,* 172-192.

Lightfoot, S. L. (1983). *The good high school: Portraits of character and culture.* New York: Basic Books.

Little, J. W. (1982). Norms of collegiality and experimentation: Workplace conditions of school success. *American Educational Research Journal, 19,* 325-340.

Lortie, D. (1975). *Schoolteacher.* Chicago: University of Chicago Press.

Macrorie, K. (Ed.). (1984). *Twenty teachers.* New York: Oxford University Press.

McLaughlin, M. W., & Marsh, D. D. (1978). Staff development and school change. *Teachers College Record, 80,* 1.

McLaughlin, M. W., Pfeifer, R. S., Swanson-Owens, D., & Yee, S. (1986). Why teachers won't teach. *Phi Delta Kappan, 67,* 420-426.

McPartland, J. M., Epstein, J. L., Karweit, N., & Slavin, R. E. (1976). *Productivity of schools: Conceptual and methodological frameworks for research.* Baltimore, MD: Johns Hopkins University, Center for Social Organization of Schools.

McPherson, G. H. (1972). *Small town teacher.* Cambridge, MA: Harvard University Press.

Powell, A., Farrar, E., & Cohen, D. (1985). *Shopping mall high school.* Boston: Houghton-Mifflin.

Purkey, S. C., & Smith, M. S. (1983). Effective schools—A review. *Elementary School Journal, 83,* 427-452.

Rosenholtz, S. J. (1985). Effective schools: Interpreting the evidence. *American Journal of Education, 93,* 352-388.

Rosenholtz, S. J. (1989). *Teachers' workplace: The social organization of schools.* New York: Longman.

Rutter, M., Maughan, B., Mortimore, P., & Ouston, J. (1979). *Fifteen thousand hours: Secondary schools and their effects on children.* Cambridge, MA: Harvard University Press.

Schwab, J. (1978). *Science, curriculum and liberal education.* Chicago: University of Chicago.

Scott, W. R. (1988). *Work units in organizations: Ransacking the literature.* Stanford, CA: Stanford University, Center for Research on the Context of Secondary School Teaching.

Shulman, L. S. (1987). Knowledge and teaching: Foundations of the new reform. *Harvard Education Review, 57,* 1-22.

Sizer, T. R. (1984). *Horace's compromise: The dilemma of the American high school.* Boston: Houghton-Mifflin.

Summers, A. A., & Wolfe, B. L. (1975). *Equality of educational opportunity quantified: A production function approach.* Philadelphia: Federal Reserve Bank of Philadelphia, Department of Research.

Waples, D., & Tyler, R. N. (1930). *Research methods and teachers' problems.* New York: Macmillan.

Wiley, D. E. (1976). Another hour, another day: Quantity of schooling, a potent path for policy. In W. H. Sewell, R. M. Hauser, & D. L. Fetterman (Eds.), *Schooling and achievement in American society* (pp. 225–266). New York: Academic Press.

PART I
Sociocultural Contexts

2

Social and Community Values and the Quality of Teachers' Work Life

KAREN SEASHORE LOUIS

Current discussions about how to improve teachers' lot tend to center on either structure (how to reorganize schools or the profession to bring about desired results) or people (how to change or motivate teachers so they will be more able to bring about desired results). I argue that, before we debate what to do, we need to incorporate a broader examination of our educational value system into the discussion of teachers' work. The concept of a value system should include interconnected ideals, customs, and institutions that relate to education and about which we have a strong affective regard.

My argument is premised on three assumptions. First, the educational value system is a major factor affecting teachers' working conditions and the way in which they evaluate these conditions (Cooley, 1963; Stewart & Cantor, 1974).[1] Values can have direct, visible effects, such as by providing a specific set of constraints or opportunities for teacher action. They may also have important "invisible effects" by conditioning broader strategies for structuring and improving schools.

Second, public discourse about educational reform usually touches directly on values, and discussions about schooling invariably involve debates about the balance between socialization and knowledge transmission, equity and excellence, or the emphasis on vocational versus personal developmental goals.[2]

Third, despite this attention to values, only a tiny fraction of the values that condition education are ever examined. The most deeply

The preparation of this chapter was supported, in part, by the University of Wisconsin-Madison, Center for Effective Secondary Schools, which is funded by the U.S. Department of Education, Office of Educational Research and Improvement (Grant No. G-008690007). Any opinions, findings, and conclusions or recommendations are those of the author and do not necessarily reflect the views of either of the supporting agencies.

embedded values are rarely discussed, because they are viewed as given rather than as issues for debate. Such absence of serious reflection on our deepest values, however, limits our consideration of alternatives for improving both education and the quality of work in schools.

Looking at the way in which social values affect the nature of school improvement strategies, the following three categories seem to have a particularly strong effect:

- *Basic cultural values*, which are central to the average citizen's views of how school "ought" to work
- *Professional values*, which govern educators' preferences about the internal structure of schools and how the people who work in them "ought" to relate to one another
- *Community values*, which are the specific expectations and demands that emerge from the specific community settings in which teachers find themselves

This chapter should be viewed as a preliminary analysis. The specific values discussed are not the only ones or even necessarily the most important. Rather, they have been selected because they illuminate some of the debates that are currently most prevalent in the United States. The discussion is based on analysis of a variety of case studies and reports that describe some of the ways the foregoing three types of values may affect the lives of teachers.

Comparative data are particularly useful in illuminating our own infrequently discussed system of deeply held values. The data used here are derived from 3 years of involvement in a collaborative effort among researchers from the United States and several Western European countries. The project was funded and coordinated by the Organization for Economic Cooperation and Development (OECD) in Paris. The values reviewed here were discussed at length with representatives of the various countries and are presented in somewhat greater detail in Louis and Loucks-Horsley (in press). In the discussion of community values, only materials from the United States were used.

The concern in this chapter regarding the quality of teachers' work life is based on considerable evidence that improving the quality of work life for individuals will affect their commitment, motivation, and, in many cases, productivity. A review of relevant quality-of-work-life constructs in the general literature (which is based primarily on studies of industry) suggests seven criteria particularly applicable to teachers and schools:

- Respect and status in the larger community (National Education Association, 1988; Sederberg & Clark, 1987)
- Participation in decision making that augments teachers' sense of influence or control over their work setting (Cohn, Kottkamp, McCloskey & Provenzo, 1987; Firestone & Rosenblum, 1988; Sickler, 1988)
- Frequent and stimulating professional interaction among peers within the school, such as collaborative work/collegial relationships (Little, 1984; Miles, Louis, Rosenblum, Cipollone, & Farrar, 1986)
- Opportunity to make full use of existing skills and knowledge and to acquire new ones (self-development); the opportunity to experiment (Newmann & Rutter, 1987; Sederberg & Clark, 1987)
- Structures and processes that contribute to a high sense of efficacy and relevance, such as mechanisms that permit teachers to obtain frequent and accurate positive and negative feedback about the specific effects of their performance on student learning (Rosenholtz, 1985)
- Adequate resources for carrying out the job; a pleasant physical working environment (Cohn et al., 1987; Public School Forum of North Carolina, 1987)
- A sense of congruence between personal goals and the school's goals, or a low degree of alienation (Cohn et al., 1987; Louis & Miles, in press)

Although all of these theoretically contribute to "teacher quality of work life" (TQWL), they are not equally important. Research on quality of work life among a variety of occupations suggests that the most critical factor is likely to be social respect and status (Kahn, 1974). There are three additional indicators that appear to relate to TQWL and commitment, in a potentially linear fashion (that is, the more the teacher experiences them, the better off they are likely to feel). These include teachers' opportunities to influence the immediate conditions of work, opportunities to engage in meaningful collaborative work that is directly related to improving their classroom performance and student learning, and increases in their ability to know and understand the relationship between student performance and what teachers do in the classroom.[3]

On the other hand, the factors of "adequate resources and a pleasant physical environment" are likely to be important primarily when they are absent. Increasing resources beyond some level of perceived adequacy is unlikely to have a big impact on TQWL.[4] This is, we believe, also likely to be true for the opportunity to develop and use new skills. In this case, more is not always better: Too much involvement in innovation may be perceived as an unreasonable overload, detracting from performance of more important tasks (Cohn et al., 1987). Other factors are simply less problematic for most teachers: Alienation (as we have defined it) is generally lower for teachers than for factory workers, because teachers tend to be drawn to their jobs for idealistic reasons.

In the remainder of this chapter, the ways in which the three different categories of values affect the seven hypothesized dimensions of TQWL will be explored.

BASIC CULTURAL VALUES

Goodlad (1985) has remarked on the dull uniformity of American schools. Equally striking is the superficial similarity of schools in different countries. Basic grade structures are organized into elementary, lower secondary, and upper secondary; major curriculum areas and instructional approaches are similar; the model of one teacher working with 25 to 40 students in a self-contained classroom predominates. But, as many informal and formal observations have shown, these similarities are deceiving.

One area that affects the teacher's sense of "real school" (Metz, 1988) is the dominant public definition of what quality education is like, what aspects of education are most in need of improvement, or what a "good school" would look like, and these vary widely between countries. To give just one example, a U.S. visitor to the Scandinavian countries would be surprised at the relatively low level of governmental and public interest in minimum achievement standards—or in testing achievement levels at all. Similarly, a typical Scandinavian visitor to the United States would find the level of current attention to matters of student socioemotional development in junior high and middle schools surprisingly low. This section concentrates on a discussion of a limited number of deeply held cultural values that have significant implications for the structure of schools and teachers' work.

Homogeneity Versus Heterogeneity

The question of homogeneity versus heterogeneity in schools is an important one for today's TQWL discussions, because it may involve trade-offs between the clarity of feedback and teachers' sense of efficacy, and their ability to experiment and use new skills. In comparative policy research much is made of the distinction between educational systems that are structurally either centralized or decentralized. There are trends in most of the developed countries, even those that are traditionally more centralized, toward policies that put more responsibility directly within the purview of the school. Both Sweden and France, for example, have recently attempted significant new policies to take some curriculum improvement functions away from the national ministries and to give more responsibility to local authorities and schools (Caré, 1986; Wallin & Hamber, in press). In the United States, the revised federal compensatory education program, Chapter 1 of the 1981 Education Consolidation and Improvement Act (ECIA), has given schools and school systems more influence over how federal monies for education are spent, and quite a few states have developed their own improvement programs, focused on the school level (Anderson et al., 1987; Berman, 1983). On the other hand, there are also strains toward greater centralization. The Netherlands, for example, has recently proposed a common curriculum for its largely private junior secondary schools, which were previously free to set their own curriculum (WRR, 1986). Not surprisingly, these changes produce heated debates. Thus, there is no doubt that the question of centralization has a place in the discussion of school policy.

But, among the more deeply held value assumptions that affect teachers' work, an important but rarely discussed distinction is the degree to which schools and the people in them are normatively viewed as homogeneous (that is, very similar across different units, and in different parts of the country) or heterogeneous (that is, different between schools, a quality often coupled with the ability of parents to choose schools).

To give an example, the Swiss have traditionally had a strong preference for homogeneous education, at least at the elementary level, although their system is rather decentralized (Huberman, in press). In most cantons identical curricula are used in each school, including, in some cases, uniform texts and materials. Teachers are viewed not as employees of the school but of the cantonal educational system. School improvement, with the exception of a small pilot program (Huberman, 1984), has tended to be seen by cantonal authorities as synonymous with curriculum review and revision.

In sharp contrast, the Netherlands appears on the surface to be considerably more centralized than Switzerland (van den Berg & van Wijlijk, in press). There is a large national ministry and much discussion of national reforms, and some secondary schools report directly to the national ministry. Yet the value system, embodied in the constitution and in educational codes, encourages diversity because of the full funding of private education and the relatively limited role that the state or region plays in its regulation.

The implications of homogeneity/heterogeneity for the quality of teachers' work life is not a simple matter. On the one hand, a homogeneous school system tends to have well-specified expectations that permit teachers to assess better how they and their students are doing, compared to other similar teachers and students. This can improve teachers' sense of efficacy. On the other hand, a heterogeneous educational system may provide greater rewards for teachers who innovate, try out new ideas, or use their skills more broadly, activities that in themselves promote heterogeneity within and between schools.

Another implication of the homogeneity/heterogeneity distinction for teachers' work concerns the availability of support given for improving their own performance, as well as the type of support. This can be illustrated by contrasting the way in which governments try to reform schools and teaching. In Switzerland and other relatively homogeneous systems, educational improvement usually focuses primarily on curriculum development (in which representative teachers usually participate in cantonal committees) and not on organizational or individual development. There is typically more emphasis on content than instruction. In contrast, in the heterogeneous Netherlands, there is a long tradition of helping schools and teachers to deal with their individual issues and needs and of offering a broad system of school support agencies (the equivalent of five or more of our regional laboratories to serve a population the size of the greater New York metropolitan area), which are generously funded to serve all public and private schools. A major purpose of these agencies, from the government's perspective, is to persuade schools and teachers, particularly those in the private sector, to go along with national reforms (Jansen & Mertens, in press). However, the main consequence from the teachers' and schools' point of view is the availability of help with developing and tailoring their own school plans.

In the United States, public opinion has formally supported heterogeneity, but more in theory than in practice. Recently the underlying preference for homogeneity has become apparent: The most frequent response to the current "crisis in education" has been to standardize curricula, performance criteria, and testing programs within states and districts, rather than to experiment and maximize the search for different options. Standardization is coupled with efforts to increase accountability to externally developed measures of educational performance. Interest in working with individual teachers to develop alternative educational models seems to be declining, and public officials talk more about the curriculum/content than about instructional practices.

The implications for overall quality of teachers' work life are not yet clear. Even if teachers' satisfaction with clearer expectations and feedback increases, there will nevertheless be a simultaneous decrease in their sense that their jobs provide them with the flexibility to use all of their skills and to experiment. Teachers who have come to expect that their careers would include a large measure of self-development work may find difficulty adjusting to a system in which experimentation with new skills is less valued than performance within a stricter operations protocol (Lightfoot, 1988).

Parental Values and Choice

Intertwined with the homogeneity/heterogeneity issue is the question of whether parental values are integrated into the school's curriculum. Do parents expect their own values to be reflected in the schools, and, if so, do they expect to be able to make choices between schools? This basic question reflects the degree to which schools are expected to be responsive to community and social interests that do not overlap with a geographic area, but it may also affect the respect that is accorded to teachers.

In Great Britain, for example, some heterogeneity is valued. Schools are relatively autonomous and are therefore expected to vary between and within local communities. In addition, there is a strong tradition of religious and secular private education. For most parents, however, the choice of which school their child attends is usually determined by where they live and, in upper forms, by examination results. As in the United States, much attention is often paid to the selection of community residence, or even geographic areas within communities, since it is only in this way that parents may "choose." In contrast, in the Netherlands and Belgium, parents may choose the school that they wish for their child, whether it is public or private, and much attention is devoted in local newspapers to coverage of the opportunities for and process of choosing.[5] Choices tend to be made on the basis of perceived educational quality, the climate of the school, and the frequency of communication with parents, although proximity is also a major factor for elementary children (Sociaal Cultureel Plan Bureau, 1982).

The implications of choice for teachers are enormous. A preliminary look at the various countries suggests that parental choice may be linked to public support of teachers and schools. In the Netherlands, parents believe that the school reflects their own values and are typically contented with the teachers. Since teachers are usually employed in a school whose religious or other pedagogical preferences are compatible with their own, this sense of satisfaction is mutual. In Great Britain, in contrast, confidence in public education appears relatively lower; parental dissatisfaction and conflict with schools and teachers is more similar to that observed in the United States; and the social status of teachers, in terms of public confidence as well as salaries, is believed to be eroding.

In the United States, there are deeply embedded suspicions about choice, which is often viewed by researchers, politicians, and others as a potential threat to the U.S. Constitution, an attack upon the obligations of the state to preserve the interests of children (Moshman, 1985), or a threat to equality of educational opportunity. As a consequence, choice experiments in this country have been limited to options within the public school system. Even these have not been strongly supported by teachers' unions, which have voiced concerns about the implication of choice for teacher control over assignments, evaluation, and other matters. Some policies that are associated with choice, such as the recent legislative action in Minnesota that permits cross-district enrollment, do not particularly reflect a commitment to incorporating parental values, as they do not affect intradistrict student assignments.

Nevertheless, cities that have experimented with magnet, options, or alternative programs, usually for purposes of desegregation or prevention of white flight, have found that teachers benefit. Teachers are pleased with the increased control that they have over their own work in settings in which both they and parents have the ability to choose a specific educational program (Reywid, 1985).[6] Furthermore, some choice programs have been found to increase parent and general local support for education, thus producing a generalized sense of respect and support for teachers (Rand, 1981). Blank, Dentler, Baltzell, and Chabotar (1983) report that teachers believe that students in magnet schools are more motivated, and that the opportunities to teach and use their special skills are more frequent than in nonchoice schools. Metz's (1986) study of magnet schools indicates that teacher involvement and empowerment in the design of the schools will affect the benefits that they derive. Magnet programs, however, are only one of the socially acceptable mechanisms for incorporating parental values and choice. Here is a clear-cut case in which our system of deeply held values has discouraged a full discussion of policies and structures that may benefit teachers.

Stability Versus Change

Countries vary a great deal in the degree to which the general population views change in education as a sign of health or with general suspicion. This variation has implications for teachers' sense of efficacy and the match between personal and school goals, as well as the more obvious relationship with the opportunity to learn and apply new skills. In Switzerland and France, for example, the general population has relatively conservative views about change:

> One changes the part when the part breaks; if it's not broken—and the Swiss are wizards for maintenance—one doesn't fix it. The notion of change as a vehicle for reducing the gap between stated objectives and ongoing practice is an esoteric one in the social sector. In a sense, good maintenance of whatever is now in service is the overriding objective. If a school system needs "reform" there is a subterranean suspicion that it has been poorly maintained. [Huberman, in press]

> In France, the educational system has always been considered as an institution of national (cultural) preservation. This function of preservation and stability is to be encountered both in the vocabulary used and in deep-seated mentalities. In its institutional capacity, national education tends to act as a brake. [Caré, 1985, p. 42]

At the other extreme, perhaps, lie Denmark and the Netherlands, where change and movement are viewed almost as necessary signals that the patient is alive (Olsen, in press; van den Berg & van Wijlijk, in press). Being innovative—looking for new educational models—is a sign that parents often look for in a school, even where the movement is "back to the basics."

Other countries fall in the middle. In Japan, for example, there is high cultural value placed on constant group assessment and improvement. This does not usually lead to invention, however, but to small-scale, incremental change within school practice (Bollen, 1985).

The United States clearly belongs among the change-valuing countries. What are the implications of this for teachers' work? The demand for change and innovation is also a demand for energy. Change that is imposed from outside may conflict with a teacher's own deeply embedded ideas of how a "real school" should operate and may cause considerable personal confusion as needed adjustments take place. Burnout or stress may be more of a problem. The need for reflection may also be higher, as teachers are asked to grapple with new instructional practices or with innovations such as reading in the content areas. As innovations come and go, teachers may also become disillusioned about the possibility of achieving enduring results from their investment in their performance and in improving education.

The degree to which teachers are embedded in a support structure may also vary. Countries that are more change oriented also tend to invest in a variety of structures outside of the school that are intended to prod, support, or otherwise insure that teaching will be responsive to the change imperative. In the Netherlands, the demand on schools for improvement and change has reinforced the perceived need for a very extensive network of support agencies. In countries with relatively low pressure for change, there tends to be either no formal system for providing help for teachers in making improvements and changes (e.g., Sweden and the Federal Republic of Germany) or a system that is oriented primarily toward subject-matter in-service training (e.g., Switzerland, France). In the United States, the district office is seen as the major source of support for change. Whether district offices actually function in this way for individual teachers and schools is, however, highly questionable. As Farrar (1987) has indicated, despite good intentions urban districts often serve more as constraints and brakes rather than as supports for innovative teachers. Other research suggests that district office staff rarely communicate with teachers at all, even when they have information relevant to the improvement of classroom practice (Louis, Dentler, & Kell, 1984).

PROFESSIONAL VALUES

Professional values are of greatest concern to educators who work inside schools. Occasionally these values are examined by noneducators, but they are rarely within the arena of either general or political debate. Here professional values will be derived primarily from writings of administrators and professors, since these have tended to dominate the discussions (Callahan, 1962). They are not necessarily congruent with the values of teachers, whose voice has historically been less prominent.

How the Teacher Is Viewed

Values regarding the role of teacher vary widely between countries and appear to have important consequences for the way in which teachers perceive the relative importance of technical skills versus craft skills, and collegiality. The main questions are as follows:

• *Is the practice of teaching largely a scientifically or artistically based activity?* In other words, is it possible to anticipate, classify, and understand the general problems faced by teachers at work, and to codify a range of solutions to them? Or, conversely, is it more likely that

teachers will face a huge range of unanalyzable problems that they must creatively solve on the job?
• *Is the teacher viewed primarily as an autonomous professional, or as a member of a collective body?* This question is of course relative, since almost all teachers have high levels of autonomy while they are actually interacting with students.

How these questions about teachers are answered will vary between primary and secondary school, but for the present discussion we will ignore this distinction and focus on the case of the primary school.

Let us look, for example, at the case of Denmark, which has traditionally emphasized two characteristics of teachers—their collective responsibility in carrying out their job and their special craft knowledge. Teachers in local schools are responsible for designing a curriculum plan within very general governmental expectations. The fact that teachers are assigned to follow the same group of students from Grades 1 through 10 (except for specialized subject matters in secondary school) is evidence that craft and personal knowledge built up within the school conditions the types of behaviors that they will choose, not a set of specialized or scientific principles of teaching. A corollary assumption is that only teachers can decide what they need to know in order to improve. At a logical extreme, it is assumed that teachers—rather than policy makers, professors, or in-service experts—should be responsible for the design of improvement efforts (Anderson & Olsen, 1985). Although Olsen (in press) indicates that teacher-designed improvement strategies have not always been successful, this is nevertheless an objective toward which the system strives.

This stands in strong contrast with France, where teaching is viewed as comprised of highly analyzable skills, which means it can be taught to any suitably qualified person. Teacher autonomy outside and inside the classroom is protected by civil service and union regulations; for example, senior secondary school teachers are only required to be in the school for approximately 15 hours a week. As Caré (1986) notes, under these circumstances there are strong constraints on what may be required of experienced teachers (largely limited to technical changes in content), even though the system is officially very centralized.

Japan represents another model. Cultural traditions support a view of teachers as good technical experts imbued with strong norms of collective professional behavior. The response of teachers to a perceived need for improvement in the school is often to form a study group voluntarily, which may meet after school or on Saturdays!

The United States is less collective in its orientation than Japan, but more so than France (Hofstede, 1984). This modestly collective orientation means that it is relatively easy to generate interest in getting teachers to work in groups, thus increasing the possibility of satisfying desires for professional collaboration. On the other hand, because the school is not unambiguously viewed as a unit of collaborative self-management, it has been difficult to sustain the administrative enthusiasm and resources that would permit more opportunities for working together. Collaboration is nice, but not absolutely necessary. Many teachers, of course, have experienced pseudocollaboration, in which they serve as representatives on committees that are dominated by administrators. This reduces their interest in more genuine collaborative work.

This ambivalence about teachers' collective role emerges, in part, from the tendency of the U.S. educational establishment to view teachers from the scientific rather than the artistic model and moreover, within that framework, to view them more as lab technicians than principal investigators. This is probably a consequence of the development of strong administrative/management ideologies described by Tyack (1974), and the subsequent efforts on the part of curriculum developers to professionalize and distance themselves from teachers. The ultimate expression of this social distance was the attempt in the early 1970s to create "teacher-proof" curricula, such as programmed books and materials that did not require the creativity of the teacher for their use.

Lightfoot (1988) argues that this conflicting set of values in this country may have real consequences for the support of superior teaching. Drawing on her data from "good" high schools, she claims that maintaining commitment to teaching over the professional life cycle depends on a delicate balance between respect for artistry and autonomy within the classroom, on the one hand, and an enduring sense of connectedness with the school as a collective body, on the other.

How the School Administration Is Viewed

School-based administrators exist in nearly every country, with the exception of many primary schools in Switzerland, but their roles vary enormously. These variations are probably related to broader cultural values about authority and work relationships (Hofstede, 1984). One of the main impacts of this variation is on the degree of control or influence teachers expect to exert over their work.

In many countries (e.g., Japan, Great Britain), teachers and others in the educational system view the head of the school as the most powerful actor in the educational system. These figures have traditionally had the authority to control virtually everything that goes on in the school, from the specifications of curriculum to the disposition of all cases of teacher assignments that are not specifically covered by union contract (Arai et al., 1986; Birchenough, Weindling, Earley, & Glatter, 1986). In other countries, school leaders are powerful, but only in a more constrained arena. In France, for example, they are the official interpreters of governmental regulations within the school. However, both custom and civil service regulations limit their role in teacher evaluation, in introducing innovations that affect teaching practice, and even their right to call staff meetings to discuss school improvement issues (Caré, 1986). Finally, in some countries, the school leader might be better thought of as a first among equals, or as the head of the team. In Sweden, for example, the leader is often responsible for several buildings and must therefore delegate substantial responsibilities to others within the staff (Stegö, 1986).

The United States operates with an ambivalent attitude toward the power of the principal. Verbal value is given to the principal being in control within the building, but in practice this value has been subordinated to district policies and, in some cases, teacher contract agreements (Farrar, 1987). The increasingly ambiguous role of principals as middle managers may contribute to a relative leadership vacuum at the building level, as well as role strain for the principal. Recent calls for "principal leadership" do not address the structural and value constraints that may fail to promote principals with strong leadership potential or to encourage the development and exercise of leadership once in office. Current reports of efforts to change the role of principals through school-based management suggest that this ambivalence is deeply embedded. Many principals actually fear the consequences of increased authority. In Madison, Wisconsin, for example, principals rejected a recent district office proposal for school-based management. Other assessments of existing programs have indicated that real authority over critical management variables (e.g., personnel and budget) is not being delegated by the district office (Clune & White, 1988).

For teachers, the poorly defined principal's role increases the ambiguity of the work environment. Unlike countries with weak school leaders, teachers rarely feel that they have either individual or collective control over many of their immediate work conditions, at least, not those outside of the classroom. Unlike countries with strong school leader models, they rarely feel that the principal can provide them with the kind of support, encouragement, and feedback that could occur if the principal had real authority over the building and staff.

COMMUNITY VALUES

In recent years, research related to the effects of community on teachers has often emphasized structural differences in school district size and organization (Samuels, 1974), or the need for parent involvement (Epstein, 1985; Leichter, 1978; Lightfoot, 1978). While these are both important in terms of quality of teachers' work life, they do not tell the whole story. In fact, both are likely to be a result of broader community issues. Community values can affect all areas of perceived quality of work life, but they have the most obvious impacts on the respect and status accorded to teachers and hence on teachers' sense of efficacy and relevance.

There are many definitions of community. For simplicity's sake, Hunter's (1975) threefold classification will be used: (1) community is a functional spatial unit, (2) community is patterned social interaction, and (3) community is any unit of collective identity.

Cohesive Versus Fragmented Values

In a cohesive community context, all three definitions of community coincide. The impacts of cohesiveness on the educational experience are vividly described by Cremin (1978), in his analysis of early New England:

> The close linkages between families, between families and schools and between families and the congregations and politics into which they were organized go far in explaining the educative basis and power of the colonial New England community. It was not merely a matter of spatial arrangement, of close physical proximity. . . . [I]t was also a matter of timing, . . . a dense collective experience. . . . [C]ommunal life itself becomes educative, with social institutions complementary and mutually supportive of a particular version of character. [p. 689]

While it is rare to find communities where the value cohesiveness is this dense, there is still variation in modern community settings. For example, in relatively homogeneous suburban towns and in rural areas we may find an approximation of overlapping value communities of families and schools described by Cremin. Coleman & Hoffer (1987) claim that contemporary parochial schools recreate, in miniature, the "social capital" implicit in the previous description.

The opposite situation exists in a fragmented community, where the three different types of community do not overlap at all. Tyack (1974) refers to the educational consequences of this as "the corporate model" of education, in which education becomes more exclusively the purview of professionals; there is distance between school values and family values; there is an emphasis on standardizing education, irrespective of the community values and needs; and the school is seen as a "compensatory institution," providing children with experiences and skills that were lacking in the general community and family. This corporate model may be to some extent reflective of all contemporary American education, but again it varies a great deal between different spatial and social settings. Value fragmentation may be most characteristic of urban school systems, in which students are drawn from a wide and noncontiguous geographic area and from many ethnic groups and religious backgrounds, and in which there is little consensus over the values that should be part of the educational experience. Peachy (1987) calls these "delocalizing" communities.

The impact of cohesiveness or fragmentation on teachers occurs at a variety of levels. Value fragmentation clearly increases professional autonomy for teachers, as well as professional and occupational identification. We need only contrast the deep concern of small communities with the dress and behavior of their schoolteachers with the typical urban situation, where a teacher's life outside of school takes place in what is both figuratively and often literally another community.

But value fragmentation also increases the dependence of teachers on their students. In such a setting, teachers lack appreciative, adult "audiences" who will provide them with positive feedback about their work. Their ability to depend on adults outside the school to reinforce the messages that they deliver is also diminished, often producing a sense of moral isolation. In the worst cases, teachers are locked into situations where the only source of feedback about performance is a group of students whose values they do not understand and whose in-school performance they believe to be unsupported in all of the community contexts that they encounter outside of school. This fosters a sense of the meaninglessness of their work (Hemmings, 1988). As Lightfoot (1978) points out, "The greater the difference between family and community culture and school norms, the greater the need for parents and teachers to work hard at knowing one another" (p. 189). But, in a deeply fragmented community, the task becomes even more difficult, because finding and defining the community with whom one should work is difficult.

Educators often view families as the intractable source of this problem. Yet, in recent studies of urban high schools, it is not impossible to find schools and teachers who have begun to create solidary communities in very unpromising settings (Lightfoot, 1984, 1988; Louis & Cipollone, 1986). As Epstein's (1985) work indicates, it is to a large extent the teacher's effort that pulls parents into schools rather than the parents' initiative or interest. Active effort can pay off in terms of status and relevance: "Teachers who worked at parent involvement were considered better teachers than those who remained more isolated from the families of the children they taught" (p. 21).

Coalition Versus Interest-Group Communities

Ravich (1974) describes the evolution of the New York City school system as the product of competing interest groups, each of which is eager to seize control of the schools as a means of increasing their power. The main point suggested by her analysis is not that coalitions produce conflict between school and community; in fact, school/community conflicts exist periodically in all settings, even those where there are cohesive values. The point centers on the process of framing value issues.

In both cohesive and fragmented communities, conflicts that affect teachers often arise as a product of shifting concerns rather than deeply embedded values. A taxpayer revolt may involve the unlikely alliance of blue-collar homeowners and high-tech businessmen, a coalition that will dissolve after the precipitating events have passed. Similarly, an outcry over school closings may involve neighborhoods that may be highly supportive of education on other issues, or a threatened or actual strike may temporarily divide a community in which parents and teachers are normally close.

However, the community in which educational politics focus on semipermanent coalitions bolstered by well-articulated,value-laden philosophies provides teachers with a no-win value environment. No matter how they behave, teachers and schools are viewed as captives of one or another coalition. As a consequence, there is no way in which teachers can obtain community respect and support from all sectors. Teachers may find themselves drawn to developing closer linkages with the dominant coalition, only to find that school board elections change the ownership of the schools and they are faced with powerful groups that see them as the opposition. Teachers have been fearful of coalition politics that promote increased community control and thus have found themselves with a much eroded base of localized public support as a consequence. The risk is that teachers may come to be perceived as an interest group— one that is not sensitive to the needs of any of the other parties to the conflict. This may in turn cause them to act as an interest group, in self-protection. The consequence is that some major segment of the community views teachers and their values as part of the problem, further diminishing teachers' sense of the relevance of their own work.

IMPLICATIONS OF VALUES FOR TQWL

There are several gaps in this analysis that should be explicitly mentioned. Perhaps the most obvious is that only a few important values have been touched upon in each section, and we have not yet arrived at a taxonomy of values that would help us to create an exhaustive list. A serious discussion of teachers' values is also necessary, since it was speculated that they are distinct from those found in the academic and administrative literature. Finally, theories about how the values in each of the categories are developed or changed, and the processes by which they affect the practice of education in schools and classrooms need to be outlined.

Despite the preliminary nature of the discussion, the line of reasoning adopted here is not an academic exercise. If values occupy a central position determining the ways in which our schools function and the quality of teachers' work life, there are important implications for practice and policy making. It is useful to illustrate some of the ways in which values should be considered during efforts to improve TQWL.

Practice

TQWL will never really improve without a broad value consensus that supports education and teachers. The most critical aspect of TQWL is relevance and status. Status can be addressed, in part, through technical policies such as raising salaries. Relevance, however, relies fundamentally on the presence of positive feedback from the various communities that the schools relate to. Educators cannot solve the problems of fragmentation or coalition politics at the community level. But, if they do not view *themselves* as the most significant actors in an effort to build community around the school, quality of work life will continue to decline.

Teachers' associations have increasingly emphasized quality-of-work-life issues that are broader than working conditions such as hall and lunchroom duty, or salary. There are, however, underlying value conflicts that must be discussed among teachers if TQWL issues are to be more directly incorporated. For example, Farrar's (1986) description of one urban system's master contract illustrates what can happen to teachers' work when seniority rights (a basic union value) permit senior teachers to choose their preferred school with no constraints. When this happens, the opportunity to develop stable collaborative relationships is undermined by teacher turnover, as is the principal's willingness to support experimentation and skill development among those staff who are likely to transfer.

Teachers' associations develop policies in response to a perceived lack of concern with teachers' needs on the part of school, district, or state policy makers and administrators. When district and state administrators develop improvement strategies that embody the value of teachers as low-level technician (such as those that promote very specific curriculum and pedagogical requirements or require certification testing of all experienced teachers), TQWL may be undermined, even when other presumably compensatory actions (increased salary) are proposed. Teachers quite reasonably react by demanding more autonomy. These value conflicts must be discussed and quality of work life put at the forefront of teacher-association and administrative agendas, if change is to occur.

Policy

Almost all policy makers agree that teachers' working conditions, including pay, are inadequate. Some aspects of the quality of teachers' work life may be altered with little regard for broader cultural and professional values. We may, for example, deal with both the smaller and larger resource problems that make teachers' lives difficult with a simple infusion of dollars targeted for supplies, telephones, and the like. To raise teacher salaries meaningfully would require reaching more deeply into the purse but would represent a critical symbol of our desire to improve their relative status. Genuinely improving quality of work life in other areas will, however, be difficult or even impossible without more basic changes.

A look at value systems will help to explain why some past reforms, such as alternative school programs, did not become institutionalized or widespread, although they were known to be beneficial for teachers and students. We can predict that, in this current round of attempts to improve education and teaching, other useful reforms may not stick if they are caught between conflicting values. For example, efforts to increase school autonomy and "empower teachers" appeal to our espoused preferences for participatory democracy and decentralization but run into conflict with the actual value system that emphasizes homogeneous schools, principals as middle managers, and teachers as technicians. Unless a clear consensus for value shifts can be enacted, conflicting values will permit an erosion of efforts to change.

Policy makers should not avoid a responsibility for directly confronting this issue. Value systems are stable but are not entirely fixed, and policy makers play a major role in shaping value discussions. Debates about values may permit adjustments and resolution of differences over time, but these debates are less likely to occur if value issues are not explicitly raised as part of the policy-making process and the relevant parties are not involved. Diagnosis of problems and needs will be more thoughtful if values are addressed before policies are fully designed and implemented, not after. This approach to policy making is more prevalent in some European countries than it is in the United States, where the development of "constructive educational policies" (those that attempt significant shifts in value systems) evolves over the period of a decade or more.

More important, policy makers should be sensitive to the fact that, although they can have an impact on the value system surrounding education, regulation is a blunt instrument for changing values. Values change slowly, and specific policies erode rapidly if they are too disjointed from the dominant value systems at all three levels discussed earlier. If policy makers wish to make a real impact on teachers' work, their own efficacy will be increased if they bring value dimensions into higher levels of public scrutiny.

Open discussion does not, of course, insure agreement, but unwillingness to confront conflict will reliably prevent stable improvement policies. Policy makers should learn from the experience of other countries that purport to enact educational policies only after serious efforts at consensus building, and recognize that this approach can be very time consuming (Louis, 1986). The hope that major institutions can be reformed within an electoral cycle or two can only result in loss of confidence on all fronts.

NOTES

1. Cooley (1963) argues for the importance of ideals and moral sentiments as primary forces in shaping society. His theory suggests that opinions and group beliefs are organic social structures, rather than simply the aggregate of individual beliefs and values. There are, of course, many other social theorists who suggest that values are largely a consequence of social structure. This chicken-and-egg disagreement is irrelevant for the purposes of this paper, as, with the exception of extreme structuralists, theorists generally accept that values exert some independent force of their own in society.

2. Kimball (1984) presents an excellent analysis about how the moral debates in the Greek city-states have influenced discussions of education throughout Western history.

3. This hypothesis is based on a preliminary analysis of case studies being done as part of the Teacher Working Conditions program at the Center for the Study of Effective Secondary Schools. It is also important to note that these three

work characteristics may imply the most significant need to restructure the school.

4. For example, some recent discussions have suggested that the availability of telephones is a real issue for many teachers. We hypothesize, however, that teachers would be satisfied if they had access to a reasonably private place in which to make phone calls, with a ratio of teachers to phones that would permit access when needed. Thus, giving each teacher a telephone would likely be overkill. The basic theoretical assumption is that the *absence* of this factor is a stress factor for teachers.

5. Student choices are made primarily by parents, but are of course affected by teacher evaluations at the secondary level.

6. Teacher satisfaction is higher in "whole-school" options or alternatives rather than schools-within-schools, largely because of higher levels of staff friction in the latter (Rand, 1981).

REFERENCES

Anderson, B., Odden, A., Farrar, E., Fuhrman, S., Davis, A., Huddle, E., Armstrong, J., & Flakus-Mosqueda, P. (1987). State strategies to support school improvement. *Knowledge: Creation, Diffusion, Utilization, 9,* 42–86.

Anderson, H., & Olsen, T. (1985). *Supporting school improvement: The Danish puzzle.* Unpublished manuscript.

Arai, I.,Maki, M., Makita, A., Nakatome, T., Okuda, S., & Takahashi, S. (1986). Japan. In C. Hopes (Ed.), *The school leader and school improvement: Case studies from ten O.E.C.D. countries* (pp. 209–250). Leuven, Belgium: Acco Press.

Berman, P. (1983). *Improving school improvement: A policy evaluation of the California School Improvement Program.* Berkeley, CA: Berman Weiler.

Birchenough, M., Weindling, D., Earley, P., & Glatter, R. (1986). England and Wales. In C. Hopes (Ed.), *The school leader and school improvement: Case studies from ten O.E.C.D. countries* (pp. 111–140). Leuven, Belgium: Acco Press.

Blank, R., Dentler, R. A., Baltzell, D. C., & Chabotar, K. (1983). *Survey of magnet schools. Final report: Analyzing a model for quality integrated education.* Washington, DC: James H. Lowrey.

Bollen, R. (1985). *School based review in Japan: Four field visits.* Amsterdam: Algemeen Pedagogish Studiecentrum. [Photocopy]

Callahan, R. (1962). *Education and the cult of efficiency.* Chicago: University of Chicago Press.

Caré, C. (1985). *External support for school improvement in France.* Unpublished manuscript.

Caré, C. (1986). France. In C. Hopes (Ed.), *The school leader and school improvement: Case studies from ten O.E.C.D. countries* (pp. 141–180). Leuven, Belgium: Acco Press.

Clune, W., & White, P. (1988). *School based management.* New Brunswick, NJ: Rutgers University, Center for Policy Research in Education.

Cohn, M. M., Kottkamp, R. B., McCloskey, G. N., & Provenzo, E. F. (1987). *Teachers' perspectives on the problems of their profession: Implications for policymakers and practitioners.* Unpublished manuscript.

Coleman, J., & Hoffer, T. (1987). *Public and private high schools.* New York: Basic Books.

Cooley, C. (1963). *Social organization.* New York: Schocken.

Cremin, L. (1978). Family-community linkages in American education: Some comments on the recent historiography. *Teachers College Record, 79,* 683–704.

Epstein, J. L. (1985). Home and school connections in schools of the future: Implications of research on parent involvement. *Peabody Journal of Education, 62*(13), 18–41.

Farrar, E. (1986). *Charles W. Eliot Junior High School: The dilemma of improvement in the cities.* Buffalo: State University of New York, Educational Organization, Administration & Policy.

Farrar, E. (1987, April). *The role of leadership at the school and district level.* Paper presented at the annual meetings of the American Educational Research Association, Washington, DC.

Firestone, W., & Rosenblum, S. (1988). The alienation and commitment of students and teachers in urban high schools: A conceptual framework. *Educational Evaluation and Policy Quarterly, 10,* 285–300.

Goodlad, J. (1985). *A place called school.* New York: McGraw-Hill.

Hemmings, A. (1988, April). *"Real" teaching: How high school teachers negotiate national, community and student pressures when they define their work.* Paper presented at the annual meetings of the American Educational Research Association, New Orleans.

Hofstede, G. (1984). *Culture's consequences.* Beverly Hills: Sage.

Huberman, M. (1984). *SIPRI: Un bilan, quelques reorientations et une vue de l'avenir.* Berne, Switzerland: Conference Suisse des Directeurs Cantonaux de l'Instruction Publique.

Huberman, M. (in press). Perspectives in external support in Switzerland. In K. S. Louis & S. Loucks-Horsley (Eds.), *Supporting school improvement: A comparative perspective.* Leuven, Belgium: Acco Press.

Hunter, A. (1975). Loss of community: An empirical test through replication. *American Sociological Review, 40,* 537–552.

Jansen, H., & Mertens, H. (in press). The school's perspective: Practical problems in supporting schools. In K. S. Louis & S. Loucks-Horsley (Eds.), *Supporting school improvement: A comparative perspective.* Leuven, Belgium: Acco Press.

Kahn, R. L. (1974). The work module: A proposal for the humanization of work. In J. O'Toole (Ed.), *Work and the quality of life* (pp. 159–204). Cambridge, MA: MIT Press.

Kimball, B. (1984). *Orators and philosophers.* New York: Teachers College Press.

Leichter, H. J. (1978). Families and communities as educators: Some concepts of relationship. *Teachers College Record, 79,* 567-657.

Lightfoot, S. (1978). *Worlds apart: Relationships between families and schools.* New York: Basic Books.

Lightfoot, S. (1984). *The good high school.* New York: Basic Books.

Lightfoot, S. (1988, April 11). *Teachers with voice and vision: Perspectives on autonomy.* (Available from the University of Minnesota chapter of Phi Delta Kappa).

Little, J. W. (1984). Norms of collegiality and experimentation: Conditions for school success. *American Educational Research Journal, 19,* 325-340.

Louis, K. (1986). Reforming secondary schools: A critique and an agenda for administrators. *Educational Leadership, 44*(1), 33-37.

Louis, K. S., & Cipollone, A. (1986, April). *Reforming the urban high school: Reports from a survey.* Paper presented at the annual meeting of the American Educational Research Association, San Francisco.

Louis, K. S., Dentler, R., & Kell, D. (1984). *Exchanging ideas: The communication and use of knowledge in education.* Boston, MA: Center for Survey Research, in collaboration with Abt Associates.

Louis, K. S., & Loucks-Horsley, S. (Eds.). (in press). *Supporting school improvement: A comparative perspective.* Leuven, Belgium: Acco Press.

Louis, K. S., & Miles, M. B. (in press). *Improving the urban high school: What works and why.* New York: Teachers College Press.

Metz, M. (1986). *Different by design: The context and character of three magnet schools.* New York: Routledge & Kegan Paul.

Metz, M. (1988). Some missing elements in the educational reform movement. *Educational Administration Quarterly, 24,* 446-460.

Miles, M. B., Louis, K. S., Rosenblum, S., Cipollone, A., & Farrar, E. (1986). *Managing change in the urban high school: Preliminary guidelines.* Boston: University of Massachusetts, Center for Survey Research.

Moshman, D. (1985). Faith Christian vs. Nebraska: Parent, child and community rights in the educational arena. *Teachers College Record, 86,* 553-571.

National Education Association. (1988). *Status of the American public school teacher.* West Haven, CT: NEA Professional Library.

Newmann, F. M., & Rutter, R. A. (1987). *Teachers' sense of efficacy and community as critical targets for school improvement.* Madison: University of Wisconsin, Center for the Study of Effective Secondary Schools.

Olsen, T. P. (in press). Denmark: School improvement and support structure. In K. S. Louis & S. Loucks-Horsley (Eds.), *Supporting school improvement: A comparative perspective.* Leuven, Belgium: Acco Press.

Peachy, P. (1987, August). *Toward a post-liberal theory of community.* Paper presented at the annual meeting of the American Sociological Association, New York.

Public School Forum of North Carolina. (1987). *The condition of being a teacher.* Raleigh: Author.

Rand Corporation. (1981). *A study of alternatives in American education: Conclusions and policy implications.* Santa Monica, CA: Author.

Ravich, D. (1974). *The great school wars: 1805–1972.* New York: Basic Books.

Reywid, M. A. (1985). Family choice arrangements in public schools: A review of the literature. *Review of Educational Research, 55,* 435–467.

Rosenholtz, S. (1985). Effective schools: Interpreting the evidence. *American Journal of Education, 93,* 352–388.

Samuels, J. J. (1974). The effect of school district size in teacher autonomy. In P. L. Stewart & M. G. Cantor (Eds.), *Varieties of work experience* (pp. 97–110). New York: John Wiley.

Sederberg, C. H., & Clark, S. M. (1987, April). *Motivation, incentives and rewards for high vitality teachers: Organizational and administrative considerations.* Paper presented at the annual meetings of the American Educational Research Association, Washington, DC.

Sickler, J. L. (1988). Teachers in charge: Empowering the professionals. *Phi Delta Kappan, 69,* 359–362.

Sociaal Cultureel Plan Bureau. (1982). *Sociaal cultureel rapport.* The Hague: Staatsuitgevering.

Stegö, N. E. (1986). Sweden. In C. Hopes (Ed.), *The school leader and school improvement: Case studies from ten O.E.C.D. countries* (pp. 295–336). Leuven, Belgium: Acco Press.

Stewart, P., & Cantor, M. (1974). Cultural and social control. In P. Stewart & M. Cantor (Eds.), *Varieties of work experience.* Cambridge, MA: Schenkman.

Tyack, D. (1974). *The one best system: A history of American urban education.* Cambridge, MA: Harvard University Press.

van den Berg, R., & van Wijlijk, W. (in press). Supporting school improvement: Strategies, structures, and policies: The Dutch case. In K. S. Louis & S. Loucks-Horsley (Eds.), *Supporting school improvement: A comparative perspective.* Leuven, Belgium: Acco Press.

Wallin, E., & Hamber, H. (in press). The school improvement support system in Sweden. In K. S. Louis & S. Loucks-Horsley (Eds.), *Supporting school improvement: A comparative perspective.* Leuven, Belgium: Acco Press.

WRR (Wetenschappelijke Raad voor het Regeringsbeleid). (1986). *Basic education: Summary of the twenty-seventh report to the government.* The Hague: Author.

3

How Social Class Differences Shape Teachers' Work

MARY HAYWOOD METZ

A notable contrast exists between, on the one hand, conceptions of the nature of schools and of processes crucial to their functioning in the literature of the educational reform movement and, on the other hand, such conceptions in a significant portion of the basic research literature written for sociologists, anthropologists, and educational researchers. The current educational reform movement, especially its first wave, takes only minimal notice of the effect of community contexts on schools, including the effects of the social-class positions or ambitions of parents and students. It emphasizes the formal structural and technical character-istics of schools and pays little attention to actors' interpretations of their participation in these structures. It places its faith in the ability of formal structural reforms to create changes in the quality of experience and the amount of learning accomplished in schools. This emphasis allows the reform movement to treat all schools alike, expecting them to be equally responsive to broad changes that can be applied across the board through increased curricular requirements, external monitoring, or internal struc-tural changes.

In contrast, sociologically oriented basic researchers have empha-sized important ways in which schools are differentiated according to the social class of their communities and their students (Anyon, 1981; Bowles & Gintis, 1976; Connell, Ashenden, Kessler, & Dowsett, 1982; Metz, 1978; Morgan, 1977; Weis, 1985). They have also noted that the nature of school knowledge itself is problematic, socially constructed, variable (often

This chapter was commissioned by the Center for Research on the Context of Secondary School Teaching at Stanford University. The gathering of data on which it is based was supported by the National Center on Effective Secondary Schools at the Wisconsin Center on Education Research, which is supported by the Office of Educational Research and Improve-ment, Grant No. G-00869007. The writing of the chapter was also supported by a grant from the Spencer Foundation. Any opinions, findings, and conclusions expressed here are those of the author and do not necessarily reflect the views of any of the sponsoring agencies.

depending on social class or ethnicity), and subject to change over time (Anyon, 1981; Apple, 1979, 1987; Bourdieu & Passeron, 1977; Heath, 1983; Kliebard, 1986; McNeil, 1986). Anthropologists analyze schools as reflections of the cultures of those who establish and run them (Henry, 1963; Spindler, 1973) and more proximately of those who staff them (Leacock, 1969; Heath, 1983; Lubeck, 1985; Philips, 1983). The same authors often analyze the ways in which schools are scenes of cultural contestation between staff members who belong to dominant cultures and students who belong to minority subcultures. Basic researchers concerned with organizational dynamics of schools have found that their formal structures by no means simply determine the activity that takes place within them (Burlingame, 1981; Meyer & Rowan, 1978). Like many other organizations, schools are open systems, very much affected by their surroundings (Gracey, 1972; McPherson, 1972; Metz, 1978, 1986; Scott, 1981; Smith, Prunty, & Dwyer, 1981).

In dealing specifically with teachers' lives, the reform literature has emphasized research and lay analysis that compares teaching to other occupations and concentrates on such matters as pay and career trajectories. The first wave of reform, especially, has neglected aspects of the same body of research showing that teachers find intrinsic rewards most satisfying (Biklen, 1983; Jackson, 1986; Lortie, 1975). It has separated social arrangements shaping teachers' careers from those shaping their daily experience on the job. It ignores the latter set of influences, most of which are grounded in teachers' relationships with students, parents, and building administrators. This perspective also encourages the view that designs for reform mandated from the top can be equally effective everywhere.

This chapter attempts to identify important social influences that shape high school teachers' perspectives, goals, experiences, and practices. It is based on a study of teachers in eight schools of varied social class. It questions the primacy of structures that are formally similar across high schools, arguing that teachers' lives differ significantly with the social class of the community surrounding a school and with the aspirations and achievements of students, which at the high school level are strongly affected by social class. Furthermore, it shows that these influences, while crucial, are not the only ones that affect teachers' lives. Other influences from teachers' own backgrounds and from administrators' and teachers' individual and collective actions within the school modify the effects of community pressures on the school—though they cannot expunge them. This chapter is designed to increase our understanding of the ways in which these varied influences interact to create the social contexts within which teachers in particular schools define and pursue their daily work.

METHODS

The study discussed here brought together questions and research styles from policy research and ethnographic sociological research, to create a hybrid project. It is one of several projects that constitute the work of the National Center on Effective Secondary Schools. Originally formulated and designed as part of the center's overall mission to discover school site levers that affect students' engagement with academic work, this individual study was intended to investigate ways in which schools facilitate and obstruct teachers' ability to be engaged with their work, on the assumption that teachers' engagement will affect students' engagement. The center's obligation to describe and analyze a broad spectrum of schools led us to select eight diverse schools to study in one year.

The schools were located in two midwestern metropolitan areas. Six were public schools; of these, two were in high-socioeconomic-status (SES) areas, two in middle-SES areas, and two in low-SES areas. The other two were Catholic schools, one serving a predominantly middle-class student body and the other a predominantly working-class clientele. This chapter will discuss just three of the public schools, one in each SES bracket, though a very brief description will be given of the ways in which each was similar to and different from the other schools serving students of roughly similar social class.

We visited each school for 2½ weeks with a team of two persons.[1] Starting each visit with a meeting with the principal, we were given an overview of the school from his or her point of view; we collected a set of documents about the school ranging from student test scores to faculty and student handbooks and the master schedule for teachers. The team then visited the classes of six students, half in Grades 9 and 10 and half in Grades 11 and 12. There was one high, one middle, and one low achiever in each group of three. We thus saw a range of classes at the outset and got to know a varied group of teachers. We then spent a full day with each of eight teachers of core academic subjects, chosen to constitute a sample diverse in age, gender, race, experience, and philosophy.[2] We interviewed these teachers at length after observing them, using a standard but open-ended interview guide. We also conducted shorter interviews with 10 other teachers in each school, chosen because they had special perspectives as chairpersons, union leaders, informal faculty leaders, new teachers, and teachers in special education and vocational education. Another team of two persons from the center studied the same schools at the same time, asking how administrators attempted to facilitate teachers' work. They spent most of their time with administrators, while we spent most of ours with teachers.[3]

The strength of the design lay in its comparative potential. We attended classes and interviewed teachers in situations that were formally parallel across the eight diverse schools. There are few studies that have allowed the same researchers to use the same design for research in schools of differing social class in the close succession that comes from visiting eight schools in a year. We obtained a much more vivid experience of the differences in schools that arise from the different circumstances and lifestyles of their communities than single researchers usually do. While our visits were short compared to those on which full ethnographic studies of school culture are based, they were long compared to most site visits or case studies in policy research.

THE FRAMEWORK OF ANALYSIS

As we thought about the striking differences we were seeing in the eight schools, in the context of the reform movement's assumption that high schools are fundamentally alike, we began to recognize that they are indeed alike in a familiar litany of ways. They use time and space in similar ways and teach students in groups of similar size. The curricular scope and sequence in traditionally defined subjects are nearly standard. High schools use the same texts in similarly labeled courses, even with very different students. Teachers' roles vis-à-vis students, colleagues, and administrators are defined similarly.

As we watched the schools in daily action and talked with the actors who gave them life, it seemed that the schools were following a common script. The stages were roughly similar, though the scenery varied significantly. The roles were similarly defined, and the outline of the plot was supposed to be the same. But the actors took great liberties with the play. They interpreted the motivations and purposes of the characters whose roles they took with striking variation. They changed their entrances and exits. Sometimes they left before the last act. The outlines of the plot took on changing significance with the actors' varied interpretation of their roles.

What made the schools we were visiting such different places, and specifically such different contexts for teachers, was that the actors around them and inside them imbued their similar structures with different meanings. Important variable meanings included parents', staff members', or students' values and their assumptions about the nature of knowledge; about the place of high school in a life trajectory; about the roles of teachers and students; and about the inherent nature of adults and adolescents, men and women, blacks and whites.

Meanings that are shared by groups are at issue here. They are located within a series of nested subcultures. Comparative analysis of education finds that whole societies share assumptions about education that may seem quite strange in other societies (Rohlen, 1983; Spindler, 1973). Similarly, within a single society, groups of the same social class develop common assumptions about education that highlight, deemphasize, or subtly transform generally accepted societal understandings (Anyon, 1981; Connell et al., 1982; Cookson & Persell, 1985). The communities around most schools, especially in metropolitan areas, are relatively homogeneous in social class; community interaction may increase the homogeneity of their perspectives. Teachers and administrators may be similar to or quite different from community members with regard to perspectives bred by their own educational backgrounds, income, and occupational status, as well as by interactions in the communities where they themselves are residents. Though professional norms and interaction may be weaker in teaching than in full professions, teachers still take on some common beliefs and values from their shared exposure to similar socialization, professional literature, and professional organizations.

Within individual schools teachers develop common perspectives (sometimes two or more competing ones) that are distinctive to that school, which they create out of their similar experiences there and their long-term interaction. They then tend to socialize newcomers into those perspectives (Metz, 1978, 1986). Because high schools are large and their teachers oriented to their separate subjects, diverse perspectives and subgroups dividing a faculty are likely. Administrators may take a part in forming, may share, or may dissent from this faculty perspective, though in the last case they are likely to try to change it. High school students' perspectives in a particular school are likely to be a blend of those fostered in the community (or subunits within it), those fostered by the school staff, and those developed and fostered by the student body (and its subgroups) as it also socializes newcomers (Cusick, 1973; Lesko, 1988; Schofield, 1982; Sullivan, 1979).

This chapter explicates the context of meanings surrounding teachers at three schools of differing social class, as they attempted to enact the common script of "The American High School." It examines five sources of meaning shaping teachers' contexts: (1) the community, including parents; (2) the student body; (3) teachers' own personal backgrounds, networks, and lifestyles; (4) the principal's efforts to shape teachers' ideas and practice, and administrative treatment of students and parents; and (5) teachers' collective perspective, or perspectives, on the elements of their work.

These five elements fall into two natural groupings. The first grouping includes the backgrounds of the community, the student body, and the teachers, all of which are beyond the direct control of individual public schools. School staff must accept them and then attempt to work constructively with them. The second grouping, the principal's strategies and the faculty's collective perspective(s), may move with or against the grain of the community and students and may even work with or against the grain of perspectives fostered by teachers' backgrounds. Though they cannot control outside influences, school staff can have some effect on parents', students', and teachers' ideas about schooling and the particular school and about their relationship to school participants. As we shall see, teachers' perceptions of the community and students often vary within a faculty. Perceptions about the community and the students among teachers have as much effect on teachers' actions as the "real" characteristics of these groups. Perceptions are, however, far more amenable to school reform.

It is equally important for district, state, or national policy makers to remember that, while community and student characteristics may appear to be unalterable realities not subject to policy manipulation, student bodies are determined by attendance policies. Policy decisions create linkages between schools and communities by legal and administrative fiat. These decisions can be altered. It is possible to create very different patterns of assignment of children to schools and so to create very different kinds of school communities and student bodies from those we have now. School desegregation plans have made precisely such changes.

As I analyze the three schools chosen for this chapter, then, I will show how the community, the student body, and teachers' backgrounds all affected teachers' definitions of their work. Analyzing the effects of these factors will illuminate *processes* through which social class makes a difference in the life of schools. I will then show how, within the school, the principal's strategies, teachers' collective perspectives, and students' responses to these staff attitudes and actions created the texture of school life that surrounded individual teachers. Here it should become clear that the importance of social class in shaping school life does not preclude school staffs from making a significant impact on it as well.

A word should be said about the concept of social class. It points to an important part of reality in industrial societies, but also to a vaguely defined and complex one. In accordance with mainstream sociology, social class here is defined as a composite of educational background, income, and type of occupation. The three do not always vary together, however. For example, one of our high-SES communities ranked higher in the metropolitan area in income than in educational and occupational standing, while the reverse was true in our other high-SES community. These bare statistical differences were indicators of real differences in the kinds of people who chose to live in each community and of the common consciousness that developed among them, to which the schools responded. Still, both can fairly be called high-SES communities, in comparison to those surrounding our two middle-SES schools.

Finally, the focus here is on schools as contexts for teachers' work, rather than individual teachers' actual practice. Individuals could and did respond to their contexts with varied amounts of energy and independence, but the subject at hand is the social pressures that act on teachers, not individuals' diverse responses to those pressures. Now, consider Cherry Glen, a school in a high-income white-collar suburb; Pinehill, a school in a stable blue-collar and middle-income white-collar suburb; and Charles R. Drew, a school in a poor neighborhood of a very large city. (Note that all proper names in these school and community descriptions are pseudonyms, and some inessential details have been altered to protect the identities of the communities.)

CHERRY GLEN HIGH SCHOOL

The Community

The Cherry Glen School District and the Pinehill School District both belong to suburbs of The City, a midwestern industrial center that is one of the nation's thirty largest cities, in a primarily agricultural state. The City was a prosperous and stable community with a heavily blue-collar but well-paid labor force until the recession of the 1980s closed many plants and reduced the workforce at others. The metropolitan area is heavily racially segregated. While the city's population is nearly one half black, there are negligible numbers of nonwhites in its suburbs.

The Cherry Glen School District lies to the north of The City, in an outer ring of suburbs beyond the county line. The district includes the town of Cherry Ridge and a smaller, more elite suburb, Glen Hollow, as well as a small piece of a community yet further north that tends to a blue-collar population. There are two high schools in the district, which has a population of nearly 50,000: Cherry Glen North, the original high school, dating from the 1950s, and the newer Cherry Glen South. We studied Cherry Glen North High School, henceforth referred to simply as Cherry Glen.

We chose Cherry Glen as a high-SES district. The principal and teachers perceive it as one, and figures from the 1980 census, presented in a publication of a metropolitan citizens' group, show it having the second highest household income (just under $40,000) among the school districts in its metropolitan area. Among the adults over 25 years old in its population, 53% have attended college; 36% of the population are in managerial or professional occupations as defined by the census. The community ranks fifth in the metropolitan area in these indicators of SES. The Cherry Glen area has a reputation—and voting record—indicating political conservatism.

Both administrators and teachers speak of the parents as including many doctors, lawyers, and business executives. Glen Hollow, totally contained within the Cherry Glen School District, is a small exclusive community with very expensive housing. Most of the high-status professionals and executives in the district are probably concentrated there; they make themselves disproportionately visible in the schools. We found in each district that school staffs' perceptions of the community were often slanted. Teachers at all the schools seemed to overstate the homogeneity of the communities they served. In the communities with high status, and certainly in Cherry Glen, they tended to overestimate parents' income and the status of their jobs. In the poorer communities, many tended to underestimate them. As we shall see at the other two schools, variations in teachers' individual backgrounds also led them to characterize the communities—and therefore the students—from varied perspectives and so to respond to them differently.

The portraits of parental attitudes in each community, as given in this chapter, are based mainly on the accounts of teachers, counselors, and administrators, though we did have some limited opportunities to see parents in action. We tried to elicit descriptions of specific actions that could give substance to our informants' general characterizations and to be sensitive to discrepant accounts, in order to see beyond teachers' subjectivity. In any case, teachers' beliefs about the community and students were as important as the objective reality, since perceptions that are believed to be real create as much pressure as reality.

Parents in Cherry Glen were interested in an education that would equip their children with a sound training in basic academic subjects, understood as a set of technical proficiencies. They were also interested in their children accumulating good records of grades. Many made quick inquiries when students' grades were low. The school had a system allowing parents of students having difficulty to request weekly reports on students' performance from all their teachers.

Parents, or at least active and visible parents, brought expectations for hierarchical authority over others to their relations with the schools. They expected to see clear written documentation justifying grades, and they demanded explicit statements of teachers' expectations. When they were displeased, they often went straight to administrators without speaking directly to the teacher, expecting administrators to see that complaints were dealt with and difficulties straightened out. While parents respected teachers' expertise, the onus was on teachers to demonstrate that they had brought that expertise to bear in any situation in dispute.

Not only did these parents—or the vocal few among them—expect the school to operate hierarchically, with teachers in the role of middle-level staff, they also perceived themselves as entitled to what they considered a satisfactory outcome. Several teachers told of conflicts with parents in which lawsuits were either threatened or actually brought.

Parents also expressed an attitude of family entitlement vis-à-vis the schools and their staffs, by their readiness to take 1- and 2-week vacations with their children during term time. At an open house for parents, one teacher warned that this practice often permanently damaged the student's ability to keep up, especially in cumulative subjects like mathematics. Other teachers told of parental insouciance in giving excuses for students' absences.

Some parents insisted that their children be moved up into "accelerated" classes, despite staff judgments that they did not have the requisite ability. Fewer parents moved them down to easier classes in hopes of obtaining better grades. Parents felt entitled not only to affect their children's placement in classes, but to put pressures on the form of the curriculum as well. These pressures, at least as teachers saw them, increased external credentialing at the cost of making the curriculum less complex and challenging and more easily encapsulated by textbook work stressing clear right and wrong answers. Science teachers were perturbed that parents had successfully lobbied to excise the requirement for a laboratory project from advanced science classes. Both they and foreign-language teachers looked askance on parental pressures for Advanced Placement classes, which colleagues in other schools told them would undercut the school's emphasis on laboratory work in science and on oral work in some foreign languages.

The Students

Cherry Glen North High School enrolls 1,400 students in four grades of high school. Test-score data indicated that students did well; nearly

50% scored in the top quarter on a nationally standardized test, and less than 5% scored in the bottom quarter. In 1985, 71% of the 382 graduates went to 4-year colleges and another 12% to 2-year colleges or technical schools. However, even though highly selective private universities and colleges had recruiters at the school during our October visit, only 17% of the previous year's graduates had left the state, almost all to go to public universities or to little-known private institutions.

On the whole, the students were polite, cooperative, and diligent in class. They arrived on time and paid attention to the tasks the teacher set before them for the whole class hour. When some teachers allowed time to start on homework, most students would work, though individual conversations would arise. In study hall, most but not all worked with academic books. There was very little talking.

There were about two sections of accelerated English, math, and science at each level; and there were advanced electives, taken mostly by stronger students. In these classes, the level of intensity was remarkable. Classes proceeded briskly, and students gave nearly absolute attention to their teachers for the whole hour.

The principal emphasized the fact that many students were highly involved in extracurricular activities, so that they left home at 7 A.M. and returned at 6 P.M., with a couple of hours of homework ahead of them. One leading teacher who worked with seniors said she told her students they would never again have to work as hard as they did in high school. Since extracurricular activities are voluntary—though important for college admissions and prestige among peers—students themselves chose this highly stressed life, though they did so under pressure from both parents and the school.

In classes that were not accelerated, students were also attentive but less intensely so. They were more likely to question requirements for work, or at least to ask teachers to justify them. Some students were surly, if compliant, when teachers departed from plans in the book or from established procedure. For example, when a geometry teacher told students to insert a step not asked for in the book, several students asked questions in tones that approached sullenness. The teacher patiently explained the reason that the extra step would be helpful to them. One girl then said, "If we aren't going to follow the book, why do we even have it?" When students questioned requirements in these ways, teachers often told them that certain procedures would be required to get a good grade. Students accepted these constraints, but did so with an air of compliance under duress.

The students, then, like their parents, wanted clear-cut, technical skills from the school. Like their parents, they placed great importance on grades. They obeyed their teachers and paid attention to their lessons because these behaviors were necessary to get good grades. Most worked hard.

At least some students shared the slightly condescending attitude of many parents toward teachers. Their surliness over discretionary changes by teachers was an expression of this view. A few teachers spoke of slighting comments, made by students to each other loudly enough for teachers to hear; for example, after a disagreement with a teacher, a student growled to his friend, "Those who can, do. . . ." When I was in the halls during passing time and would try to break into heavy traffic from a side aisle or to get onto a crowded staircase, students did not notice an adult and yield the right of way, as they did at other schools. I had to push my way in just like the students. Several teachers spoke of not liking to walk through the mob scene in the halls between classes, a comment not made at other schools. Apparently, students did not yield even to known teachers. This was a subtle sign of lack of respect, which teachers preferred not to endure.

Cherry Glen students could be far from the diligent, polite students they usually seemed in those relatively rare situations where a teacher was not skillfully in command. We saw a few classes where students were restless and even rude with teachers who seemed not to know how to check this behavior. We also heard about unruly behavior with substitutes.

The school also had a number of problem students of various kinds. The student body was less homogeneous than an overall impression of the majority of classes at first suggested. Some deviant students, like the "druggies," whom teachers described as usually reasonably able students who withdrew rather than becoming disruptive, did not disturb regular classes and were simply referred for counseling assistance. However, the student body also included some deviant students who did not fit in so easily, such as markedly less able students; students with visible signs of working-class allegiance such as leather jackets, tight skirts, and heavy makeup; and some seriously rebellious students. Overlap among these groups made some students significant problems. The school found a variety of ways of segregating them from the mainstream. Less able students were tracked into special low-achieving sections or cycled back into elementary courses such as earth sciences, and they were referred to fields such as fine arts and vocational education. In the upper grades, many participated in work/study for half of each day. There was a flourishing special education program that took students with learning or behavioral problems. Finally, rebellious students could be channeled to the district's alternative high school, which drew about 100 students from the population of the two high schools together.

Teachers' Backgrounds

We obtained systematic data on teachers' lives outside school only from the eight teachers we both observed and interviewed. None of them lived in the community. Five lived in a small city to the north that had more blue- than white-collar neighborhoods and that was clearly less expensive to live in than Cherry Ridge. Two lived further out in the country, and one lived in a suburb equivalent in status to Cherry Ridge.

Four of the teachers in our sample were not far from the community in social class. Two had attended private colleges and had done graduate work at demanding institutions. All four mentioned parents or siblings who were in careers that demand at least a college education. Often their siblings and the friends they made in private life worked at jobs either requiring more education or giving more income than teaching, or both. Their leisure activities were likely to be those that are associated with people who are well educated, such as attending the symphony or theater. In a word, their education, associates, and lifestyle suggested membership in the upper middle class.

Three of these four teachers had a somewhat more sophisticated view of knowledge than did the community. They were concerned with content and with ambiguity and complexity. They were less oriented to grades and credentials than was the community. They also were somewhat critical of community values, especially what they believed to be concern with money, appearances, and status striving, though they rarely used such harsh words.

The other four teachers were educated at branch campuses of state universities and had done less work beyond the bachelor's degree. All four lived in the predominantly blue-collar small city north of Cherry Glen. Their parents, siblings, and friends were engaged in blue-collar work, clerical jobs, small businesses, or technical fields such as engineering. Three had regular second jobs, either year-round or in the summer, while only one of the first group did, and he alternated summer work with exotic travel and sometimes taught at the college level for his summer job. This second group went bowling or fishing, not to the symphony. These teachers seemed to be on a border between the working class and the middle class, in their origins and associations outside of school and in their lifestyle. All of the teachers in this group were men.

More than the other group of teachers, they spoke frequently, and with resentment, of the money in the Cherry Glen community and of the condescension toward teachers expressed by students and parents.

The Principal

Principals are expected to work at the borders between communities and school staffs, balancing their perspectives and accommodating their differences. Mr. Coyne was unusually active in this role. He enacted many of the Cherry Glen community's expectations. He spoke of striving for excellence, of maintaining high standards of courtesy and conduct as well as of academic performance. He said that this community had the resources to make good education possible, and he told his faculty that such education could be accomplished here, if anywhere.

Mr. Coyne had shaped the school through careful recruitment of faculty, at least in the early days of the school when there were fewer restrictions on hiring. Many of the older teachers told of being sought out to apply for a position. Mr. Coyne told of consciously cultivating a perspective like his own among the faculty in the early years of his principalship. Later, as only a few new faculty were hired each year, continuing faculty taught the common perspective to new recruits. The school had not given in to changes fostered in the 1960s, he said. When the district moved the ninth grade from junior high schools into the high schools four years before the study, a large group of junior high school teachers were transferred with the students. Mr. Coyne worked hard, he told us, to socialize this large group of persons, who had not really chosen the high school or been chosen by it, into the perspective he had previously fostered among the faculty.

Mr. Coyne chose an extremely hierarchical role in administrative matters; he demanded attention to fine points and full and meticulous reporting on all aspects of other staff members' activities. He had written a detailed teachers' handbook and another describing the duties of all cocurricular leaders' positions. He developed a system of forms for reporting on a wide variety of standard activities and special events, to keep himself thoroughly informed of all school operations. These forms were taken seriously by the staff and filed regularly as requested.

He enacted measures to assure that grading of students was documented and defensible and that a clear, articulated curriculum was uniformly enacted. He expected teachers to grade students daily, if possible, or at least several times a week. At the end of a year, they handed in their gradebooks, which were kept for years in case any questions subsequently arose about a student's performance or a teacher's fairness.

Individual teachers were asked to fill out a form for each course they taught, at the beginning of each year, in which they stated their goals and their methods. All teachers were observed several times a year, either by Mr. Coyne or by one of the two assistant principals. In case of parental question, Mr. Coyne had at his fingertips each teacher's statements about the goals and methods used in the course, the past grading patterns, and reports of repeated administrative observations over a period of years.

At the same time, he regarded teachers as curricular experts and delegated decisions in that area to them and then supported their curricular autonomy. He expected hard work and dedication from them in their role as experts, while encouraging and facilitating their involvement in associations in their disciplinary areas and supporting their engagement in further study. When they developed innovative projects or participated in unusual activities outside the school, alone or with their students, he saw to it that they received publicity and implicit congratulations in a newsletter the school produced. He thus used the generous financial resources the community made available to facilitate teachers seeking further development or public recognition. He then was able to speak to the community of their excellence and expertise and so to forestall some parental attempts to second-guess their efforts.

The district and the principal required coordination of syllabi and assignments between sections of a course. This policy turned the crucial professional decisions of the staff into group decisions, arrived at collegially. They thus could not be dismissed by parents as a matter of individual whim (unless a teacher were the only one who taught a course), but rather stood as the product of a professional consensus.

Teachers who talked about serious conflicts with parents reported that Mr. Coyne was very supportive of the teachers, as long as they could document what they had done and why they had done it in a reasonable way. He seemed to take a very active part in these crises, interposing himself between the conflicting parties. It was noteworthy also that Cherry Glen had no individual parent/teacher conferences, as the other schools we studied did twice a year.

In all of these matters, the faculty found the principal fair, consistent, and straightforward. His control over school policy was less direct and so more problematic for the faculty. In such matters (e.g., whether to have a homeroom period or to allow candy sales), the administration often formally consulted the faculty. There was an array of standing and ad hoc faculty committees related to such policy issues. But the teachers we talked to were all but unanimous in saying that after these consultations the administrators followed their own judgment, regardless of teachers' advice. Teachers were only mildly affronted by this behavior, however.

They dismissed it as an annoyance, saying that the administrators should simply make decisions themselves, rather than pretend to consult them on schoolwide policies, if they intended to ignore their advice. Administrators' control of student-life issues allowed the principal to maintain a delicate balance between community pressures for constant performance and students' restlessness. For example, the principal initiated—and protected against some faculty criticism—an open study hall for juniors and seniors in good academic standing which became essentially a social hour.

In short, Mr. Coyne accommodated the Cherry Glen community by defining the school as a hierarchical organization; teachers were to follow many rules and to document their activities for his perusal. He thus could present himself to the community as consistently knowledgeable and in charge. While going through the forms of faculty governance, he kept control of schoolwide policies and could fine-tune their accommodation to the community and the students. At the same time, he carved out some freedom for teachers as subject-matter experts, some of whom taught in ways the community might not have preferred. By using the labels of *excellence* and *expertise*, by facilitating teachers' pursuit of outside professional activities through monetary support and public praise for their activities, and by encouraging teachers to seek prizes for both curricular and cocurricular work with students, he helped them to legitimize their efforts in the community's eyes.

Teachers' Shared Perspectives—Schoolwide

On the whole, the Cherry Glen teachers felt supported by the Cherry Glen community and grateful to be working with its students. They found parents mostly cooperative and students mostly reasonably capable and ambitious. Apathetic students could usually be coaxed into a facsimile of diligence, via the power of grades. Teachers who taught lower-track classes found their students less industrious and amenable than others, but we met no teachers, except special education teachers, who worked only with low-ability students.

Teachers were well aware that Cherry Glen was a high-status community; in fact, they overstated its income and the accomplishments of its parents. They felt some reflected glory from their association with such a community. The principal's rhetoric about striving for excellence in the school as a whole and for expertise in their role as teachers further enhanced their sense that they were doing important, effective work. The prestige conferred by such a definition of their tasks made them willing to shoulder the burden of the steady, conscientious effort it entailed. Both our observations in the school and the accounts of our interviewees about their work habits inside and outside the school suggested that this faculty put in by far the most hours of preparation of the three faculties described in this chapter. The norms of the school environment called on them to use constructively the two preparation hours their union had negotiated for them. Most teachers did in fact work during those hours, though some went to lounges where they switched back and forth between work and conversation. They also arrived at school early, and the parking lot was nearly full more than 1 hour after school and still was not empty 3 hours afterward.

Most of the faculty accepted much of the community's definition of school knowledge as technical and highly skill oriented. They also saw their relations with students as hierarchical ones, where they were experts supervising the acquisition of skills. As a group, the Cherry Glen teachers taught their subjects as facts and skills to be accumulated. Almost all of them were serious in their attempt to help students gain as large a quantity of knowledge as they were capable of absorbing. A vision of school knowledge as a matter of accumulating correct information or acquiring definable skills was consistent with the requirement that every teacher grade every student as close to daily as possible.

In following six students through their classes and in spending a day with eight teachers, we saw only two teachers who purposely drew students into discussions where they contributed ideas or thoughts not included in the readings or previously presented by teachers. One of these teachers was teaching health, a course designed to deal with feelings and experiences. The other was teaching a humanities course. When the interviewer mentioned to the latter that she "seemed to draw the kids out as people more" than other teachers, she replied defensively: "I never want to shortchange the technical. And that's a hard thing, to maintain these standards of excellence and technique at the same time that you want them not to be frightened and to communicate."

Teachers' Shared Perspectives—In Subgroups

Departments. The Cherry Glen faculty were expected to come up not only with common curriculum guides for each department but with common syllabi and grading practices and similar pedagogy in each course taught by more than one person. Consequently, they were administratively pushed into considerable collegial conversation and cooperation within departments and subgroups of departments. Furthermore, the math and science teachers had a common office with many comfortable amenities such as a coffee pot and a microwave oven. Some other departments also had smaller common offices that separated them from most other teachers but threw them in contact with one another. Departmental relationships became relatively close and intense.

There was some variation among departments in their orientation to knowledge and to the community. Departments most in tension with the community were those whose members' conceptions of knowledge were somewhat more complex and sophisticated than the community's. These teachers were no less subject oriented than others, but they had had contact with outside groups that encouraged open-ended or at least nontraditional approaches to skill acquisition. The school had for years been a test site for a federally funded experimental curriculum in one science subject that teachers of that subject had enthusiastically embraced, but the community was less enthusiastic about the emphasis on independent projects and laboratory exploration that it encouraged. A subunit in another department had been strongly influenced by experiences at the university learning about new methods of instruction in their area. They also practiced these with enthusiasm, but some parents and some of their colleagues voiced skepticism, since the new methods broke with tradition and did not produce as much "textbook" knowledge.

Informal status and background differences among the faculty. There was an unstated hierarchy of prestige among the faculty. Those high in prestige were more likely to be on school policy committees, had more demanding and visible extracurricular assignments with students, and numbered the most department chairs in their ranks. The price of high status was hard work, most of it not rewarded by increased pay, or at least not by pay commensurate with the duties. There was some tension over this issue; we noticed that the topic of "sharing the load" was a popular one. There was both an administrative and a faculty norm that all teachers should have some responsibilities beyond the classroom. Practice seemed to depart from this norm of equal load, however. While all of our interviewees did something, both the hours and the amount of initiative and involvement required by their extra duties were quite unevenly distributed.

We also noted that, within our sample of eight teachers, high-status teachers were more often ones with upper-middle-class social networks. They described their obligation as one of doing a good job, rather than one of working conscientiously for a given number of hours. In our sample, most of the teachers with lower status who did not work as hard on preparation and did fewer extracurricular activities also had friendship and family networks on the border of the middle and working class or in the working class. Some of them argued that it was unreasonable to expect them to work substantial hours outside the school day. A definition of reasonable expectations for effort, which our small sample suggested was class related, was closely associated with informal status inside the school.

Teachers who differed in status both inside and outside the school also differed in the sophistication with which they talked about teaching itself. Compare the following two quotations. The first is from a low-status teacher who was asked if discussions about curriculum or teaching methods were helpful and if they made a difference to his work.

> They're helpful, yeah. I'm not sure if they make a great difference, but they're helpful. You find out that what you're doing is what the other person is doing. You find out you're on the right track. You basically are covering the same material at the same time with the same sort of tests. And you find out that you're not, quote, too easy, too hard.

The second, high-status teacher had more complex comments:

> I was on a learning styles committee. . . . We were teachers who were interested in students' learning styles. Our students were tested and we were tested . . . to see how we learned, and how that affected what we did with our students. . . .
>
> It was funny for me, because I am a very structured person in the classroom, but taken out of my professional role, I am not structured at all. So it was very interesting to [see] how we do things—how we force ourselves to do things—that just are not the way we would normally operate.
>
> So, at any rate, I think that probably made me a lot more aware, too. While I did not know what I was doing from an academic point of view, I think my previous teaching experience fit in very well with the learning style committee that I served on. I don't know that I was necessarily aware when I would change activities, or when I would have them work in groups, or when I would have them stand up and do something, or when I would have them write rather than speak, that I might be appealing to someone else's learning style. I was doing it from a foreign language teacher's point of view. You work on listening, speaking, reading, and writing. You work on all of these skills, and you do every single one each class period. I think this committee was interesting to me from the standpoint of, "Oh, my gosh, you mean I was doing all these things and at the same time, I was meeting every one's learning style?"—supposedly.

There seemed to be a circular process at work. Energetic young people who had been stimulated by challenging training and who came from social networks that expected dedication to a job beyond its literal requirements were attractive to the principal as recruits for the school. Once recruited, they either volunteered for committee and extracurricular assignments or were asked to take them on. These gave them contact with colleagues, administrators, and parents, an experience that helped them develop a vision of the school that extended beyond the classroom and so stimulated their efforts. The assignments also made them visible to others and raised their status. They were encouraged to engage with groups beyond the school, which in turn fed them new ideas and increased their ability for leadership.

Other teachers did not volunteer for significant extra duties and were not singled out for special assignments. They became low-status, less visible teachers. They thus did not feel as much a part of the school as a whole and found participation with other teachers less rewarding, since their status was lower. When we observed at this school, these processes had been at work for many years, and there was a tacit but very real hierarchy among the faculty. Its sources had become hard to identify with confidence,but it tended to be self-reinforcing. Since all of the teachers in our sample of eight who had working-class lifestyles and associates had come from the junior high, one might suspect that coming from there was the important variable in these processes. But one former junior high teacher in our sample of eight had upper-middle-class associations and high status, while one long-term high school teacher had middle-class associations and relatively low status.

The relationship of the faculty to the community was expressed in their reluctance to speak of this informal hierarchy to us. In fact, at Cherry Glen more than any other school except possibly Drew, we were treated with caution. The principal made sure he knew exactly with whom we were speaking, and leading faculty and administrators were very aware of when we were present and with whom we spent our time. Teachers expressed surprise—not altogether pleased surprise—when they encountered us after the few days that constitute the usual stay of outside visitors. Administrators and especially leading teachers made careful efforts to give us the same good impression of well-organized, energetic excellence and expertise that this staff gave to parents and the community.

Cherry Glen and Other High-SES Schools in This Study

The other two high-SES schools in this study were Maple Heights, a public school, and St. Augustine's, a Catholic school. Maple Heights was a small school of less than 1,000 students in a suburb of 14,000. Its district had a higher proportion of adults who had attended college and participated in professional or managerial occupations than did Cherry Glen, but a drastically lower family income. It was influenced by a branch of the state university just beyond its borders and had heavy proportions of well-educated but poorly paid adults. St. Augustine's was located in The City, but near its northern border, and drew heavily from northern suburbs close to Cherry Glen as well as from the middle-class areas of The City around it. It had a fairly diverse but still heavily college-bound and mostly middle-class student body, which was also 90% Catholic.

Cherry Glen resembled the other schools that could be called roughly high SES, in that (1) its parents felt entitled to have a say in school affairs and to be advocates for their children and (2) its students were mostly capable of doing the work adequately and were diligent and cooperative most of the time in class. The other faculties were like Cherry Glen's original faculty in having had some contact with universities and colleges that were more demanding than average and having social networks of private associates who were college educated and had middle-class lifestyles. The other schools also honored teachers' expertise. Maple Heights gave them resources and encouragement for engaging in continuing broadening study and to be active in subject-related groups outside the school. The other schools, like Cherry Glen, had school structures and administrative and peer expectations that encouraged collegial contact and discussion of curriculum and pedagogy.

Both the other schools allowed individual teachers more scope than at Cherry Glen and regarded them more as creative artists and less as technicians working together. The other schools also regarded knowledge as less technical and less given, more as something fluid and constantly recreated that was therefore open to students' contributions and discussion. Especially at Maple Heights, more students went out of state to prestigious private colleges. At the other schools, teachers knew their students better as persons and took more interest in their individual development. Students there were rarely condescending to teachers. At Maple Heights, many teachers lived in the community and others wished they could. There was much more similarity and continuity between the teaching staff and the community than at Cherry Glen. The other schools differed from Cherry Glen in giving teachers more say in school governance.

The similarities among these schools may point to commonalities, or at least frequent characteristics, of schools in their class settings. Their differences underscore differences within each social class; here, especially, the effects of high SES in terms of income versus high SES in terms of education and occupational experience can be seen. The small size of Maple Heights and its intense community life also interacted with class, as did Cherry Glen's larger and more fractionated community. Though St. Augustine's was larger than Cherry Glen, theological concerns and school community were high priorities there, and they helped to create a much stronger sense of staff and student unity than at Cherry Glen.

All of these schools were given distinct advantages by the social class of their parents and students. Parents placed a high priority on education and were vigilant in looking for high quality, though how each community defined this was somewhat different. The public school communities could express their value on education with reasonably generous monetary support for the schools. These resources, together with a cooperative student body that did not require heavy supervision of the halls, translated into two class hours formally allocated to preparation and consequently to more time and opportunity for collegial contact than in other schools. Funds also facilitated teachers' contact with colleagues outside the schools. Principals had a large say in hiring and had significant pools of applicants from which to choose when hiring. They also could and did dismiss untenured teachers who did not work out well. (At Cherry Glen, with a shrinking student body and transfers of tenured teachers from the junior high, these powers became moot, however.) All these schools had a majority of students whose skills were thoroughly adequate for high school work and who thought learning and doing well in high school would bring them future benefits. Many students appeared even to find the work interesting, especially at Maple Heights and St. Augustine's. Teachers consequently could find their efforts rewarded with students' progress and could feel relatively successful.

The consequence of these patterns was that these three schools had already moved in many of the directions suggested by the initiatives for restructuring teachers' roles in the second wave of reform. Their teachers engaged in considerable collegial discussion, participated in continuing education outside the schools, and, especially at Maple Heights and St. Augustine's, maintained close contact with students. At the latter two schools, they also played a larger role in school governance than anywhere else; at Cherry Glen the community's and the principal's emphasis on hierarchy undercut formal moves in this direction. It seemed that patterns tending toward suggested restructuring depended upon the kinds of community and student support just described. As we will see, these were not available to the schools in lower-SES communities.

PINEHILL HIGH SCHOOL

The Community

Pinehill is one in a set of predominantly working-class suburbs, extending out from the western side of The City, where most of its heavy industries are located. A relatively new suburb, Pinehill has grown through unplanned housing development; its only high school was built in the late 1950s. Some of the heavy industry in the town, neighboring suburbs, and The City has recently closed its doors or reduced its workforce. While we were at the school, rumors were reported in the papers that one of the remaining major factories within Pinehill might be closed. At the same time, the community is experiencing an expansion of commercial and service establishments. Pinehill reflects the story of many blue-collar communities in the Rust Belt. The teenagers whose parents were well-paid factory workers must search harder for a shrinking pool of equivalent factory jobs or accept much lower pay in service jobs.

The population of Pinehill is less than half that of the Cherry Glen School District, or about 20,000. Only 25% of adults in the community have ever attended college, and only 16% are engaged in occupations the census counts as professional or managerial. In Cherry Glen, more than twice the proportion of adults have attended college and hold professional or managerial jobs. The average family income is just over $25,000, compared to Cherry Glen's $40,000. The blue-collar suburbs surrounding Pinehill have average incomes just below or just above it, with similar rates of college attendance and proportions of adults in professional or managerial jobs.

There were a few clear community priorities for the schools. First, they were not to be too much of a burden on taxpayers. The school board was proud that the district had one of the lowest per-pupil costs in the state. When new programs were added, others had to be cut. While salaries were low, they were not markedly lower than in other districts in the metropolitan area, especially for the experienced teachers who formed the bulk of the Pinehill faculty. Most of the financial pinch was felt in the area of supplies. New textbooks could be ordered only about every 10 years; lab supplies were limited; computers had only recently become available. Support for planning curriculum was available only occasionally for departmentwide efforts, not for the development of special courses. Money for special projects or for travel to professional meetings was virtually nonexistent. These constraints were demoralizing for the most professionally and intellectually engaged teachers, but apparently hardly felt by the majority.

While the evidence was less clear, we gained the strong impression that the community cared about cleanliness and order in the school. The building was kept in good condition, and a high priority was placed on student decorum. Students and parents alike accepted punishments for misbehavior with little debate, including the staff's heavy use of a relatively new in-school suspension room picturesquely known as The Freezer.

Parents seemed to be concerned about students' grades and their progress toward graduation, but they were much less concerned about the level of challenge they were exposed to or the content of the curriculum. Teachers and counselors told us that, when students were not doing well, parents often requested that they be moved to a lower track where the work would be easier. Parents seemed to have fewer concerns about the internal operation of the school than did Cherry Glen parents, and they seemed not to feel entitled to give unsolicited advice or criticism as easily as did the Cherry Glen (and other upper-SES) parents. We heard about only two strong parental complaints, one about a counselor who steadfastly argued against moving a student she judged to be capable from a challenging class to a lower track, and the other about a teacher's failing a student in a high-track section of a required course.

The school board was concerned about high failure rates for the student body as a whole. They were in the process of establishing a special program for at-risk students. They also pressured the principal to lower the rate of failures in the classes of a few teachers with unusually high rates. Community concern with failures was in part a response to a new state requirement of 22 credits for graduation. The school had previously required only 18 credits, so students could afford to fail a few courses and still graduate. Some students who previously would have graduated despite three or four failed courses now found their graduation in jeopardy.

The Students

Pinehill High School enrolls about 1,250 students. In the 2 years before our study, just under 45% of graduates had enrolled in 4-year colleges, with another 9% to 12% enrolling full-time in a local 2-year technical college and others taking some courses there. Of those who went to college, more than 90% stayed within the state to do so, and most of the rest went to neighboring states, all of them to public and little-known private institutions. The test scores for Pinehill students were, however, relatively high. In the eighth grade, before entering high school,

34% had scored in the top quartile on nationally standardized tests, while 11% had scored in the bottom quartile.

On the whole, our team was impressed with students' orderly and pleasant behavior in the school at large, for example, in the lunchroom and the halls. In interacting with adults, students were generally polite and cooperative. But students were less compliant when academic effort was expected of them.

They seemed quite diverse in their skills and diligence. The school was correspondingly the most heavily tracked of the three described here. Students in the bottom tracks were restless and visibly lacking in concentration and effort. Teachers considered themselves successful if only a quarter to a third failed a class, although they said that, even in these classes, most students had difficulty more from lack of effort than lack of basic skills or comprehension. With many of their teachers, regular-track students had negotiated a standard practice of giving over the last half of a period for doing "homework." This time actually became a social hour during which virtually the whole class engaged in private conversations on social topics. This time had come to be considered a right in many classes; we saw students demand it when teachers working before an observer carried on the lesson for a longer time than usual. In some high-track classes, where teachers less often yielded this "free" time, some students kept up a running guerrilla battle of bantering, teasing, or openly hostile and distracting comments aimed at the teachers.

While we thought gender differences played a part at most schools for both students and teachers, gender issues were typically subtle and nearly impossible to identify clearly in a 3-week visit. At Pinehill, however, gender was a category unmistakably crucial to relationships and individual behavior, for both students and teachers. We noticed a visible absence of boys in demanding, high-track, classes in the upper grades, especially in humanities subjects. We also noticed a preponderance of male students in the lowest tracks. Boys, when they were present in high-track classes, were the most likely to hector teachers. There was scattered evidence that some of the boys defined serious involvement with the school's academic agenda as unmasculine, the more so when teachers were women.

Pinehill (and the other two schools with predominantly working-class student bodies) differed from other schools in students' regular participation in public displays of affection in the halls. Several times each day that we traveled from class to class with students, we saw couples standing intently kissing, often right beside the door to a classroom students were entering for class. We witnessed such students' adamant resistance to teachers' attempts to break them apart—an exception to their otherwise orderly hall behavior. Since we only once saw a pair of students engaged in this behavior in the relative privacy of a lightly used stairwell rather than in the midst of heavy student and faculty traffic, these activities seemed to be intended as much to be public statements as private interaction. They proclaimed each student's prowess as a budding young man or young woman, and, more important, they distanced each from the role of student. Such behavior claimed adult status for students. It also reflected what seemed to be a community vision of school and work as but one activity in adult life, to which family life and leisure pursuits are at least coequal. This is a perspective that has often been discussed in sociologists' treatments of working-class values (e.g., Connell et al., 1982; LeMasters, 1975; Rubin, 1976).

Teachers' Backgrounds

Teachers at Pinehill had relatively homogeneous backgrounds that were closely connected to, or at least similar to, life in Pinehill. A number of the long-term teachers had grown up together in a neighboring suburb. At least four of the eight teachers we interviewed at length had grown up in the nearby suburbs and come "home" or "back" to teach, sometimes after a few years teaching in some other part of the state. Only three had studied outside The City's metropolitan area, and only one, who came from a rural area in another state, had studied at a private college. All but one of the eight now lived in Pinehill or one of the immediately adjacent blue-collar suburbs. The eighth lived near her husband's work, to the north of The City.

Several teachers were the only one of their siblings to attend or finish college. All but two, when asked about friends' and siblings' work, mentioned jobs that did not require a college education. One of the two exceptions spoke of a family of teachers, and the other of a wife who was a nurse and a close friend who was a "middle manager," a term that we found often referred to people without college educations.

As we tried to make sense of the perspectives and actions of the Pinehill faculty, there were patterns that puzzled us. They became more comprehensible when we looked at them in the context of values and behavior common in working-class families and communities, which have been consistently noted in a number of studies by sociologists (Komarovsky, 1962; LeMasters, 1975; Rubin, 1972, 1976). While these teachers were all college graduates and many had master's degrees, their community and often their family backgrounds were blue collar, and many of their family and friends were still participating in blue-collar work. It made sense that they continued to hold perspectives associated with blue-collar experience.

The faculty members were aging. Six of the eight teachers we interviewed at length appeared to be, or told us they were, over 40, most over 50. While there were younger teachers, they were in a minority position in a faculty dominated by older teachers with 20 and more years of experience in the school. Most of the dominant teachers had gone to college before the changes introduced during the sixties with regard to class, race, politics, and sexual attitudes. Many of them spoke openly and frequently of finding it difficult to deal with changes in the student body over the years.

The Principal

There was far more continuity between the community and the school at Pinehill than at either of the other schools discussed in this chapter. Like the majority of teachers, the principal of Pinehill, Mr. Taylor—more often referred to by teachers as Jake Taylor—had grown up locally and currently lived in a neighboring suburb. He was a regular participant in community business clubs, such as the Lions and Kiwanis. His relations with local leaders brought tangible benefits for the school, especially donated equipment and facilities.

Mr. Taylor seemed to reflect the community's values, priorities, and style. In the tour of the school he gave us the first day, he was clearly pleased with its clean and quiet halls. He greeted aides who had the responsibility for surveying the bathrooms and giving him a daily count of cigarette butts in each location, so that supervision and prevention could move to where it was most needed. Cleanliness and order were high priorities and ones he spent time and energy supporting.

Pinehill was a social world where trust was based on personal knowledge in long-term, stable relationships. The first principal of the school had come from Millerton, a stable neighboring suburb that was older, smaller, more densely populated, and somewhat poorer than Pinehill. He brought many teachers to Pinehill whom he had known there as students, young teachers, or both. Mr. Taylor was one of these, brought on to serve as one of the assistant principals. He and several teachers, all of them now in their early fifties, had gone to high school in Millerton during the same years. They had been working together in Pinehill now for more than 20 years.

Mr. Taylor was supportive of students and sympathetic with their concerns as whole persons, in keeping with community priorities. He asked us if we found our days following student schedules tiring, and when we said we did, he said that teachers tend to be unsympathetic to that fatigue as they pile on homework. He found it hard to get them to understand the issue from the students' point of view. At the same time, this was the only school where part-time job openings in local service industries or as babysitters were read as part of regular school announcements, with an invitation for interested students to get more information in the office.

Mr. Taylor did not take a directive stance with teachers in many matters. Teachers agreed that they could get in trouble if they sent large numbers of students to the office for discipline rather than handling those matters themselves. They also thought they could get in trouble if they failed too many students. Indeed, in light of the community's pressures on this issue, Mr. Taylor had instituted intensive observation and conversation with some teachers who failed unusually large numbers of students. Teachers said that otherwise they were more-or-less free to teach as they liked, and several complained that others did not follow departmental curricula and were not reprimanded.

We wondered, however, whether the principal was directing the faculty more than he seemed to be by meeting with them individually and in private. Intriguing possibilities are raised by the following comment from a male chairperson of a department in which he both denies community influence on his teaching and mentions more intervention from the principal than we usually heard about (albeit exercised through the chair). The teacher had been asked whether he had to consider the wishes of parents or the school board in deciding what to teach. He said he did not, but, when asked whether he or other teachers got any complaints, he said,

> In my [many] years as chairperson, I've never had the problem of the principal calling me and saying, "Hey, one of your teachers is teaching this unit. What the hell is going on? Why is that being done?" But we've had dozens and dozens of problems of, "Why are your teachers giving an exam during this week? Why are they counting it that much for the kids' 9-week grade?" And, "The other teacher doesn't give that final or doesn't give that big of an exam." That type of thing. That's not the curriculum. That's just grading policy or evaluation procedures.

We see here the community's lack of interest in the substance of the curriculum, and we see the principal's adherence to community priorities and his greater involvement in teachers' work than they are ready to admit.

The principal also became involved in teachers' work through support of teachers who had initiatives or ideas for special courses or programs or who were simply energetic. Both a special education teacher and a teacher who had developed some innovative courses for high-track juniors and seniors said that the principal's support was crucial to their work and very helpful to them personally. The principal had also recently appointed three new chairs of departments, all of them more academically lively than most members of their departments and ready to take some initiative to get the department involved with new ideas.

The principal's efforts to support the quality of instruction, then, were mostly exerted through support of individual teachers and through delegation to active chairpersons. These ran against the current in Pinehill in subtle ways and seemed to be the only part of his efforts that did. That the community, through its budgeting priorities, did not support a concern for more than routine curricular effort was evident in the limited budget for books and extra supplies. The faculty had for the most part come to accept this. Several teachers, however, who went beyond their required duties to develop a new course or to learn new techniques or pedagogy, spoke with real bitterness of the principal's denying them the small amounts of money they requested for these efforts.

Teachers' Shared Perspectives—Schoolwide

Teachers at Pinehill universally assumed that adults define the content of what students are to learn. Curricular aims were always spoken of in terms of information to be acquired and skills to be learned. The few teachers who also spoke of awakening sensitivities or stimulating awareness of events in the larger world assumed that those sensitivities and awarenesses would be homogeneous. No teacher talked of nurturing differing perspectives or encouraging diverse points of view.

All teachers directly or indirectly expressed a desire to teach obedience and hard work as values. Despite students' negotiation of free time in class, teachers were greatly concerned that all students turn in all work. Several had elaborate systems so that absent students would be able to make up work with as little disruption of a class as possible. Others spent considerable class time with students needing to make up work. Some of the teachers spoke explicitly of their desire to teach obedience and responsible work habits. Asked what were the most important things that students needed to know from his courses, one teacher who held this perspective to the extreme said,

Attitudes. Forget about content, because they're going to forget it fifteen minutes after June 10th. They're going to forget 90% of it, anyways. . . .

First of all, I think the attitude towards authority is important—the fact that they are going to always have someone in authority, and they have to learn to respect it. And if they don't respect it, they're going to get themselves in trouble.

Most teachers did not make statements as extreme as this; however, several implied that they did not expect students to find their subjects interesting, and that they did not find the material they were teaching very interesting themselves. Still, most expected students to feel a duty to be obedient and diligent and were morally angered when they were not. Students did not share teachers' beliefs that hard work and obedience are moral duties, however. Most were neither eager to learn the material nor willing to learn in the belief that either knowing it or having good grades would benefit them later. They expressed their distance from academic pursuits in a number of ways, for the most part short of active rebellion. To elicit cooperation, teachers used authority, occasional coercion, and negotiation in which they reduced demands for time on task and difficulty of assignments in return for a measure of academic effort.

Many teachers described relationships among the faculty as supportive, as characterized by friendliness and camaraderie. For those with the longest tenure, that camaraderie had been nurtured in the earliest years when the school was small and the faculty all came to athletic events and centered a common social life around the school. There still was an annual faculty party that many teachers referred to with pleasure. Most had worked together over 10 or 20 years in close quarters, despite some significant differences on some issues. Forced intimacy made cordiality important and, at least on the surface, they did get along pleasantly.

There were some teachers who seemed to be marginal to that camaraderie, however, among them those who were extremely enthusiastic about their subjects and who tried hard to infect their students with their enthusiasm, sometimes successfully. Though their backgrounds were like those of other teachers, they had found their college experience and later experiences with continuing education to be absorbing, exciting, and liberating. They had some difficulty in bringing their students with them, especially those who were not in high tracks, and especially boys, but they succeeded with some and persisted. They paid a price in isolation from their peers, though the principal supported them in most things.

They found aid for their efforts and compensation for their isolation through involvement with groups outside the school. One was deeply involved in the local ecology movement, though it was fading and his social support was disappearing with it. Another had taken a semester off to study at the university in The City and then had become involved with the area writers' project.

Teachers' Shared Perspectives—In Subgroups

Departments. Departments varied a great deal in their cohesiveness and style. The vocational education departments seemed to be solidary, each somewhat separated from the rest of the faculty. With increased academic requirements for graduation and significant failure rates among students, especially ninth graders, students had fewer and fewer elective courses, so these departments had to struggle to maintain their programs. They seemed to form strong internal bonds and, where they appealed to the same sex of student, to feel strong competition with each other. Academic departments were less unified and solidary. Some had little interaction or coordination, while others at least contained pairs and small groups who discussed strategy and coordinated their efforts out of their own initiative or that of a chairperson.

Gender as a basis of solidarity and division. It seemed that the most important, or at least the most visible, subgroups and divisions in the faculty were based on gender. The social life of the faculty within the school was strongly segregated along gender lines, both as to who interacted with whom and as to the content and perspectives expressed in their interactions. The teachers' lounge had one large and two small tables. The men sat at the two small tables, where they played cards or talked about sports. Any mention of students or school affairs seemed to be informally forbidden at these tables.

The large table was the territory of women. Conversation there was sometimes general, in a group that numbered up to 14 when the table was full. This group sometimes broke into separate interactions involving 2 to 4 women. Talk at this table flowed without markers from topic to topic, including fashions, preparation for a wedding of a daughter or niece, illnesses of various friends and relatives, work in college classes, news from the newspapers available in the lounge every day, problems students were having, problems teachers were having with students, and curriculum. Thus, while much of the talk was traditional women's social talk, equivalent to the men's talk about sports, some was job related.

Some of the women teachers said that informal discussion among women teachers was important to getting mutual assistance with problems with students or pedagogy. There were several groups of women, often within a department, who discussed curricular or pedagogical matters on a more regular basis and even developed common approaches to mutually taught courses. A few mixed-gender pairs of teachers cooperated in their work on a shared course or special program.

Although there were strong and weak teachers of both sexes, there were many more men who seemed to have withdrawn their commitment from teaching and to be walking through their classes, while there were more women actively engaged in trying to reach students. The activities of the strongly segregated informal groups based on gender reinforced this difference. At least some of the women were aware of and could articulate these differences. One, a department chairperson, worried aloud in an interview about the future of a promising young man in his first years of teaching; she feared his participation with older men in the card games and conversations of the lounge would lead him to alienation and lack of effort.

A number of patterns we observed—complemented by the literature on working-class values, family, and work—offered a partial explanation for the men's greater withdrawal from teaching. We saw a great deal of evidence that both sexes accepted gender segregation and embraced very traditional definitions of sex roles. Several of the men said explicitly in their interviews that they did not like to talk about their work, that it was a relief to go to the lounge to play cards or talk sports, and that their friendships with other men outside of school centered around common interests in golf, hunting, and fishing. Two said that they refused to talk about their work to their wives, even though one wife was angered by this silence (cf. Komarovsky, 1962; Rubin, 1976). For these men, work was a duty, something that could be tolerable or even enjoyable from time to time, but still a necessary burden that one laid down as soon as possible. Even though several of the women were single and had to support themselves, for many work seemed to be an expression, a challenge, as well as a way to earn their bread. Again, this attitude seems to be typical of blue-collar women, in contrast to their husbands (Rubin, 1976).

The experiences of the men and women in the classroom were probably more central to their differences. The men who were the most withdrawn from their work and said most vehemently that they did not like to talk about it had a very negative view of the students, which seemed to be stronger than the women's and seemed exaggerated to us. Two of the eight teachers we followed all day were particularly expressive on this point. They told us repeatedly during the day, as well as in formal interviews, that the students had lost all interest in learning and all respect for adults. For example, one said,

It's their attitude. I was just talking to a girl. She couldn't understand why she failed. . . . She's typical of many of the students
here, at least 30, 40%. I would be explaining something to them up
in front of the class and she would be turning around talking to
her friend about her date last night. When I'd say, "OK, Sharon,
pay attention," she'd turn around and in effect say, "Don't bother
me with your dumb-assed education bit; I'm more interested in
what happened last night." And that's the attitude. . . .

The low levels [students in lower-track classes] . . . have the
attitude that, "Well, he's an adult. What the hell does he know?"
Why should they [pay attention], because they probably go home
at night and the old lady's telling the kid to get lost because she's
shacking up with some other guy. And the kid doesn't know up
from down. So no one listens to her. Why the hell should she listen
to her mother, or you, the teacher?

Another teacher said he had learned early in his teaching career not
to try too hard to teach content:

I tried to be content oriented. And it doesn't work. . . . You get
out of college and you're so full of useless knowledge. I mean,
you've got tons of useless knowledge that these kids don't give one
damn bit about. So, "Oh boy, I'm really going to teach them this
[subject]. I'm really going to pound this [subject] into them."
Until, all of a sudden, 5 minutes later all the heads are banging
down, and then you wake the kid up and then he harasses you,
and you harass him. And you wind up in all kinds of bad shit. And
I've [said], "Hey, hold it, these kids don't want this stuff."

Both of these men seemed to us to have given up serious efforts to
teach, though one still taught some reasonably interesting material for 15
or 20 minutes in a class period while our observer spent the day with him.
The other showed what he himself called a "boring filmstrip" and engaged the students in minimal recitation about it.

Both these and other male teachers complained that students were
absent so much it was impossible to develop continuity in class. Women
complained about this, too, but mostly in the lowest-track classes. Men
complained more broadly, as in the following:

Our absentee rate is just incredible. . . . If you opened up my
gradebook and you looked at the "a" of kids who are absent, then,

you know, out of a class of 25 kids, the page is just nothing but
"a" all over.

Two teachers showed us gradebooks indicating that, in a middle-
track class, two or three students would miss 1 to 2 days a week, and two
or three others would miss five to ten classes in a 9-week marking period.
While such rates of absence constitute a serious inconvenience and annoyance for teachers, the page was far from "a" all over. When I asked if
some students might not be sick a good deal, they dismissed that as an
excuse for absence. It seemed that students' absence was not just a
technical and logistical burden but a symbolic statement. These teachers
understood students' absence as their way of expressing the low value
they placed on the class and, by inference, on the teacher's efforts.
Because it was so insulting, moderate rates were experienced as rampant
absence.

The Pinehill men experienced a challenge to their claim to classroom
authority as a threat to their status as worthy adult males. At Pinehill,
where the content of what was taught was for the most part traditionally
defined and not subject to debate, these teachers' authority was more like
that of a traditional father than like that of an expert. They expected
students to do as they were told because the teacher was the teacher, the
adult in charge, not because the teacher justified directives on the basis of
expertise in the subject, which he could explicate if asked. When students
expressively ignored these teachers through absence or through chatter
during class, the teachers perceived this behavior as a rejection of their
claim to authority as an adult, as a respected person.

Such a rejection was a serious personal insult. It was especially
serious in the context of a blue-collar world where fathers were often still
expected to wield unquestioned control over their wives and children, an
expectation that had been the norm when these teachers were boys and
young men. These teachers talked about the moral depravity of students
in terms of historical change, especially of the loss of habits of diligence
and respect for adults and society. One may question, though, whether
the past they remembered was more mythic than real, a matter of
precept rather than practice, even in their youth (Rubin, 1976).

For women teaching at Pinehill, such a questioning of their authority
was less threatening. It was far from pleasant or convenient, and it was a
challenge to their competence as teachers and perhaps to their status as
adults, but not to them as women. In general, blue-collar mothers do not
expect their word to be law, especially with teenaged boys who are
beginning to assert their male ascendancy. Successfully dictating limits to
behavior is more a father's than a mother's responsibility, in their eyes

(Kohn, 1977). Women temper their directives; they not only command but discuss, persuade, and cajole. The women teachers at Pinehill were often angered or annoyed by students' unwillingness to be cooperative, attentive, or diligent, but they saw this behavior not as moral depravity but as something that could potentially be changed by their efforts. Consequently, they made more active, varied, and persistent efforts to teach and to control students' behavior than did the men, and as a group they were much more successful in getting students to pay attention and do their work. Their experiences were then less frustrating than the men's, and they had all the more reason to view the students less negatively and to persist more actively in teaching them.

There was one more way in which authority was important to the teachers' common perspective at Pinehill. Some teachers, especially the most alienated men but also some women, were critical of Mr. Taylor for not disciplining other teachers who they said failed to abide by various rules (e.g., leaving early or not following prescribed curriculum). Many teachers also looked to the principal to provide more leadership in giving them a clearer, more articulated curriculum. As believers in authority and hierarchy, they saw him as responsible for both providing curricular initiative and enforcing adherence to curriculum guides.

While they believed in strong authority, in practice they wanted it exerted over other people, while they themselves would not accept it. Two women told us that, on the rare occasions when Mr. Taylor held faculty meetings, some teachers were not politely attentive but engaged in whispered side conversations—rather like their students. Furthermore, when a new superintendent was hired with a mandate from the board to discipline or build cases against weak teachers, even though he concentrated most of his efforts on other buildings, the high school faculty were indignant over his repeated observation of some teachers and his reprimands for such things as leaving early. This administrator was engaging in the enforcement that teachers said they wanted, but, in practice, they considered it harassment.

Comparison with Other Middle-SES Schools

Our other predominantly blue-collar public school, Quincy, was located in a small industrial city a short way from The City, but in the same state. St. Theresa's, a private Catholic school serving a mostly blue-collar clientele, was close to an industrial area inside The City. In both contexts, economic opportunities for students were declining. Also at both, parents and the community expected students to earn credentials and to follow rules. They made few inquiries about curriculum and few

efforts to intervene in school practice on behalf of their children. They
also provided only modest financial resources. As at Pinehill, many students were uninterested in the subject matter they were taught, unim-
pressed with the prerogatives of the role of teacher, and expressive of
their distance from the role of student through various kinds of inattention, badgering of teachers, and public displays of affection with the
opposite sex in crowded halls.

At St. Theresa's, very small size and a division of responsibilities
between two figures made it difficult to compare the principal's relationship with faculty to that at the two public schools. At Quincy, the
principal, who was nearing retirement, took a laissez-faire approach to
many issues. As at Pinehill, many teachers argued that he should be more
active and should enforce more standards for teachers.

Teachers' characterization of students' reluctance to learn and behave with desired civility varied between schools. Teachers at St. Theresa's were a diverse group brought together by a religious mission, and
they blamed students' inattention and sporadic incivility on a shift in the
origins of the student body over a period of years and on the increasing
family problems with which students had to cope. At Quincy, where
most teachers had working-class families and associates, students' inadequacies were construed in terms of "some students who don't want to be
here," without whom teachers thought both they and other students
could function more constructively. At Quincy there also was talk of
"being realistic." The teachers argued that most students would not go to
college, even if they expressed a desire to do so; therefore teachers
thought they should give them the kinds of practical knowledge useful to
workers in local factories. In this context, it is important to note that
Quincy was part of a district desegregation plan and was more racially
and socially diverse than Pinehill. Some of these despairing comments by
the overwhelmingly white staff appeared to have had special reference
to black students, though that was never made fully explicit.

At these schools, like Pinehill, some teachers became frustrated and
withdrawn, while others persevered and drew some diligence and interest from students. The division lay less clearly along gender lines in these
other schools, though it was still somewhat correlated with gender. Some
departments had strong influences that overcame gender differences. In
the teachers' lounge at Quincy, the other public school, there was also a
continuing, all-male card game where talk of work was banned. But the
other group that met there and talked of many things included a minority
of men as well as a majority of women. Also, teachers at Quincy who
were fired up with enthusiasm for their teaching—including one whole

academic department—were more admired than isolated. Most teachers at Quincy were conscientious in presenting material in class but seemed distanced from the effort and the students. They appeared not to expect much of what they taught to be learned or to engage students.

Three lessons seem to stand out especially vividly from these schools, providing fuel for further exploration. First, it seems that blue-collar and lower-income white-collar communities are rapidly changing, so that their young people see little practical gain from schooling. Such students try to maintain their dignity as budding adults by resisting school staff in ways differing only in degree from the more open rejection of people in much more polarized situations. (See Ogbu, 1978, for discussion of this phenomenon among members of an excluded minority, and Willis, 1977, among the English working class.) The recent reports of alienation of up to 70% of students, summarized by Sedlak and his colleagues (Sedlak, Wheeler, Pullin, & Cusick, 1986), need to be considered in this light. As the schools affect the economy, so the economy has effects on the schools.

Second, we need to think about the effects of this alienation of students on the morale of teachers. Many teachers see obedience and diligence as virtues for their own sake, so students' attempts to distance themselves from the student role appear immoral. Such apparent immorality makes teachers inclined to reject students, rather than to want to work to reengage them in the academic task. Furthermore, many teachers, perhaps especially those who share a working-class perspective, perceive their relations with students in terms of authority based on the teacher's position, rather than on expertise. The teacher's role is thus perceived more as that of an adult relating to children rather than as that of an expert working with clients.[4] Students' rejection of teachers' efforts will not only make their work harder and more frustrating, throwing doubt upon their competence as teachers, but it will also call into question their very claim to adulthood and their worth as persons and, for men, their manhood as well.

Third, it seems that, as both of the first two conditions lower teachers' morale, teachers are likely to withdraw from collegial contact and discussion as well as from students. They may also limit their effort; only the most dedicated and successful teachers at Pinehill and Quincy took much work home or even worked during preparation hours. Furthermore, teachers with these perspectives and experiences may emphasize the hierarchical responsibility of the principal for all school functioning, including curriculum, and then rebel if a principal or other administrator actually uses hierarchical constraint.

CHARLES R. DREW HIGH SCHOOL

The Community

Charles R. Drew High School serves a very poor area of The Metropolis, one of the half dozen largest cities of the country, in a different state from The City. The population of the area in which Drew is located quickly turned from white to black in the early 1960s. It is now part of a solidly black portion of The Metropolis that is far larger than Drew's attendance boundaries.

Because Drew serves a neighborhood in a diverse city, we were not able to get the kinds of data on education, occupation, and income that we obtained for the suburbs of The City. It is safe to say, however, that Drew's neighborhood is one of classic urban poverty. A drive through the area reveals many boarded-up windows, dusty streets, and aging buildings that speak of low incomes. Free lunch is served to 44% of the students at the school. In a state summary of statistics about the school, 60% of students are listed as "low income," compared to 45% for The Metropolis and 24% for the state. (Figures for the Cherry Glen and Pinehill districts, which may not be calculated in the same way, are 2% and 4%, respectively.) While we were at the school, we heard of ills commonly associated with urban poverty: Welfare dependency, early pregnancy, family crises of health or violence, and house fires. A drug dealership that had been operating in an empty building across the street had been broken up the previous year. Gang members attended the school, and gang signs were visible in graffiti on the walls, though everyone agreed that the gangs were not active within the school. Although the school building and its parking lot were considered safe, teachers avoided dismissing students from activities so late that they would have to go home in the dark, because they feared for their safety.

Several teachers told us that students could fill all their practical needs within the extended neighborhood in which they lived. Many literally never ventured beyond its borders. Several of the teachers said that one of their major aims was to broaden students' horizons so that they would roam farther afield in the city, and, more important, become aware of cultural and economic opportunities that were neither available nor visible within the boundaries of the neighborhood. The community also had a self-sufficient character, as expressed in its broad-based network of personal acquaintances and its reliance on personal ties to spread news and to help with the tasks of daily living.

Drew had a solidly black administration, and three-quarters of the teachers were black. Black staff members talked about "the community" as a cohesive, coherent, and stable group. We heard from many teachers how Mr. Crawford, the assistant principal in charge of discipline, had extensive ties in the community and had taught the parents of many students and the grandparents of a few. While families might change addresses frequently, many stayed in the neighborhood long enough to allow three generations to attend the same high school.

In striking contrast, some white teachers told us it was impossible to get any support from parents or even to find them because they moved so frequently that their phone numbers were never current. Since this is the more common account from school personnel in such areas, we realized that the black staff and those whites who had learned from them were familiar with community patterns that were not evident to outsiders. They could trace families through the word-of-mouth network. Many black and a few white teachers told us about forging cooperative relationships with the parents of their students, especially their homeroom students, whom a teacher would keep for 4 years. In contrast, the white teachers who could not find parents also complained that parents would not come to school to pick up report cards or to have conferences, and that they were uninterested in their children's education. The community was experienced very differently by teachers, depending upon how wise they were to its ways.

Drew's staff had to be responsive also to a "community" that stretched beyond its neighborhood and the parents of its students. Drew's surrounding community was a much more complex and interconnected entity than those at the two suburban schools discussed so far. All the schools in our study had to be responsive to public opinion and a bureaucratic apparatus in the school district, as well as to pressures from their neighborhood and from parents. At suburban schools in districts with one or two high schools, however, these groups were nearly coextensive, while at Drew they were emphatically not. Drew was under the control of a school board and school administration that functioned as a single unit in serving a city of several million. Although the city is becoming poor and minority, it includes representatives of many classes and races. Drew as an individual school had to answer to the scrutiny of a board and administration that had little contact, and often little in common, with its students' parents.

The community of The Metropolis could also take the form of citizens' groups that included persons living in the suburbs who wanted to improve the quality of the city labor force. A citizens' group published a report highly critical of city schools in poor areas, just as we were finishing our stay at Drew. The school administrators were girding themselves for one more in a long series of skirmishes with such groups.

Because The Metropolis is such a large city, its schools are often discussed in the national press. We became part of a stream of visitors concerned about urban education beyond The Metropolis who pass through the school and form part of the community that its staff must treat as environment or audience. At Drew, unlike most of our schools, we initiated contact for the research through the central office; we were assigned to Drew by a central office official. It seemed likely that Drew got more such visits than other schools. While it could not be called a showplace school, in a district that also contained magnet and specialized schools, Drew provided an example of an "ordinary" neighborhood school where positive efforts were being made with some effect.

From the school's point of view, the complexity of the community is also reflected through the huge bureaucracy of the central office and the equally large teachers' union, which bargains conditions for all schools in the city. The principal at Drew had much less control over hiring, materials, and maintenance of equipment than did those at the suburban schools.

The Students

The students at Drew were not only considerably poorer but considerably less academically skilled than those at Pinehill or Cherry Glen. When standardized tests were administered to tenth graders, after some dropping out had already occurred, only 3% scored in the top quartile, while 58% scored in the lowest quartile. There were 566 freshmen, 779 sophomores, but only 208 seniors. The large number of sophomores reflects a pool of third-year students without sufficient credits to be promoted to junior status. The principal estimated that 57% of students drop out.

The absence rate at Drew was noticeable. Especially in classes for freshmen and sophomores, the number of students in the room might be half the number on the roll for the class. Even in classes for juniors and seniors, five or six students might be missing in each class. Teachers told us of students who were proud of missing only one day a week of class.

Students were as tardy as they were truant. There was a steady trickle of students arriving from 5 to 10 minutes after the bell rang, and some students arrived up to 20 minutes late, in a 40-minute period. Despite the presence of supervising teachers and security guards in the halls, there was constant traffic during class hours, especially during the first 20 minutes of the day, while students could still arrive late to class without a school-level penalty. After that, students in the halls without a pass were supposed to be "swept" into a special study hall. With so many students out of class, it was difficult for supervising adults to herd stragglers to where they should be, or to punish students for violation of rules about promptness with enough sting to make an impression (cf. Metz, 1978).

Despite these problems, Drew was far from a disorderly school in the sense of tension or conflict. That it was not disorderly was something of an accomplishment, given the conditions fostering disorder that were present. There were some volatile students in the school, and the open and hidden spaces of its architecture provided many opportunities for individual or collective conflict. The lockers were all in one crowded space where jostling could easily spark off tempers. Our team concerned with administrators saw the assistant principals deal with one student altercation that drew a crowd and with some intense conflicts between individual students. Partly because the assistant principals and security guards were efficient in getting to trouble spots quickly and effective in dealing with the offenders, these problems were defused quickly without much impact on the rest of the students.

In the classrooms and halls, relations between and among adults and students were pleasant and courteous almost all of the time. While there were graffiti on the walls of the few unlocked bathrooms and signs of graffiti washed off or painted over in stairwells and even classrooms, their messages were for the most part not hostile. The school was considered a safe environment by all the teachers with whom the subject arose in our conversations. Even as strangers, all of us white, we felt courteously welcomed by those around us. Students engaged us in friendly conversation after classes more often here than in most other schools.

Despite the difficulties Drew students had in playing the traditional student role, even during our brief visit, with its focus on the teachers, we noted some strengths in these students that are rarely mentioned in the media's discussions of such schools. While the written work we saw confirmed that students had weak writing skills, we were impressed that many of their oral comments, especially in literature and history classes, seemed insightful and certainly more sophisticated and more competent than their written work. We saw and heard some very good aesthetic productions from students in advanced art and music classes.

Teachers' Backgrounds

The teachers at Drew were a more diverse group than those at Cherry Glen and Pinehill. They differed not only in class and gender but in race and regional origin. Furthermore, they had moved among schools far more than teachers at the other two schools; that movement reflected both voluntary and involuntary transfers among district schools. There were also teachers who had been laid off or had come in conflict with administrators in shrinking suburban systems.

Based on a visual census of the teachers at the faculty meeting we attended, we calculated that the faculty was about three quarters black and half black women. Since many of the whites were women also, the faculty was dominated by blacks and women. Our sample of eight teachers on whom we obtained relatively full background data was constructed to be roughly representative of the faculty. Five were women and three were men; five were black and three were white. Although three had less than 5 years of experience at Drew, all had at least 10 years of experience as teachers, and most well over 20. Our sample may have been somewhat older than the faculty as a whole.

Only three of the eight teachers had grown up in The Metropolis. Of the five black teachers, four had grown up in the South, and though one had gone to college in The Metropolis, all had gone to historically or predominantly black colleges, some of national stature. Two of the white teachers had gone to private universities with some national reputation, while the third had gone to a local teachers' college no longer in existence.

All of the eight teachers had some graduate work; five had master's degrees, mostly from local institutions emphasizing teacher training. Those asked about their associates (all but two) reported that most siblings and friends were in occupations requiring a college education or more. Some seemed to include both college- and noncollege-educated associates in their circles. The group seemed more highly educated and more oriented to the middle class than the teachers at Pinehill. There was some class variation in both racial groups, though overall perhaps the blacks had more educated lifestyles than the whites. Four of the eight teachers moonlighted or worked in the summer, but their work was related to their teaching; it consisted mostly in teaching summer school for the public schools or night or summer classes at local 2-year and 4-year colleges. Those not engaged in extra work spent their summers in study, leisure, or travel.

These teachers' ties to the school did not overlap their personal lives very much. Most of the black teachers lived in the same section of the city, but at some distance from the school; they were not neighbors, but simply lived in the same general region of the city. The white teachers and one black teacher lived in suburbs on the same side of the city as the school. Thus, teachers' residence did not create close ties to one another or to the school's neighborhood. Only one had out-of-school friendships with a small group of teachers from the school, and one other associated mostly with teachers from elsewhere.

The Principal

The principal of Drew, Dr. Catherine Thayer, was a sophisticated black woman active on several national advisory committees concerned with secondary education. She had to accommodate the many constituencies that made up the school's "community," as she directed its efforts. She seemed responsive to all of them, with the result that the tensions and inconsistencies among their expectations became part of the life of the school. There were three main elements to her initiatives directed toward students. One was an attempt to accommodate the local culture enough to get and keep the students involved in the school enterprise. A second was an attempt to accommodate metropolitan and national expectations in strengthening the traditional academic requirements and curriculum, at the expense of vocational education. A third was the introduction of a series of nationally visible innovations. The first two had the most impact on the school. They expressed—and reinforced—a tension that was central in the life of the school.

Dr. Thayer clearly had both empathy for and knowledge of the ways of the community immediately surrounding the school. One of her initiatives for ninth graders consisted of meetings with them that she called "chapel." None fell on a day when we were observing in the school, but as she described them they were secular inspirational and hortatory addresses, in the style of church services with which most students would be familiar.

Much of her initiative for all grades during the year we visited centered around keeping students in class or getting them back in once they started cutting. Dr. Thayer set a policy that tardy students must be accepted by teachers during the first 20 minutes of class. Her reasoning was that students who miss classwork or tests because of tardiness will fall behind, get poor grades and get discouraged. She thought that much of students' cutting of individual classes was the result of their giving up on a class in which they had already become lost or gotten poor grades. Starting in the year of the study, freshmen were to receive a P, for "pending," in any class in which their grade was D or F. They had until the end of summer school before their sophomore year to make up work so that the grades could be C or better, before the P would be changed into the original D or F. Again, the logic of this strategy was to keep students from becoming so discouraged with the transition to high school that they gave up on particular courses or on school altogether.

While Dr. Thayer adjusted to local realities and to the characteristics of the students in these ways, she also kept an eye on the expectations of the larger metropolitan area and the nation. First-year teachers said she asked them to make 80% a requirement for a passing grade. She instituted graduation requirements higher than those for the system as a whole. Students had to take 4 years of English, 4 of mathematics, 4 of science, and 3 of social studies. Starting with the class of 1988, 20 credits were required for graduation, up from 18. A year of art and a year of music, as well as 2 years of physical education were also required, leaving students with just one other elective credit within the minimum 20 credits. With a nine-period day, those who wished to take more courses could. (Many students had double periods of academic courses, however, in freshman remedial courses and in more advanced courses where they might take, for example, "algebra with support." "Support" was an extra period of class for those who needed help.) As a consequence of these requirements, the vocational areas of the curriculum were losing staff and courses.

Not only did students take a heavy load of academic courses, those courses had demanding descriptions. Students moved from unified science to biology, chemistry, and physics. The courses in earth sciences and ecology—with which weaker students at Cherry Glen, Pinehill, and several other schools met science requirements—were not available. Furthermore, very few subjects were tracked, though there were remedial and support classes for Grades 9 and 10 and a few honors sections. The English curriculum moved from ninth-grade English to American literature, British literature, and world literature, rather than to diversified electives. British literature used a text we saw at other schools with far more skilled student bodies, as did American history. In world literature, students read seven major works during the year, including Sophocles's *Oedipus*, Dante's *Inferno*, Shakespeare's *Hamlet*, and Huxley's *Brave New World*.

This demanding curriculum was part of the principal's argument that Drew's students were inherently as capable as students anywhere, but they simply lacked background and confidence and so needed extra assistance and perhaps extra time to complete a high school program as challenging as any. Dr. Thayer, with the cooperation of most faculty, set the formal sights at Drew for the whole student body higher than those at Pinehill, where such work was expected only of high-track students.

Consequently, the principal's position was somewhat paradoxical. She tolerated tardiness and cutting of classes and initial low grades, in an attempt not to discourage students who were alienated from school or had weak skills and were unused, unable, or unwilling to abide by expectations for prompt and regular attendance. She adjusted to the immediate community in so doing. But at the same time, she required and fostered an extremely demanding formal curriculum, more difficult than most students at Pinehill were willing to undertake. She wanted students to leave high school with a record as impressive as that which students took away from the affluent suburbs of this large, heavily stratified metropolitan area. In setting both policies simultaneously, she reflected the contradictory pressures that play upon schools like Drew.

These pressures were directly visible in classes for juniors and seniors. We saw teachers working with students on the basic mechanics of writing a business letter, in the same course where they had just read Huxley's *Brave New World*. We saw students in physics—who had taken but not necessarily passed biology and chemistry and who might not yet have reached trigonometry—being taught how to work with exponents. The teacher we observed said she hoped to have them attain a really good grasp of mechanics by the end of the year, but they might not progress much beyond that point, one reached by Christmas in physics courses we visited at other schools. With the principal's strong encouragement, then, Drew teachers of advanced courses tried to deal with contradictory community expectations, both by working with students on skills they should have acquired earlier and by teaching classic advanced material. This strategy seemed to be a compromise between meeting students' distinctive academic needs and following a pattern that city pressure groups and the teachers themselves understood to be the stuff of a "real high school" (Metz, in press).

While the principals of the suburban districts had some role in the hiring of teachers, principals in The Metropolis were supposed to accept whatever new or transfer teachers the district personnel department sent them. In our initial meeting, Dr. Thayer talked at length about how she tried to regain some control over recruitment, despite her formal obligations. In a city run for decades by machine politics, bureaucratic patterns were tentatively established. Dr. Thayer knew how to operate in this system. She spoke of engaging in practices that were not part of formal procedure, such as simply sending a teacher back to the central personnel office with a firm refusal to accept him or her, even though she had no right to do so. She also took formal steps to have teachers transferred or dismissed. We observed and heard about actions she took that rewarded and punished individuals, in ways designed to encourage those who could help with the school's work as she saw it and to induce those who could not to take advantage of the school system's voluntary transfer program.

Teachers' Shared Perspectives—Schoolwide

The faculty at Drew was large, diverse in background, and separated by the architecture of the building and departmental divisions so that many teachers had little contact with each other. While diversity is the major theme in understanding the meanings that motivated these teachers' practice, there were nonetheless some striking commonalities in their perspectives and rhetoric. These attested to the possibility of social-izing even a diverse faculty in some important ways.

The courtesy with which teachers spoke both to and about students was the most striking common feature of the faculty. This pattern did not hold at our other low-income school. Teachers at Drew rarely made sharply critical or demeaning statements about students, even in their absence. They consistently referred to girls as "young ladies," a small linguistic device that signaled a broader courtesy. Their approach to students was not merely civil, but gravely courteous. While, for most teachers, this courtesy apparently stemmed from genuine respect, for others, it seemed more a pragmatic strategy for keeping the peace and the following of an established group norm. The students responded with civility most of the time, and very rarely with hostility.

There clearly was an understanding among adults that students were to be regarded as similar to any other high school students. Teachers spoke about their academic deficiencies or their social problems in spe-cific contexts, for example in talking about their teaching strategies in particular courses or in talking about an individual student's unwilling-ness or inability to concentrate on schoolwork. They did not volunteer characteristics of the student body as academically deficient or sunk in social problems. At least in public discourse, teachers did not speak of students as inherently different from other students, but rather as having particular skill deficits and problems to overcome; hope persisted that with a little more assistance and time they could catch up and perform as well as other students. Still, this position was for some teachers more a public stance than a private belief. While our longer conversations and interviews made it seem that some teachers genuinely saw their students as essentially like all students, with a few incidental difficulties to deal with, others seemed to think it prudent to say little about problems that they thought were fundamental.

Similarly, race was rarely mentioned at the school in any way. In part, that practice reflected the school's being predominantly of one race, so that being black could be assumed except for a relatively small proportion of adults. But it seemed also to be a tacit social agreement, a taboo. It served both to mute potential conflict between races and to bolster the image of students as having relatively easy access to the mainstream. Even though there was some tension and division between teachers of different races, they almost never talked about one another in openly racial terms. We heard no racial epithets during our visit.

At the same time, the curriculum was overwhelmingly oriented to white experience. Except for some short excerpts by black authors in anthologies, the few pieces of literature in the English curriculum that dealt with blacks were written by whites. The last specifically black course, one on Afro-American history, had recently been dropped from the curriculum. Symbolically, the school expunged race as an issue.

Finally, at this school we noted that teachers who were working hard to be successful with the students put a good deal of effort into establishing personal relationships with them. It was visible in their classes, but even more in their talk about their strategies as teachers. Some spoke most of developing close relations with particular promising or difficult students whose potential they were attempting to foster, while others spoke more of their relations with classes as a whole. In either case, it seemed that the students' academic difficulties and consequent lapses into discouragement, their limited acquaintance with academically successful exemplars, and the difficulty of life in the community put them particularly in need of personal support as an aid to turning their energies to academic pursuits.

Teaching at Drew was a difficult, demanding, and discouraging task. It could easily have been a demoralizing one, and was for some teachers. Some started to come late to class, like their students. Some gave students highly routinized, undemanding work. Some improvised their way through the class hour. But many worked extremely hard with their classes and seemed to put much thought and energy into planning their strategy, as well as into daily interactions that would bring reluctant, hesitant, or angry students into the academic enterprise. These different approaches stemmed from varied causes and were only partly explained by the many social divisions that ran through this diverse faculty.

Teachers' Shared Perspectives—In Subgroups

Departments. Because the school was large, departments also were. Most included teachers with diverse backgrounds and orientations. We encountered none that were solidary units, though there were strong cliques within some departments; in one, such a clique was large and dominant. Departments did unify around some tasks and issues, though we also encountered at least three where there were visible group or individual rivalries. Still, departments offered each teacher a wide choice of associates, and most teachers were best acquainted within their departments.

Racial groups. There was some distance and difference between the black and white teachers. The small lunch room for the faculty had three tables. During all three lunch hours, we noticed that groups at each table were predominantly of one race and very often exclusively of one race. The cliques and broad factions that we became aware of in the school also seemed to be of one race or predominantly of one race. These divisions were probably imported from the city where racial succession in housing has traditionally been accomplished through panic selling that transforms the racial composition of neighborhoods within months or even weeks, and where conflict over school desegregation has been going on for two decades. In this context, it probably is most appropriate to stress the lack of visible racial tension among the faculty and the small amount of open criticism of each group by the other.

Although it seemed to us that race made a difference in teachers' relationships with the students, both races were restrained in talking about race and about students' academic deficiencies and social problems. None of the teachers spoke about students with the blunt, directly critical language used by Pinehill's male teachers as they reflected on their work. This restraint was probably born both of the desire not to appear racist or to inflame potential racial tensions in the school and of greater caution with us. In the much more complex and intrusive world that surrounded Drew and that was constructed among its diverse staff, teachers had good reason to be more careful in choosing their words and guarded in what they said than did teachers in Pinehill's homogeneous context. While this caution constituted a methodological problem, it also was in itself informative about the social setting.

Even whites who made statements disparaging black students' skills, willingness to cooperate, and social behavior seemed to restrain their criticisms lest they be labeled racist. Blacks did not want to add to stereotypes by criticizing students, nor did they want to inflame relationships with the outside world by criticizing social structures or practices in elementary schools that a few glancingly referred to as sources of students' problems. The courtesy of the school had elements of southern politeness, but it was also a "veneer of harmony" (Clement, Eisenhart, & Harding, 1979) that smoothed the school's functioning in a situation where conflicts between adults and students, among adults inside the school, and between the school and the outside were always a possibility. Such a veneer keeps relationships smooth, but makes underlying problems less visible.

Some of the white teachers seemed to respond to students in much the way that the Pinehill men had responded to theirs, except that they used far more moderate language to talk about their difficulties and their feelings. One such teacher in our sample of eight had taught for years at a school that was in a white neighborhood near the edge of the city and seemed to have much in common with Pinehill. He had been laid off from there 5 years earlier and had found the loss of his connection to that school a tremendous blow to his personal and professional life. He expressed considerable frustration with the students at Drew, saying they were hard to teach because they lacked diligence, skills, and ambition. He spoke of these qualities as reflecting historical change—as "kids today." But he did not seem to have regarded his students at his old school 5 years earlier in the same way. Some of the other white teachers we interviewed and observed in the classroom also obliquely or directly complained about students' diligence, obedience, and skills, sharply enough to suggest that the teachers considered them to be less than morally worthy, to be persons undeserving of respectable teachers' efforts. These teachers also failed to make energetic efforts in their teaching. Some made very little effort at all, while others were conscientious in fulfilling regular duties but did not go beyond that level. A few disparaged students' efforts or abilities in class, though always in indirect ways, never as a frontal criticism.

Other white teachers took their efforts to teach very seriously and were energetic. Some of them were active in the principal's various innovative programs, and some belonged to supportive white cliques of teachers who put in long hours beyond what was required. These teachers were optimistic about the abilities of at least some of the students. They worked hard to develop students' skills, though one complained bitterly to me in full hearing of his class that students were no longer tracked and his task in an advanced class was therefore impossible. These teachers seemed especially eager to acquaint students with classical culture and to help them gain access to mainstream opportunities.

The majority of black teachers worked hard at their teaching, though there were black teachers who were unskilled with or indifferent to students and who did very little teaching. Most spoke of their students in sympathetic though also frustrated terms. Some, many of whom had spent their early careers in elementary school teaching, were more comforting than demanding, but others were extremely firm task masters. We found the black teachers often were able to use subtle forms of communications to get good attention from their students. More than once we saw a simple raised eyebrow bring a roomful of restless students to full attention.

Black teachers spoke very matter-of-factly with us about students' deficiencies in academic skills and about the personal problems that distracted students from their schoolwork. One aide, a black woman, joined a conversation I was having with a black teacher and soon explicitly expressed the attitude we sensed in many of the black teachers. She said first, with moderate heat, that students now are "lazy," the harshest statement we heard from a black adult. But then she started to talk about the difficulties their families must overcome in finding steady incomes and safe, well-maintained housing, and she finished by telling me that I should "walk awhile in our shoes" before trying to describe or judge the students. The black teachers, even those from much more economically comfortable and secure backgrounds than the students, seemed to be close enough to their students' experience to be able to walk in their shoes, and to believe that most of the students had the potential someday to walk in the teachers' shoes. Most of these black teachers were at least 40; they had been teenagers before the gains of the Civil Rights movement and had good reason to see race, as well as class, as a barrier that students had to overcome. They were willing to offer the students effort and sympathy, even when they made a teacher's work difficult. They were far more patient and persistent in trying to overcome the students' discouragement, distractedness, and noncompliance than the Pinehill men, at least, were with students—also similar to themselves—who presented less severe inattention and uncooperativeness.

Indeed, for many black teachers the work seemed to be a matter of passionate dedication both to individual students and to a larger cause, although they were very restrained in talking about these feelngs. For example, one who had just come to the high school level from elementary teaching spoke with real bitterness, but little concrete detail, of some schools she had been in where administrators and teachers made no serious effort to help students learn. She taught ninth-grade remedial classes with tremendous energy and attention to individual patterns of progress and difficulty. During her homeroom, she spoke quietly and seriously with students, who seemed to be drawing on her personal resources. At the close of her interview, answering questions about her life outside the school, she said she sometimes feared she had short-changed her own children because she went home too tired from helping "these children" to have the energy to be fully responsive to hers.

Other bases for grouping. In the complex world of Drew there were yet more cross-cutting allegiances. There were more women than men in the school, and women seemed to dominate the high-status positions the principal controlled. Some black men commented on this pattern and thought it reflected conscious choice. The principal may indeed have found herself most frequently in close agreement with women, especially black women, and so have appointed them to positions of power. The assistant principals, all black men, also played a larger role than in most schools, however.

There was an old guard of black teachers who had been at the school for a long time, since before it had moved into its current building. They seemed to feel a strong loyalty and obligation to the immediate community of parents. They set less store by the desires of the larger surrounding community and so differed with the principal over some policy issues. For example, they were sympathetic to parents who were concerned about the fading of the vocational education program resulting from standards for graduation that required more academic work. On such issues, neither parents nor old-guard teachers could get a sympathetic hearing from the principal.

These teachers had little regard for actions taken for the sake of public relations in the city as a whole, and they wanted strict discipline within the school. Some looked with a jaundiced eye on the principal's cosmopolitan connections in The Metropolis and beyond. Her enthusiasm for nationally popular innovations drew skeptical responses from them. They also thought that teachers with similarly cosmopolitan connections or ambitions for such connections tended to receive favor. It is possible that this division in part reflected a difference between older teachers of southern origin, who had grown up in a world of ties that crossed class lines within a tightly bounded black community, and younger teachers indigenous to The Metropolis with its recently expanded mainstream opportunities for middle-class blacks. The latter group had little to say about this fault line, however.

The complexity of the community setting offered one advantage to Drew's teachers. The Metropolis contained a wealth of groups concerned with education and a wealth of resources for enriching knowledge of various subjects. Two teachers told us they derived social support and good ideas from their association with other teachers in their subject areas at the school district's meetings of representatives of individual departments from each school. Another teacher was part of a continuing noncredit seminar of teachers in her subject area, sponsored by a local university. Yet another was active in an association of teachers of his subject. A music teacher we interviewed had season tickets to the opera; an English teacher took her students to Shakespearean plays downtown. But the contribution made by these resources depended both on their availability and on the initiative of Drew's teachers.

Comparison with Another Low-SES High School

Our other high school with low SES was Ulysses S. Grant in The City. The City schools had been desegregated under a court order for over 10 years at the time of our study. With a high school population about half white and half black, all but one of the system's high schools were formally desegregated. Blacks, though a minority of the adult population, were gaining political power in The City and were using it to contest what they saw as inattention to their children's needs in City schools. While The City is smaller than The Metropolis, its schools also face complex city, class, and ethnic politics; an entrenched bureaucracy (though in this case without the machine tradition); and a powerful, heavily centralized teachers' union.

Ulysses S. Grant was 65% black, the maximum percentage allowable. It was located in a racially transitional neighborhood that was slowly going black and slipping economically. Most of the students came from the surrounding area, though some were bused in. As at Drew we could not get good data on the economic conditions of the neighborhood. Sixty-five percent of the student body was eligible for free lunch, though only half that many lunches were actually served. Upon entering school, 39% scored in the lowest 23% on standardized tests of reading, so students' skills at entrance were notably stronger than at Drew. It was our impression that these students were better off both economically and academically than Drew's students, though not as well off as Pinehill's. They were more diverse racially, economically, and academically than Drew's students. Grant's student body was less tardy, less often absent, and more conventionally attentive than Drew's, though less compliant with the school in all these respects than Pinehill's. There was more tracking than at Drew, and fewer students took courses such as advanced science and literature.

The teachers were diverse in race, but the vast majority were white. They were more diverse than the faculties of the suburban schools in their geographic background and more diverse than the Pinehill faculty in class background and current lifestyle.

The principal was a white man well into middle age, who had been appointed principal before desegregation of the school. He seemed to feel somewhat beleaguered in the face of central office demands for paper reporting. Record keeping was a priority in this highly bureaucratized city of clean government, and it was growing as a response to rising political demands to increase accountability toward black students. For the most part, the principal passed system demands along to the faculty, unaltered. He told us—perhaps only half seriously—that he was just as glad not to have any say over hiring, since he then did not have to bear responsibility for teachers who did not succeed well in the school. He was far less activist in stance than the Drew administration. The assistant principals, whom the district rotated among schools so that none remained in place very long, were also not activists or very visible to the teachers.

The teachers at Grant felt their sense of pride in teaching threatened by a student body they thought was getting steadily less skilled; they accused a nearby magnet school of skimming off their best potential students. They bolstered their image of themselves as "real teachers" in a "real school," despite students' alienation and weak skills, by raising high a banner of "standards." Through strict grading, they struggled to make their level of certification match that at other schools, even if the general performance of their students seemed not to. When the principal came under district pressures to raise grades, he responded by circulating a list of teachers' grade-point averages to all faculty. His effort backfired, as teachers with high averages—those above 2.0—felt more pressure to lower their grades, even if they were teaching advanced courses, than teachers with lower grade-point averages—in a few cases below 1.0—felt to raise them. These teachers differed from Drew teachers in expressing negative evaluations of the school, the students, and the students' prospects, in both public and private settings.

The black and white teachers led more separated lives here than at Drew, and they were more openly critical of each other. The black teachers were more sanguine about the students and their prospects in life than were the white ones.

Despite a student body that was economically and academically better off, Grant's faculty had lower morale than Drew's overall, and the school environment was less safe. We heard of several minor physical confrontations between students and teachers, in some of which students injured teachers slightly. These confrontations were usually in halls, not classes. Some teachers working with ninth graders told us they did not feel safe in certain parts of the halls of the school at particular times. Though there were fewer graffiti in the school than at Drew, more were obviously gang related and more bragged of physical prowess or were threatening.

The most important lesson to be learned from a comparison of Drew and Grant to the other schools may be that the world surrounding poor city schools is much more complex and full of difficult pressures than that surrounding schools in suburbs. Political conflicts and large, powerful bureaucratic organizations shaped the life of both low-income city schools in crucial ways. At the same time, students' histories brought them to school with fewer academic skills and less positive prior school experiences. While we obtained only a little direct evidence on the point, it appeared that the economic futures that students in these two schools anticipated, as they watched the adults around them, made them feel that little was to be gained from cooperating with the high school or even from obtaining a diploma. At Pinehill, at least the diploma did appear to have worth to students.

Faculties at these schools were also more diverse. They differed in race and had a greater variety of regional, educational, and career backgrounds than the suburban and small-city teachers. Transfer of faculty members among schools complicated faculty relationships, though teachers seemed to move more in The Metropolis than in The City. This diversity, together with the demanding and discouraging character of classroom teaching, seemed to work against cooperation around curriculum among faculty members and cohesiveness in departments. Principals also did not delegate any meaningful participation in governance of the school to these diverse and not always harmonious faculties. At Drew, some teachers were asked to be on policy committees, but these seemed to implement innovations the principal had already chosen, more often than plan them.

Most teachers who had some similarity of background with the students in these low-SES schools seemed to find them easier to teach and cared more about them than did other teachers. Some, but not all, teachers who differed in class and race from students found it very difficult to reach a common ground and were profoundly frustrated and discouraged by working with them.

CONCLUSION

Policy makers must take heed of the differences in schools born of social class, lest they prescribe across-the-board changes for all schools that are based on analysis of the needs or conduct of schools of a single social class. The results of such policies will be frustrating at best and counterproductive at worst. At the same time, it would be equally inappropriate to conclude that social class alone determines the experience of students and teachers in schools and that nothing can be changed, or that schools do not make a difference.

It is clear that class issues get into the schools primarily through community pressures and through the students. The three communities described here had different priorities for their schools' goals and daily practice. All of the school staffs, especially principals, took community priorities seriously. These priorities were visibly a part of each school's life, particularly in the overall policies of each school, but also to a significant degree in classroom teaching.

In the high-SES communities, parents and board members brought confidence, skill, and power to their relations with the schools. Both individually and collectively, parents had a great deal of impact on the schools. The public schools in high-SES communities also gave abundant material resources to their schools. Salaries, supplies, amenities, and professional support were much more easily available in these schools than elsewhere.

The nature of the community/school link was also very different with social class. In this sample, both the high- and middle-SES parents were located in suburban districts, where small size greatly enhances parents' collective and individual control. There are, of course, stable working-class and upper-middle-class neighborhoods within large cities, and differential parental power associated with social class persists within these large systems (Metz, 1986), but it is less easily exercised within the constraints of a single system. The low-SES parents in our study, like most poor families in metropolitan areas, lived in the cities, where their individual and collective control was greatly hampered by the large size of the district, the power of a rule-making central bureaucracy to which access was difficult, and the rules that limit access. In low-SES schools, although parents can have some direct influence, as at Drew, community influence is less a parental prerogative and more one of conflicting social and political coalitions who lobby the central office on various issues. Response to their initiatives is transmitted, and sometimes transformed, through passage down the channels of the bureaucracy and into the schools.

Teachers experience differences in student bodies much more directly than they experience differences in communities. At these high schools, student bodies differed significantly from one another. As a group, students had differing skills, though the difference between Cherry Glen and Pinehill was not enormous. Perhaps more important, especially in the difference between Cherry Glen and Pinehill, students had very different attitudes toward the importance of the subject matter and toward studying. These differences may very well have been based in the different trajectories they pictured their lives following and the different pressures their parents exerted upon them. Even with the limited chances we had to hear Cherry Glen students make spontaneous statements, we heard several conversations in and out of class that indicated their sense that they must be ambitious, and we heard them express consequent anxiety about their futures. Pinehill students, on the other hand, found a lot of ways to express their detachment from schoolwork and their sense that it had little impact on their lives. Cherry Glen students were consequently far more industrious and compliant than were Pinehill students. At Drew, for many students, poor skills made success in high school without intensive assistance almost an impossibility. Discouragement and disaffection from the school's tasks were evident in the behavior and demeanor of many students.

There was, of course, variation in the skills, expected life trajectories, and values of students within each school, despite the differing predominance of certain patterns at each school. Cherry Glen responded to this variation by isolating into a variety of special settings those students whose skills were weaker than average or who showed any serious rebellious tendencies. At the opposite extreme, at Drew, the administration was very reluctant to isolate industrious high achievers in honors tracks, though some honors classes did display differences from others in the direction of high-SES schools. In the middle, at Pinehill, there was the most elaborate tracking system of the three schools. It separated both the most rebellious and least skilled and the most industrious and most able from the majority. These classes also differed in the ways that schools of differing SES do, except that at Pinehill even high-track students, especially boys, expressed some of the distance from and discomfort with serious academic work that pervaded the school.

The differences between Cherry Glen and Maple Heights in particular remind us that social class is not a simple hierarchy. Income in Maple Heights is not significantly higher than in Pinehill, but, with higher education and higher participation in professional and managerial work than in Cherry Glen, Maple Heights parents and children were far more interested in the substance of education than were those in Cherry Glen. They also saw knowledge in a more open-ended light and approached it with a confidence that allowed students to question and even expect to participate in creating it. They were more self-assured, almost patrician, in their approach to education. Social class is thus a multifaceted, constantly reconstructed social entity that is as much process as structure. Full-fledged study of social class must take its complexity and fluidity into account.

It is important to recognize that teachers participate in communities and in kinship and friendship networks that also are part of the social-class system. While teachers have formally similar educational credentials and participate in a single, undifferentiated occupation, they not only come from a range of social-class backgrounds but participate as adults in networks that vary significantly in their social class. We were struck with the differences in attitude, lifestyle, and associates among our teachers. We also found that the suburban and Catholic schools seemed to hire teachers whose current social networks were not far different in social class from those dominant in the school's community. (The teachers from the junior high school in Cherry Glen were an exception to this pattern, and the other teachers were less wealthy than dominant community members.) At the poor city schools, all teachers were at least currently of higher status than parents and children, though some came from poor backgrounds.

Teachers' own class affected their definitions of their work. Teachers who associated with managers and professionals defined their responsibilities more in terms of being sure to do a good job, whatever that required, while those with working-class associates defined their responsibilities more in terms of conscientiously putting in required hours. On the whole, the first group also seemed to give work more priority in their lives and to draw their identity from it more. At the extreme, two highly involved English teachers at different schools who worked long hours outside school blamed their dedication to their work for divorces and felt they were not alone in that experience. Several teachers with working-class orientations spoke of making sure their work did not invade the hours outside school, which they considered belonged to their families.

These differences are somewhat confounded by the association of teachers' social class with that of the students. Teachers who worked with high-SES children received more intrinsic rewards from responsive children, more status from their association with their students, and more logistical and professional support from better-funded schools than did other teachers, just as white-collar professionals on the whole receive more intrinsic and status rewards at work than do blue-collar workers. These perquisites of the job make it intrinsically rewarding and quite possibly more satisfying than family life, while the reverse is true where children are unresponsive, where their social class stigmatizes the teacher, and where there are few tangible or intangible institutional supports for teachers' work. There is some evidence, however, for the independent importance of teachers' class locations in these schools. Some of the upper-middle-class teachers of long tenure at Drew (both white and black) put in long hours and worked hard to build strong personal relationships with students. Similarly, the teachers at Cherry Glen who participated in more nearly working-class networks seemed to commit fewer hours to their work and to find it a less significant part of their lives than did most teachers with upper-middle-class private networks.

Still, teachers' class was not simply determinative. Teachers at Cherry Glen whose personal networks bordered on working-class patterns worked considerably harder and longer than did teachers with working-class networks at Pinehill, and they were more willing to talk about their work to each other. Faculty socialization and administrative pressures interacted with influences from private life. Nor are class background and school socialization the whole story; there were teachers at Pinehill who were willing to face isolation to pursue their excited and committed approaches to their subjects. Most of these teachers sought social support from groups formed around their academic interests, but outside the school.

All of this is complicated yet further by the question of similarity and difference in class (and race) between teachers and students. One would expect that similarity would be helpful to teachers' engagement in work with students. Indeed, at the high-SES schools (especially St. Augustine's and Maple Heights), and at Drew, where the similarity was based on race more than class, it seemed to be so. At Grant, differences of both class and race clearly erected barriers between teachers and students.

But at Pinehill, similarity in class did not seem to help much in the men's relations with students, nor did it at Quincy. As already suggested, it may have been that either generational differences or a tension that has always existed between precept and practice in working-class families made the working-class men at Pinehill unable to deal very constructively with students' rejection of their authority in academic matters. Equally important, it may have been that students and teachers together were alienated from intrinsic interest in the curriculum, a danger that can arise when a school hires a teaching staff whose backgrounds resemble those of its alienated students.

Still, many of the women at Pinehill, and especially the handful of enthusiastic rebels of both sexes, though they had similar backgrounds to the dominant men and to the students, found intrinsic interest and extrinsic usefulness in the subjects they taught and so were able to try to pull students beyond their current cultural perspective, which was antithetical to active cooperation with the school's agenda. These teachers were similar enough to the students to be able to empathize with them and communicate effectively with them, but also had a different understanding of the academic work, toward which they could lead the students. Similarly, many black teachers at Drew understood but did not share their students' perspectives. They also could both enter into and partially alter their students' cultural point of view. To teach students outside the dominant upper-middle-class white group, biculturalism in teachers, not a simple match to students (or a simple missionary attitude) seems to be needed.

Principals stand at the border between the school and community. They are expected to moderate the relations between the two so that they are acceptable to both sides. All of the principals described here both transmitted community pressures, so that they did much to give the schools the characteristics community members wanted them to have, and resisted community pressures, so that they stood as barriers or dikes holding back a flood of community influence.

Principals did not necessarily do this self-consciously. All of the principals seemed to have important points of personal continuity with the communities they served. They were chosen in part because they fit those communities. Indeed, we did thought experiments in which we mentally moved principals from school to school. It was immediately evident that, if a very effective principal were moved to a school in a different kind of community, he or she would at least initially be bewildered and ineffective and regarded very skeptically by both community and teachers.

Still, none of the principals described here simply passed community pressures along to the school. Mr. Coyne at Cherry Glen sought teachers more sophisticated in their understanding of school knowledge than was the community, and he actively protected their curricular autonomy. Dr. Thayer at Drew blended the demands of the diverse communities she had to please in a distinctive way. Even Mr. Taylor at Pinehill quietly supported the academic enthusiasts whom the faculty isolated and many parents and children avoided. There is, however, nothing automatic in this active role of principals in buffering the internal life of the school from the community. The principals at Grant and at Quincy did very little of this.

The faculties of these schools formed collective perspectives and socialized both new recruits and continuing participants into common points of view. At all three schools there were common perspectives in the whole faculty. These arose in part from commonalities in the perspectives of the majority of teachers as they entered the school, sometimes because principals had recruited a particular kind of teacher, and sometimes because the school was attractive to certain kinds of teachers. Principals also articulated certain visions of what the school, its teachers, and its students should be like. They did this with varying clarity and insistence, and their vision took root better in some schools than others.

Teachers also formed common perspectives as their common experiences in the school led them to shared reflection and analysis and so to common strategies that, again, generated common experience. This process might or might not be made explicit. The courtesy with which the majority of Drew faculty treated their students undoubtedly played a part in the generally polite way in which students treated teachers, even though many expressed alienation from school in tardiness, cutting, and failure to pay attention to class or do assigned work. Students' general politeness reinforced teachers' courtesy. But we never heard norms for courtesy explicitly articulated, though we did see teachers' acute discomfort on the few occasions when other adults violated them in dramatic ways.

There were also subgroups in each faculty who shared specific outlooks that differed between groups. Some of these subgroups were formal. Members of departments generally interacted, and in some schools they did so intensively, either because they were thrown together in a common space or, at the high-SES schools and particularly Cherry Glen, because they were supposed to coordinate their curriculum in detail. Departments were thus important loci for social interaction and the formation of common conceptions about teaching, students, and the community.

Departments were cross-cut by unofficial social affinities that brought together informal groups. At Pinehill, gender was important; at Drew, it was race. At both schools, groups homogeneous on those dimensions socialized one another into different perspectives on their work and their relationships with colleagues, students, and parents. Their different perspectives led them to different actions with students that generated experiences that differed between groups and then reinforced their divergent perspectives. The majority of men at Pinehill, and those whites at Drew who did not learn from blacks how to interact with students effectively, had far more negative experiences with students than did the majority of Pinehill's women or most of Drew's blacks and some whites who learned from them.

These differing subgroups within the schools overlapped, and their perspectives competed. At Quincy, departments with strongly academic orientations were more effective than gender-based friendship groups in shaping the attitudes of their male members. At Cherry Glen, the continuing majority of teachers were slowly socializing the newcomers from the junior high school, but according to some of our interviewees were also taking on some elements of perspectives this large block of newcomers had brought with them. Blacks at Drew defined much of the general perspective of the faculty, but there was significant disagreement among subgroups of blacks, and some whites seemingly accepted dominant black perspectives for public expression but not private allegiance.

This account of the ways in which social class found its way into these schools has been designed to provide some sense of the impact of class upon the lived experience of teachers. It suggests that, while social class has a strong effect on daily life inside schools, it is not a simple, unitary, determining force. Rather, individuals perceive themselves as living within constraints that a sociologist would call those of class position, though participants often do not think about them in terms of either class or social structure. Individuals in similar structural positions have similar experiences and often influence one another, through their shared cultural interpretations of those experiences, to respond with similar attitudes and feelings to those events. However, as Connell and his colleagues (1982) have argued so eloquently, and as is very evident in the schools we have described, these class positions are not simply determinative of either attitude or action. Every school will have students, teachers, and administrators who bring a somewhat distinctive mix of class (and racial and gender) perspectives to the social life inside a school building. While class is a crucial element in constituting the life of every school, it never determines that life in any simple or complete sense.

POLICY IMPLICATIONS

As noted earlier, the educational reform movement has neglected the role of social class in schooling and has regarded all schools as essentially alike, subject to improvement through a single set of reforms, though in some versions those reforms are expected to consist of granting considerably increased autonomy to school staffs. But the argument advanced in this chapter suggests that the formal, structural standardization that characterizes American high schools is extremely deceptive. Schools are about meaning, and meaning is highly variable among American high schools. The meaning of school is shaped by expectations for students on the part of parents and teachers that are deeply colored by parents' social class. Students' own assessment of their life chances and so of the usefulness of school are similarly colored by their parents' status. By the ninth grade, these influences have also had a hand in creating differences in students' academic skills.

Teaching is an interactive endeavor; it requires making connection with students. If their attitudes and skills vary substantially, so must the content and style of teachers' work with them. Accordingly, the very nature of teachers' work varies with their students and so with the social class of the communities from which students come, even when teachers' own training or initial skills are similar.

The social and academic status of students attaches itself to their teachers. Teachers who work at schools of differing social class are perceived by their peers in both their professional and private lives as thereby placed in a social and academic hierarchy. Teachers at Cherry Glen basked in the reflected glory of the community and students they served. Pinehill teachers both complained to us of the limited skills and commitment of their students and comforted themselves by saying that of course things were far worse in The City. A few teachers at Drew and most at Grant complained of dealing with conditions that persons they knew in their private lives would find unimaginable. These teachers clearly felt demeaned by their association with their students.

At the low-SES schools, and to some extent at the working-class schools, the only teachers to escape the insidious drain of low status upon their morale were those who thought about their work as service, either in conveying an intellectual tradition they found exciting, or in assisting young people to whom they were for some reason committed, despite their low rank and sometimes resistant behavior.

Those concerned with educational reform are unlikely to succeed if they take restructuring teachers' roles as the crucial point of leverage in schools but leave their segregation by social class (and race) untouched. While the teachers in our schools certainly did have individual and collective effects on their students, and while the structure of their roles had effects on them, both their practice and the shape of their roles were importantly affected by the students. It seemed no accident that the schools with the most able and eager students were also the best at fostering patterns toward which reformers would like all schools to move, such as increased collegial discussion among teachers and increased roles for them in school governance. Able and eager students seemed to facilitate the adoption of expanded responsibilities and collegiality among teachers, while less-willing and less-able students seemed to dampen such efforts.

Social class differences such as those described in this chapter must be considered and publicly discussed as we think about how effectively to reform our schools. To the degree that the educational reform movement sets aside class differences as unimportant, it brackets and overlooks one of the major influences on schools. It consequently relies for all of its impact on attempting to change patterns that exert much weaker influence. To ignore the most forceful influences in a situation is rarely a prescription for effective reform. Reformers avoid the topic partly because of its extreme political sensitivity, a problem that is less pressing for academic sociologists and anthropologists, who are less subject to political pressure because they have less practical impact. Nonetheless, social-class differences are politically volatile in part precisely because class privilege and deprivation is so tightly entwined with schooling—and thus with meaningful educational reform.

I have stressed the ways in which social class generates differing perspectives related to education at each class level. If one steps further back, one can see that the simple fact of a social class hierarchy had very strong effects on teachers' work, across the board. For the society, education in general, and high school in particular, is a crucial mechanism for allocating new members to slots in higher education and the workforce. Our society gives high schools major responsibility for sorting students into ranked categories that play the most important role in determining their access to further education or the job market. Consequently, for individuals, education plays a central role in determining their life chances. The overarching intimate tie between schooling and the re-creation of an occupational and economic hierarchy in each new genera-tion has an overwhelming impact on daily school experience, for teachers and students together.

Ranking individuals and allocating them to adult roles has very little to do with education, defined in a philosophical sense. But this allocative task tends to overwhelm the task of education. Parents at all three of the schools described here tended to reduce a high school education to the credentials it generates, though the three communities regarded those credentials differently. This attitude, shared in significant degree by students, militated against teachers' ability to draw students into intrinsic involvement with academic learning at all three schools. At Cherry Glen, it pushed toward a technicized curriculum and one with right and wrong answers. At Pinehill, it led students to calculate the minimum effort and involvement needed to pass or to get a respectable grade. At Drew, it led students to give up, and it led staff, in resisting students' sense that they were not even in the game, to offer a curriculum that had striking discontinuities. At all of the schools, as a result of these attitudes, teachers who wanted to draw students into involvement with their subjects had to work against the grain not only of students' expectations but of adults' as well.

For the educational reform movement to resist this identification of public education with the process of sorting and selecting students for differential power and privilege in adult society would be to oppose deeply engrained societal patterns. But it seems that the societal sorting process is coming to dominate secondary education in ways that alienate students from engaged learning throughout the social scale. In our sam-ple, only at Maple Heights, where many parents were professionals whose work in some way involved knowledge that was not technical, and at St. Augustine's, where a religiously based moral quest and a shared effort to build community were deeply entwined with the substance of education, did the faculty as a whole seem able to experience some limited success in encouraging students to learn for intrinsic reasons.

If we want effective reform of high schools that will allow teachers and students to be engaged together in academic learning, we must consider policy that will weaken the stranglehold that ranking and alloca-tion have on secondary education. Such a reform movement might need to start with the kind of moral suasion the Reagan administration used so effectively in changing public thought about education, though the con-tent of this campaign would be different. We need a reorientation of our values to emphasize the importance of learning for its own sake. Schools should be places to create the curious, informed, and responsible citizen rather than the ready occupant of an occupational slot. If we must make learning instrumental—and Americans have a long history of doing so—then at least we need to see its importance not just for "successful" students but for all future citizens and economically productive participants in society. The alienation and discouragement visible at Pinehill and Drew preclude even the development of accomplished workers with a sense of craft. If only for economic reasons, the economic structure and the schools must be changed in ways that will raise the morale and encourage the academic involvement of students across the board. Their teachers will then have more attractive and rewarding work.

For the schools, a change in values would have to be linked with more concrete, structural changes. For example, schools might adopt experimental curricula that are not easily measured in traditional course units, or that do not fit into one period of a high school day. Some areas or periods of learning might be uncoupled from the pressures of grading. As Sizer (1984) suggests, there might be less frequent grading, and it might be based on more substantial and more individualized demonstrations of knowledge or skill by students. Of course, employers and colleges would have to adapt their current recruitment policies in significant ways.

In this perspective, it is important that reformers not take for granted or see as natural the social-class segregation of metropolitan schooling reflected in the organization of the schools we studied and in schooling in most urban areas of the United States. This segregation is not accidental. Well-educated, affluent, or ambitious parents flee to suburbs where they can place their children in well-funded schools with small class sizes and peers from similar families, in order to give them an advantage in the race for educational success. Rules about lot size, resistance to public housing, and racial steering by banks and the real estate industry keep such suburbs socially and racially homogeneous.

This chapter has shown how schools in communities of fairly homogeneous social class at high, middle, and low levels become very different places. Students and teachers have markedly different social and academic experiences in these schools, despite their common schedule, curriculum, and textbooks. For both individual students and individual teachers, the experience of life in school and the effectiveness of their academic efforts is deeply affected by the social class of the school in which they happen to find themselves. To appreciate this point, one can simply imagine individual students and teachers of various backgrounds and inclinations and then ask oneself what each would be like after 4 years of experience in each of the three schools discussed here. Neither a student nor a teacher would emerge from 4 years at any two of the schools with similar experiences, skills, or attitudes. If these schools are at all typical, it is clear that teachers as well as students will have much more difficulty in developing their academic abilities at the lower-SES schools, and that teachers and students of moderate ability will be helped to flourish in at least some directions in schools of higher SES.

The successful match of teachers' and students' aims in the high-SES suburban and private schools in our sample was accomplished by isolating the most privileged and ambitious students from the other young people of their generation. Such isolation breeds negative stereotypes and social distance across class lines, while it also stigmatizes and demoralizes the students and teachers of all but the more select schools. The social benefits of relatively trouble-free relationships and academic progress for the few teachers and students who profit from social segregation may well not be worth the costs to students and teachers in the less privileged settings to which the majority find themselves consigned. Some form of metropolitan desegregation seems the most promising vehicle for breaking up homogeneous alienated student bodies. It would be most workable if metropolitan areas were divided into districts of manageable size, shaped roughly like pie slices. Magnet schools that give parents and students choice of educational style but have safeguards against social and racial separation could make such a plan more palatable.

If such an idea seems politically unrealistic—and at the present time it does—the most important factor in making it so is the tight linkage between educational success and placement in an adult hierarchy of power and privilege. The relatively powerful citizens who currently use high-SES suburban schools to give their children an advantage in an unequal race will relinquish their advantage only if education ceases to be primarily a competition for success. That may only happen when we recognize that even children of privilege will depend as adults upon the educated abilities and enthusiastic participation of all members of society. Such abilities and attitudes are very difficult for teachers to foster in homogeneous schools set in social contexts like those shaping Drew and even Pinehill.

NOTES

1. As principal investigator, I took the lead role in fieldwork at six of the eight schools. Nancy Lesko, a staff researcher at the National Center on Effective Secondary Schools, took the lead role in two of the eight schools. Graduate

assistants Annette Hemmings and Alexander K. Tyree, Jr., alternated as the second team member. Tyree (1988) has written a paper about Cherry Glen and Pinehill from a somewhat different perspective from that given here, asking about the effects of normative and social integration and control over the work process on teachers' ability to be engaged. Hemmings is senior author of a paper (Hemmings & Metz, in press) on teachers' differential reaction to student bodies of differing social class, which concentrates most heavily on the three public schools not discussed here.

2. We also made our choices with some eye to the center's focus on teachers' engagement. We purposely excluded teachers whom we thought to be marginally competent or less, with the thought that an inability to reach educational goals would overwhelm the other issues in which we were interested. This choice rendered the sample less than fully representative of teachers, since there are less-than-competent teachers on most faculties. It also may have created a sample of teachers who were more than typically at ease with the dominant faculty and with the administration of each school; the least competent teachers often had difficult relationships with other teachers or with administrators. However, we also consciously sought some teachers who seemed in some way to be dissidents from either faculty consensus or administrative style, so that we would not be exposed only to insiders' views and experience.

3. That administrative study team spent about a week in each school. Although this chapter is based on the work of the teacher team, it draws in places on data gathered by the administrative team. The researchers for the administrative study were Richard Rossmiller, principal investigator, and Jeffrey Jacobson. Rossmiller (1988) has written separately about findings from the administrative study.

4. For a more detailed discussion of these different models of authority, see Metz (1978).

REFERENCES

Anyon, J. (1981). Social class and school knowledge. *Curriculum Inquiry, 11*(1), 3–42.

Apple, M. (1979). *Ideology and curriculum.* Boston: Routledge and Kegan Paul.

Apple, M. (1987). *Teachers and texts: A political economy of class and gender relations in education.* New York: Routledge and Kegan Paul.

Biklen, S. K. (1983). *Teaching as an occupation for women: A case study of an elementary school* (Final report, Grant Number NIE-G-81-0007). Washington, DC: National Institute of Education.

Bourdieu, P., & Passeron, J.-C. (1977). *Reproduction in education, society and culture.* London: Sage.

Bowles, S., & Gintis, H. (1976). *Schooling in capitalist America: Educational reform and the contradictions of economic life.* New York: Basic Books.

Burlingame, M. (1981). Superintendent power retention. In S. B. Bacharach (Ed.), *Organizational behavior in schools and school districts* (pp. 429–464). New York: Praeger.

Clement, D. C., Eisenhart, M., & Harding, J. R. (1979). The veneer of harmony: Social-race relations in a southern desegregated school. In R. C. Rist (Ed.), *Desegregated schools: Appraisals of an American experiment* (pp. 15–64). New York: Academic Press.

Connell, R. W., Ashenden, D. J., Kessler, S., & Dowsett, G. W. (1982). *Making the difference*. Sydney: George Allen and Unwin.

Cookson, P. W., Jr., & Persell, C. H. (1985). *Preparing for power: America's elite boarding schools*. New York: Basic Books.

Cusick, P. A. (1973). *Inside high school: The student's world*. New York: Holt, Rinehart and Winston.

Gracey, H. L. (1972). *Curriculum or craftsmanship: Elementary school teachers in a bureaucratic system*. Chicago: University of Chicago Press.

Heath, S. B. (1983). *Ways with words: Language, life and work in communities and classrooms*. Cambridge, England: Cambridge University Press.

Hemmings, A., & Metz, M. H. (in press). Real teaching: How high school teachers negotiate societal, local community, and student pressures when they define their work. In L. Valli & R. Page (Eds.), *Curriculum differentiation in U.S. secondary schools: Interpretive studies*. Buffalo: SUNY Press.

Henry, J. (1963). *Culture against man*. New York: Random House.

Jackson, P. W. (1986). *The practice of teaching*. New York: Teachers College Press.

Kliebard, H. M. (1986). *The struggle for the American curriculum, 1893–1958*. New York: Routledge and Kegan Paul.

Kohn, M. L. (1977). *Class and conformity: A study in values* (2nd ed.). Chicago: University of Chicago Press.

Komarovsky, M. (1962). *Blue-collar marriage*. New York: Vintage Books.

Leacock, E. (1969). *Teaching and learning in city schools*. New York: Basic Books.

LeMasters, E. E. (1975). *Blue-collar aristocrats: Life-styles at a working-class tavern*. Madison: University of Wisconsin Press.

Lesko, N. (1988). *Symbolizing society: Stories, rites and structure in a Catholic high school*. Philadelphia: Falmer Press.

Lortie, D. C. (1975). *Schoolteacher: A Sociological Study*. Chicago: University of Chicago Press.

Lubeck, S. (1985). *Sandbox society: Early education in black and white America*. Philadelphia: Falmer Press.

McNeil, L. (1986). *Contradictions of control*. New York: Routledge and Kegan Paul.

McPherson, G. (1972). *Small town teacher*. Cambridge, MA: Harvard University Press.

Metz, M. H. (1978). *Classrooms and corridors: The crisis of authority in desegregated secondary schools*. Berkeley: University of California Press.

Metz, M. H. (1986). *Different by design: The context and character of three magnet schools.* New York: Routledge and Kegan Paul.

Metz, M. H. (in press). Real school: A universal drama amid disparate experience. In D. Mitchell & M. Goertz (Eds.), *Education politics for the new century: The twentieth anniversary yearbook of the politics of education association.* Philadelphia: Falmer Press.

Meyer, J. W., & Rowan, B. (1978). The structure of educational organizations. In M. W. Meyer and Associates, *Environments and organizations* (pp. 78–109). San Francisco: Jossey-Bass.

Morgan, E. (1977). *Inequality in classroom learning: Schooling and democratic citizenship.* New York: Praeger.

Ogbu, J. U. (1978). *Minority education and caste: The American system in cross-cultural perspective.* New York: Academic Press.

Philips, S. (1983). *The invisible culture: Communication in classroom and community on the Warm Springs Indian Reservation* (Research on Teaching Monograph Series). New York: Longman.

Rohlen, T. P. (1983). *Japan's high schools.* Berkeley: University of California Press.

Rossmiller, R. (1988). *Secondary school principals and the quality of teachers' worklife: Final report of the field study on principals' management of school to affect teacher engagement* (Final Report, Office of Educational Research and Improvement Grant #G-00869007). Washington, DC: United States Department of Education.

Rubin, L. (1972). *Busing and backlash: White against white in an urban school district.* Berkeley: University of California Press.

Rubin, L. (1976). *Worlds of pain: Life in the working-class family.* New York: Basic Books.

Schofield, J. W. (1982). *Black and white in school: Trust, tension or tolerance?* New York: Praeger.

Scott, W. R. (1981). *Organizations: Rational, natural and open systems.* Englewood Cliffs, NJ: Prentice-Hall.

Sedlak, M., Wheeler, C. W., Pullin, D. C., & Cusick, P. A. (1986). *Selling students short: Classroom bargains and academic reform in the American high school.* New York: Teachers College Press.

Sizer, T. R. (1984). *Horace's compromise: The dilemma of the American high school.* Boston: Houghton Mifflin.

Smith, L. M., Prunty, J. J., & Dwyer, D. C. (1981). A longitudinal nested systems model of innovation and change in schooling. In S. B. Bacharach (Ed.), *Organizational behavior in schools and school districts* (pp. 160–207). New York: Praeger.

Spindler, G. D. (1973). *Burgbach: Urbanization and identity in a German village.* New York: Holt, Rinehart and Winston.

Sullivan, M. L. (1979). Contacts among cultures: School desegregation in a poly-ethnic New York City high school. In R. C. Rist (Ed.), *Desegregated schools: Appraisals of an American experiment* (pp. 201–240). New York: Academic Press.

Tyree, A. K., Jr. (1988). Belonging and work control in two suburban public high schools and their effects on teacher engagement. In M. H. Metz (Ed.), *Final report: Project on the effects of the school as a workplace on teachers' engagement—Field study on teachers' engagement* (Final Report, Office of Educational Research and Improvement Grant #G-00869007). Washington, DC: United States Department of Education.

Weis, L. (1985). *Between two worlds: Black students in an urban community college.* New York: Routledge and Kegan Paul.

Willis, P. (1977). *Learning to labour: How working class kids get working class jobs.* Westmead, England: Gower.

PART II

Organizational and Policy Contexts

4

The Conditions of Teachers' Work in Independent Schools

ARTHUR G. POWELL

During the 1980s, private schools entered the mainstream of American educational discourse for the first time in this century. They became directly relevant to issues beyond the specialized religious, social, and ideological beliefs that created them. What came to matter most about these schools was not their supporting beliefs, but their day-to-day educational practices and policies. Private school practices suddenly seemed partial remedies for some of the ills of many public schools ("Competitive State," 1989; Finn, 1989).

This did not mean that the American people enthusiastically embraced private schooling. By the end of the decade there was little evidence that schooling would become "privatized" in the sense of large transfers of students out of public schools. Such a sectoral shift did not occur during the Reagan years, despite federal policy initiatives to facilitate private school enrollments. A more probable future development is the incorporation of private school features or perspectives in public schools, to boost student achievement and engagement.

One such private perspective is to regard public education more as a consumer purchase than as a public service. The rise of opportunities for family choice among public schools or schools-within-schools is one example of consumerism. Another is expanding the number of coherent, purposeful, and specialized educational programs from which choice can be made. Actively marketing educational products to potential customers, along with developing attractive product lines, are classic ways to build educational commitment and consumer satisfaction.

A second private school feature of public school reform is the proposed "empowerment" of adults who work in schools. Reformers have advocated increasing principals' authority at the school site, while simul-

Preparation of this chapter was supported in part by the Edward E. Ford Foundation and by the Center for Research on the Context of Secondary School Teaching.

taneously increasing the authority and autonomy of classroom teachers. Much of what has been called "restructuring" refers to decentralizing and dispersing educational authority to the "building level." Additional policy emphases flow directly or indirectly from these general themes: small and caring school environments (instead of large and impersonal ones); greater parent involvement; character development as an explicit goal; and an unapologetic emphasis on academic learning, including more homework and higher standards.

It goes without saying that none of these themes is found exclusively in private schools or even in all private schools. Nor, of course, is the entirety of the contemporary school reform movement confined to these themes. But the themes do form a relatively coherent reform agenda celebrating features that many private schools regard as their most distinctive characteristics.

Two aspects of this reform agenda seem instructive. First, its ideas are not primarily derived from research conducted on private schools. The agenda happens to echo broad themes long part of private school tradition, but it is by no means a conscious effort to apply private school ideas to the public sector. The agenda arose mainly within public school practice and research. Indeed, the intellectual and political sources of the reform agenda are usually individuals, commissions, and state authorities with no special interest in or affection for private schools. Although more good research on private schools has probably been done in the 1980s than in all preceding years combined, it would be a mistake to overestimate the amount of that research or its policy impact.

Many private school proponents even regard the reform agenda as more threat than benefit. On the one hand, they appreciate the favorable publicity given to many practices they have long espoused. Yet they also fear that, if public schools emulate those policies, private schools may ironically be placed at a competitive disadvantage. When private school supporters call attention to the public school reform agenda, it is often not to take comfort but to warn. Unless they do a demonstrably better educational job, they say, the public schools may beat them at their own game ("Competitive State," 1989; Finn, 1989).

The second point is that the reform agenda has been shaped primarily by widespread concern that students of all races and circumstances are not learning enough or studying enough, and that the nation as well as the students are consequently at risk. The agenda is directed broadly at "conditions of work" for students in schools. Well-trained and committed teachers are obviously an indispensable condition of work for most students. But it has been somewhat less clear what conditions of teachers' work support effective and committed teaching. The latter question, so far, has been of secondary concern.

In these circumstances it seems useful to explore workplace conditions within private schools, as they are experienced by teachers. Just as certain private school features have been found suggestive in enhancing student learning and commitment, it is conceivable that the same or additional features might be suggestive in enhancing teacher effectiveness and commitment. Such an exploration does not assume that there are clear and unique differences between workplace conditions in public and private schools. The task is to call attention to certain types of general workplace conditions that otherwise might be submerged or neglected. One way to do this is to examine schools where those conditions of work are clearly central to institutional life.

To simplify the work of mapping the territory of conditions of teachers' work, we focus here on the type of private schools known as "independent" schools. These schools present two analytic advantages. Relative to most other private schools, they are less suffused with denominational religion and therefore more similar to the legal circumstances of public schools. In addition, independent schools are the most expensive of private schools. Although this fact makes them inaccessible to most Americans, it also permits an examination of institutions that are chosen by families who can afford any type of schooling. In many areas of American consumer life, what the few possess today is what the many will prefer—and receive—in some form tomorrow. So an examination of more privileged institutions has a potentially practical and perhaps predictive aspect.

Like all private schools, independent schools are not governed by public authority, nor do they receive appreciable public financing. But the special features just mentioned sharply distinguish them from most other private schools and make them a small minority within the private school universe—perhaps 1,500 schools out of an estimated total of nearly 26,000 private schools. They enroll perhaps 10% of the roughly 5.5 million Americans who attend private schools [National Center for Education Statistics (NCES), 1987; National Association of Independent Schools (NAIS), 1987].[1]

Their "independent" status derives first from the character of their nonpublic governance and support. Independent schools are managed by independent boards of trustees rather than by systems. Financially, they are nonprofit institutions which hardly ever receive funds from external systems such as religious denominations. They are fully self-sustaining and self-governing entities to an extent that many private schools are not. In this sense, they are among the most private of the private schools.

But their most obvious difference from other private schools—in part both the cause and effect of their self-sustaining character—is that they serve primarily higher-income families and the educational preferences of those families. They are the most privileged private schools. The median tuition for all American private schools in the 1985–1986 school year was $1,100 (calculated using each school's highest tuition level). In that year only 17% of private schools had tuitions in excess of $2,500 (NCES, 1987). Yet, in the same year, the median twelfth-grade tuition of independent private day schools was $5,338 and the average per-pupil expenditure in independent secondary day schools was about $6,000 (NAIS, 1985).

In many respects, then, the most important reference group for independent schools is not other private schools but suburban and other public schools patronized primarily by higher-income families.[2] Unlike most affluent public school districts whose student intake is regulated by residence within the district, most independent schools have deliberately sought a greater economic and racial mix in their student bodies during the last quarter century. With no funding sources from public authority— for the schools or the students who attend them—the task has been difficult. Virtually all funds must be raised from a school's own community—from its parents, alumni, and the resourcefulness of its fundraisers in generating other private support. That very narrow financial base means that schools that serve a financially well-off clientele are rarely well off themselves. Despite these constraints, some 16% of independent school students presently receive financial aid from the schools' own resources. In addition, the fraction of racial minorities in student bodies rose from 9.1% to 11.6% between 1981 and 1988 (NAIS, 1988a).[3]

Compared with private higher education and affluent public school districts, these are reasonable and even notable achievements. But they do not alter the reality that independent schooling, as presently organized and financed, is simply not affordable for most Americans. The tone of the schools is established by the educational preferences of upper-income clients. Their preferences, along with the schools' self-governing and self-sustaining organization, shape the conditions of work within them for teachers and students alike.[4]

But the nature of these conditions has not been thoroughly explored. The territory is largely uncharted, and the map that can be sketched is preliminary and somewhat speculative. Many different types of scholarly materials can help the mapping expedition, but more systematic exploration is obviously necessary in the future. The present effort will draw from many kinds of data.

Case studies of individual schools at particular moments, for example, are crucial to understanding how abstract notions like "conditions of work" acquire concrete meanings in specific school communities. Conditions of work change over time, often over quite short periods of time. They are not inherent in organizational structures, changeless and impervious to historical forces. All schools have distinct histories that must be understood. Teachers' collective memories, which compare what is to what was (or to what once appeared to be), also shape profoundly how the contemporary workplace is imagined (Lightfoot, 1983; Lloyd, 1987).

Grant's (1988) incisive account of how historical forces transformed teachers' work lives at "Hamilton High" shows how time affects conditions of work within a public school undergoing rapid transition. Independent schools also experience major change. Grant's high school anthropology students were enthralled by an idyllic picture of a stable and elegant boarding school during quiet times. But the essay they read about St. Paul's School did not fully capture the feelings of loss and liberation that St. Paul's veteran teachers held about their changing vocational lives. In its way, it, too, had been buffeted by the same egalitarian social forces that had struck Hamilton High in the 1960s. The boarding school's own historian had no problem describing the late 1960s as a "revolutionary" period for the school which decisively altered faculty conditions of work (Heckscher, 1980).[5]

Even where rich studies of individual schools exist, in the form of ethnographies or institutional histories, the situation of teachers is often shadowy or dimly sketched. The focus of attention is usually on leading administrators or, sometimes, on students. Teachers are observed or remembered for their lives inside classrooms, yet classroom practice is but one dimension of their work. Sometimes the most crucial "conditions" of their work are not visible at all when they are in the classroom (Graubard, 1981).

Surveys and other large-scale data bases can supplement case and historical studies, but it is hard to get a full sense of the work life of independent school teachers from existing survey data. Few surveys have been designed with that issue in mind. The situation will improve in the early 1990s, with the appearance of data from two projects coordinated by the National Center for Education Statistics: the Schools and Staffing Survey (SASS) and the National Educational Longitudinal Study (NELS:88). Most available teacher survey material is limited by the small number of independent schools represented, by difficulties in separating "independent" from other kinds of private schools, and by survey questions that do not probe below surface opinions (Abramowitz & Stackhouse, 1980; Chubb & Moe, 1985; Kane, 1986; Kraushaar, 1972).[6]

Within these current data limitations, an examination of the issues and literature suggests a tripartite preliminary map of the territory. Three broad themes seem to capture many important aspects of the conditions of teachers' work within independent schools. These are a workplace context of purposeful educational communities; a workplace emphasis on personalizing education; and a workplace conception of teacher authority that attempts to embrace both the idea of teacher empowerment and the idea of strong management at the school site.

These themes may be useful analytically because they contain not only concrete policies and practices but undergirding ideas, problems, and contradictions. They are part of the ongoing self-consciousness of independent schools, of how independent schools imagine themselves and present themselves to outsiders. They are, in short, recognizable themes to practitioners—bottom-up analytic categories, as it were, as distinct from top-down ones imposed on schools from the outside.

PURPOSEFUL EDUCATIONAL COMMUNITIES

The importance of reasonable agreement about school purpose or mission is a near universal theme in recent scholarly and popular writing about school improvement. Americans have been singularly unable to think of an educational purpose that they should not embrace. Educators have tried to solve the problems of competing purposes by embracing all of them. This is a practical accommodation to the realities of increased diversification of the school population, on the one hand, and decreased educational authority and agreement about what is educationally desirable, on the other hand. The result has been a tolerant do-your-own-thing institutional neutrality. The multiple "products" offered by many schools are consumed or passed up like the products available in large shopping malls. Schools typically convey no coherent message about what is most valuable; that is left for individual shoppers alone to decide (Powell, Farrar, & Cohen, 1985).

Independent schools usually constitute more purposeful communities than many public schools. Their governance and financing make them directly responsible to limited and particular constituencies whom they must constantly satisfy to stay afloat. They have no direct obligation to the whole of society (Grant, 1988). Tuition, student fees, and charitable giving constitute well over 90% of the annual income of independent day schools. They perforce must serve individual clients instead of serving social functions paid for by a multiplicity of local, state, and federal revenue sources.

What Grant (1988) calls the external policy matrix of bureaucratic orders, government mandates, court decisions, and union contracts have but a marginal impact on the cohesiveness of independent schools. To be sure, the schools are not immune from public regulations concerning safety, civil rights, and teacher certification. Nor are they unaffected by the subtle intrusiveness of publishers, external testing, and college admissions requirements. But in relative terms they remain masters of their own houses. They retain a focused identity. A recent New Jersey study concluded that "independent school teachers are almost twice as likely as public school teachers to cite the professional ethos of their school as a source of professional satisfaction" (Kane, 1986, p. 57). The "communal feeling" of their schools was second only to "autonomy" in what teachers liked best about them (p. 61; see also Chubb & Moe, 1985).

The schools' purposes embrace both objectives and the means by which those objectives are pursued. The affluent and educated parents who form their primary constituency tend to have fairly clear general goals for their children and hence for the schools. They are academically ambitious, regardless of their childrens' apparent talents. They want them to get ahead, attend the more prestigious public and private 4-year colleges, and then enter the more highly esteemed vocations. They want their children to retain at least the same position in society that they hold themselves.

They are also concerned with the personal development of their children; that is, they care about happiness, self-esteem, and the formation of sound moral character. They want schools actively to develop these qualities and to protect their children from the many dangers and lures of modern American society. Privilege does not immunize these students from behaviors such as cheating, stealing, verbal cruelty, substance abuse, selfishness, materialism, arrogance, and self-doubt. "Affluenza" in its many forms can always strike, and independent schools are expected to thwart such dangers more explicitly than are most public schools. They are rightly perceived to have many more resources at their disposal for doing so, including the power to admit and expel and the moral authority of religion.

When stated in general terms, these "bottom-line" purposes hold up across the entire national independent school spectrum. Parents, however, differ on the specifics of an appropriately ambitious academic education, definitions of character, and the types of educational processes that produce desired results. Though most independent schools claim to be purposeful communities along these general dimensions, they often vary sharply in content and process. Although many public school curricula have recently become more specialized and purposeful, and though some define their mission according to the ability levels of students, independent schools espouse a wider variety of purposeful communities.

The main independent school types exemplifying focused purposes are single-sex schools, boarding schools, schools with religious affiliations or orientations, schools that deliberately cater to particular ability levels, and schools that embrace a special educational or pedagogical ideology.

More than one-fifth of NAIS-member independent school students currently attend single-sex schools (NAIS, 1988a). Because of the rise of coeducation in the 1960s, girls no longer must attend single-sex schools because they are excluded from boys' schools. Girls' schools are now schools of choice rather than schools of necessity; consequently, these institutions have had to develop a positive ideological and educational rationale for an all-girls' environment as a marketing strategy. Gender has become a more self-conscious component of their conception of purposeful community.

About 43,000, or 12%, of NAIS-member independent school students are boarders (NAIS, 1988a). The roughly 172 boarding schools are a very specialized type of purposeful community, since students are in residence for more than half of the calendar year. While they are at school they certainly are part of a "total institution." Boarding schools are the quintessential type of prep school in the American mind, the core image of independent education. Yet boarding schools are not an area of growth within independent education. At best they are holding their own. The boarding school experience in America remains a somewhat arcane taste, and the schools' cost (median annual fees approached $12,000 in 1988) further limits their appeal, despite financial aid commitments greater than the rest of the independent school sector. Of all specialized types of independent schools, only boarding schools have so far joined together to create a separate marketing organization to widen public understanding of the advantages of residential secondary education.[7]

It is sometimes thought that independent schools are nearly synonymous with "secular" schools, since part of the usefulness of the term "independent" is to differentiate them from religious schools governed by a religious system. Indeed, the traditional influence of Protestant denominations has softened considerably in the independent sector, but even schools that have abandoned religious formality steadfastly attempt to make religion germane to character formation. Still, many independent schools retain strong religious commitments that reach significant numbers of teachers and students, even if the schools themselves are nonsectarian in spirit and free from all ecclesiastical control.[8]

Schools also differ according to the academic abilities of their student bodies. Most independent school admissions practices are not "selective" in the sense made famous by certain colleges since the 1950s. The schools typically admit those who seem reasonably committed and able to do the work, and whose parents can pay the bills. Only a handful of boarding schools and some day schools in urban areas such as New York, Washington, and Boston are regularly faced with with greater numbers of attractive applicants than they have places. These meritocratic institutions are atypical of the sector but symbolic of it in the public eye, just as Stanford and Amherst wrongly typify all private colleges in the minds of many. The fact that most independent schools are not highly selective on academic grounds, but are patronized by educated parents who have ambitions for their children, has important consequences for the work life of teachers.

Finally, independent schools sometimes differ among themselves by ideology, pedagogy, politics, or a commingling of the three. It is true that most emphasize academic propulsion and moral safety through catalogs so similar that they appear to have been written by the same advertising agency. But a thousand individual entities still contain considerable variety. There are staunchly conservative schools; schools with very particular traditions, such as a history of ethnic diversity, or a history of public service, or a history of preparation for one or another vocation; and progressive schools with strong commitments to student participation in decision making and to nontraditional curricula.

Since one of the classic arguments for these schools' existence is that they provide options and models for public education, it is easy to complain that there is insufficient diversity among them. But the range of institutional diversity—of different types of purposeful communities— remains impressive when compared to the rest of American schooling. In the public sector, diversity seems primarily a product of economic differences. There are schools for the poor, schools for the middle class, schools for the suburbanites. Within independent education and its context of general affluence, there seem to be more notions of what a decent school might be. Social class is not a sufficient explanation.

In recent years, independent schools have become increasingly self-conscious of themselves as purposeful communities. The growing acceptance of modern marketing techniques in admissions offices has made schools aware of their images within and outside the school community. They have practical incentives to be sufficiently different from their competition (public and other independent schools), yet sufficiently mainstream to avoid alienating prospective customers. The need to compete in the marketplace has led schools to discover an image, refine it, project it, inculcate it, and even change it. "Ethos" is no longer just an academic construct; it is what schools make videotapes about (Boarding Schools, 1987; Griffith, 1987).

Most writing on the theme of school purpose addresses how the absence of shared objectives, collective identity, or positive ethos adversely affects students (e.g., Grant, 1988; Powell et al., 1985; Rutter, Maughan, Mortimore, Ouston, & Smith, 1979). But institutional consensus about purpose, when it is present, is equally important as a condition of teachers' work.

Focused school purpose helps match a teacher's basic values with a particular institutional setting. There are often substantive reasons beyond accident of convenience for teachers' attraction to and retention at particular schools. Purpose links a teacher to other teachers, administrators, students, parents, and often to a historical tradition. It is a potent educational force of its own which reinforces teachers' individual, often isolated professional efforts. A purposeful community can deepen teachers' vocational identity and commitment to a school, build a web of collegial and other teacher supports, and directly assist teachers in getting the educational job done. Each of these conditions of work requires elaboration.

Teacher choice over school assignment has not received the attention recently given to student choice, but the voluntary nature of independent school teacher placement is an important condition of work. Compared with many large public school districts, independent schools have wide discretion over who they hire. Prospective teachers also have wide discretion over where they will work. No system administrators outside the schools tell teachers where they must teach, or principals who they must hire (or, for that matter, must retain).

This means that a school can freely seek out teachers whose lives have embodied some of the central purposes of that school: a successful career as a student culminating in graduation from a very selective college, or a deep faith in a particular religion, or a commitment to some specialized purpose such as outdoor experiential learning or women's studies or coaching crew. In light of the central academic purpose of most independent schools and their general freedom from teacher certification requirements, it is not surprising that one statewide study (Kane, 1986) found that the 58% of independent secondary teachers had graduated from "very competitive" colleges, in contrast with 15% of public secondary teachers.

Teacher choice also means that, from the beginning of their careers, teachers are encouraged to consider the positive or negative fit between their own values and skills and the wide variety of purposeful communities in which they might work. Despite the surface similarities of many independent schools, insiders are often impressed by what seem to be important community differences. The work of teaching, they say, is not easily portable. One is not just a teacher, but a "Putney teacher." Teaching grows out of the customs, rules, and mores of a particular place, not just out of professional classroom techniques readily transferable to other settings.

A purposeful community permits deeper patterns of colleagueship with other teachers and school professionals, as well as greater support and understanding between teachers and families. The regular routines and structures of most schools isolate adults from each other for much of the day. But when teachers share fundamental values, they are more likely to work cooperatively. According to Chubb and Moe (1985), private schoolteachers "are more likely to know what their colleagues are teaching, . . . spend more time than public school teachers meeting to discuss curriculum and students, and more time observing each other's classes . . . they have a higher level of collegiality" (p. 37). They have greater mutual respect (see also Grant, 1988; Kane, 1986; Powell et al., 1985).

The connections with families, often expressed as an "alliance" between home and school, are of equal importance. School learning occurs in many places besides school; the classroom is only one learning setting. When there is some understanding and consensus about objectives, rules, regulations, and expectations for learning at school and at home, the possibilities for successful teaching improve dramatically. The existence of supportive parents, even if they are sometimes overdemanding of schools and children, is surely one of the decisive conditions of teachers' work in independent schools (Powell et al., 1985).

A purposeful community is not just a morale booster or a pleasant setting in which decent education may flourish. It is a distinct intervention in the educational process. Sometimes parents believe it to be more important to learning than teachers' classroom skill, because of the kinds of students it draws to the school. As an educational force, a purposeful community usually assists teachers in two ways. First, it supplies a legitimated system of rules, regulations, and behaviors that are enforced by teachers and acquiesced to by students with reasonable consistency. The individual teacher does not have to be a lone enforcer. The rules constitute an instructional support system. Compliance is widespread and generally voluntary. Some of these rules concern personal behavior and civility, but many address academic behavior such as homework and classroom participation. A school's "system" by no means applies only to students. Consistent behavior is also expected of teachers regarding such matters as when homework or papers are returned and what kind of written feedback students can expect.

The other way that a purposeful community directly affects teaching and learning involves peer pressure. Students in these schools often say they obey the rules and do their work because they want to, not because of the penalties for misbehavior. Everyone does it, they say. It is "cool" to work hard; you are "out of it" if you do not. Such peer pressure among students in purposeful communities, operating generally in favor of academic learning, is a major condition of teachers' work. Students are willing to engage with the academic agenda of the teachers without overt or covert protest, if not always with enthusiasm. The absence of organized student resistance to teaching and learning is an enormous source of high teacher morale.

None of these dimensions of purpose are fixed conditions of life. In different ways, each is in constant transition, under pressure both from critical self-scrutiny and from changing patterns in independent education. Teachers actually experience these conditions in more complex and problematic ways than these brief generalizations may suggest.

A purposeful community, for example, often verges on being an isolated, narrow, and self-satisfied community, cut off from worldly currents that are as potentially exciting and educative as they are potentially dangerous and fragmenting. Impatient students call such schools "protective bubbles" and wonder about the price of limited diversity. Most schools have gradually become far more diverse in student and faculty backgrounds than they were only 25 years ago. That diversity has created tensions about curriculum, admissions policy, faculty recruitment, and other central concerns. Compared with most public schools, this diversification has been modest; however, in communities accustomed to consensus and homogeneity, strong disagreements over modest issues can lead to serious, painful, and exhausting talk (Anson, 1987; Powell et al., 1985).

At the same time, a subtle fragmentation may make the independent school notion of purposeful community more a public relations phrase or marketing gimmick than a substantive reality. Coleman and Hoffer's (1987) exploration of the communities that surround private schools suggests that the very "independence" of independent school families may undercut crucial links that sustain genuine community, and hence genuine purpose. They argue that independent school families, as distinct from Catholic school families, purchase an individual service—the academic acceleration and character development mentioned earlier. But the families often have little in common other than the school their children attend. They do not know each other outside school, in part because they do not live close to one another; hence they do not reinforce the norms of the school through contact with each other. Coleman and Hoffer's speculations conjure up an image of independent school students isolated from any functional community other than what they experience within the walls of the school. It is a chilling notion, and these authors use it to point to the significance of a third vector of community relationships beyond the two we have considered: Purposeful communities may be formed not only through within-school relations and school/family relations, but also through between-family relations.

A final problem of purposeful communities is the high expectations parents have for independent schools, which ironically complement the high expectations those schools have for their students. Independent schools, far more than public schools, are expected to produce results for individuals rather than results for groups. Many parents assume that their financial transactions with schools—their act of paying directly for the service—should somehow guarantee that their goals will be achieved. They believe that they should be able to purchase student achievement and personal development under market conditions, just as they purchase high-performance automobiles and longer-lasting outerwear.

But expectations that schools should be able to "work the miracle with each child" profoundly overestimate the transforming power of even purposeful communities, as well as the power of the educational technologies independent schools employ. Parents retain the hope anyway, and schools dispel it at their peril, since it is so central to their recruiting advantage over local public schools. An exhausting and perhaps intractable condition of teachers' work in independent schools is facing their partial or total failure to fulfill parents' dreams. Played at these high stakes, the modern game of school "accountability" has nothing to do with aggregate statistics about group performance and everything to do with the development of individual youngsters (Powell, 1980; Powell et al., 1985).

PERSONALIZATION OF EDUCATION

The educational strategy most characteristic of independent education is to provide personal attention to each student within a small-scale environment. The *personalization* of education is the heart of independent school technology. All schools, of course, profess full allegiance to the ideal of *individualized* education. In many public schools, especially secondary schools, individualization means providing greater curricular variety and removing barriers to student choice about classes and programs. Individualization thus means the freedom to do one's own thing. Very often it is a surprisingly anonymous process, carried on without much knowledge of particular individuals. Anonymous individualization is almost the opposite of personalization (Powell et al., 1985).

School professionals often say that the biggest difference between public and private school practice is that private school teachers "are being paid to know your kid." Parents and students tend to agree. A recent summary (Roeser, 1987) of the results of market research on parent and student attitudes toward 19 independent schools found that a "caring and concerned faculty" ranked first among all the attributes they desired, even above the teaching ability of the faculty (p. 25).

This parental expectation, and the various ways schools attempt to meet it, constitutes a crucial workplace condition for independent school teachers. Much institutional energy is expended to ensure that all students are known, that no one falls through the cracks and gets lost. Students with special abilities or disabilities are always easy to know and often easy to like. They gravitate to teachers, and teachers to them. But many average, normal, regular students are not distinctive in any way. It is easy for them to become neglected, invisible, unspecial—to quietly pass through school without anyone knowing or caring that they are there. Average students form a sizable part of the independent school constituency, and the schools are expected to treat each one as special (Powell et al., 1985).

How do they go about doing this, and how in particular are conditions of teachers' work affected? First, the schools' small size, small scale, and low student attrition help minimize the distance between teachers and students. Second, teachers interact with students in a wide variety of ways. Third, these interactions along with parental and school expectations, shape a somewhat distinct conception of the role of the teacher and of the desirable qualities possessed by good teachers. The result is that teachers in independent schools have no more chance of being invisible or anonymous than do students. They cannot easily escape students, any more than students can escape them. Let us now discuss each of these three dimensions of personalization.

Independent schools are typically quite small. Students are known and taught by teachers who know and talk with each other. It is very unlikely that a teacher could bring up a student's name in the presence of other teachers without most of them knowing something of the student. Over 80% of independent schools enroll fewer than 400 students. The median school size in the 1987–1988 school year was 320 and has remained stable through the 1980s (NAIS, 1988a). But school size is only one measure of environmental scale. Many independent schools span elementary and secondary grades but have separate upper, lower, and middle divisions, sometimes in different geographical locations. The actual unit with which students have contact is often smaller than the size of the school would suggest.

The size of grades can therefore offer a better perspective on the scale of independent school communities. Since these schools tend to build up their enrollments over the K–12 progression, the upper grades are usually the largest. The average number of twelfth graders in independent schools having a twelfth grade was 65 students in 1987–1988. The figures for the third, sixth, and ninth grades were 33, 34, and 50, respectively (NAIS, 1988a).

An examination of data from 656 independent high schools in 1986–1987 indicates that only 17 (fewer than 3%) had graduating classes of 200 or more. Most of these were relatively large boarding schools. Eighty-four percent of the senior classes were smaller than 100; 63% of all seniors were in graduating classes with fewer than 100 students (Powell, 1988b).

Another quite different indicator of scale is the number of students a teacher actually instructs. Despite research disagreement over how class size and student learning are related, there is very little disagreement (and none in the minds of parents) that personal attention is directly related to how many students a teacher is responsible for. The traditional student/teacher ratio gives only an indirect and confusing measure of actual student load. The current independent school ratios of 9.4:1 for elementary grades and 8.5:1 for secondary grades (NAIS, 1988a), for example, say little unless they are compared with other types of schools. Even then, one only gets a rough sense of "better" or "worse," as distinct from a feel for the actual workload of teachers.

Available secondary school data suggest that student loads significantly smaller than those carried by public school teachers characterize independent schools. In New Jersey, the average load of independent day teachers was 69, compared with 103 students for public high school teachers (Kane, 1986). Many of the recent national high school studies have reported student loads of 125 or even 150 in urban schools, though truancy may reduce the numbers somewhat. A national survey (Powell, 1986) of all independent secondary schools found that the median student load per teacher was 63. Perhaps more important, 88% of schools reported that their student loads per teacher were 80:1 or lower, which is the target student load for Theodore Sizer's Coalition of Essential Schools.

A small community and a small student load are typical conditions of teachers' work in independent schools. These conditions make it easier for teachers to know students well and in more ways than they might in large schools with large loads. A related circumstance is the relatively low turnover rate of students from year to year, which, according to NAIS (1989), is about 12%. Since independent schools are rarely "neighborhood" schools to begin with, family residential moves from one part of town to another, or from one town to another nearby do not need to result in a school change. This is one of the advantages of independent schools for parents who anticipate local but not national geographic mobility. The more students change schools, the less well they will be known by school staff (Grant, 1988).

These conditions are enabling conditions. They permit desired things to happen but do not in themselves guarantee that they will. Do teachers capitalize on these advantages in their actual interactions with students? One tentative answer is that independent school teachers may work longer hours than many other teachers, despite the fact that they have fewer students. They interact with students in more varied ways than many other teachers, and probably know them better. The New Jersey independent teachers who taught one-third fewer students than their public school counterparts nevertheless spent 7 hours more on their jobs per week (55 hours vs. 48 hours). Thus, the average time spent per teacher per student in the independent schools was 48 minutes per week, as compared with 28 minutes per week in the public schools (Kane, 1986).

But the extra hours worked by these independent teachers were not spent on additional classroom instruction. In fact, independent teachers spent slightly less time in classroom teaching (Kane, 1986). The big difference—5.5 hours a week—between the public and private teaching roles was the greater out-of-class time spent by independent school teachers in helping students, in correcting papers, and in preparing for their classes. Indeed, independent school teachers spent slightly more time on these out-of-class instructional duties than they spent on classroom teaching. Such out-of-class instructional duties should not be confused with all the other out-of-class, extracurricular, athletic coaching, advising, and monitoring activities that all teachers undertake in the ordinary course of a day. These latter responsibilities are a separate item and consumed 10 hours of the 55-hour workweek of the independent school teachers, compared with 9 hours of the 48-hour workweek of the public school teachers—an equivalent percentage of effort (Kane, 1986).

The significant time spent on out-of-class instructional duties in independent schools confirms evidence from other sources that the personal attention supplied by teachers embraces many more types of teacher/student interaction than that of classroom teaching. Classes themselves, of course, are smaller in the independent schools. (This follows from the smaller numbers of students per teacher and the fact that independent schools tend to follow public school patterns regarding the number of classes teachers have per week.) But what is the most distinct about the independent teaching role is the variety of ways teachers interact with students.

Instruction in independent schools seems considerably less specialized in function than in public schools, where there are far more programs funded from different sources, governed by different rules and agencies, and employing different types of personnel. Regular classroom teachers in independent schools are more likely to coach sports, advise clubs, and work on student publications and drama productions. They are far more likely to spend time preparing written summary evaluations of student performance, a tradition that rarely turns up in public schools. They are also more likely to discuss with other teachers the progress of students who are not in dire academic or personal trouble. Such schools often spend entire faculty meetings reviewing the situation of every student. Just as students must participate more in the varied activities of independent schools simply because there are fewer of them and they are needed, teachers must be generalists, too (Kane, 1986; Powell et al., 1985).

Perhaps the best example of the less-specialized nature of the independent school workplace is student advising. In the departmentalized world of high schools, it is very easy for no one to have an across-the-board picture of how a student is progressing. This is understandable in public schools, where responsibility for such in-depth understanding usually rests with specialist guidance counselors, each often burdened with 400 students. These busy individuals have time to advise only that small minority with distinct problems of one sort or another. For the rest, advising too often consists of signing study cards to insure that formal requirements have been met.

Independent schools, in contrast, assume that student advising is a proper job for teachers. In New Jersey, nearly half of the independent day teachers had advisees, compared with 14% of the public school teachers (Kane, 1986). But the skills of the teacher/advisor are not those of the specialized psychological counselor. Independent schools describe the role as an adult friend who pays particular attention to an individual student, or a ready listener who cares. Advising is one more extension of the task of knowing all students well and taking a genuine interest in their lives. This is a far cry from the "neutral, facilitating professional" function that Grant (1988, p. 65) describes at Hamilton High. While the former may be amateurish, it is also more involved (Powell et al., 1985).

Over the years the pervasiveness of personalization has helped shape a particular image of the "good" independent school teacher. This emphasizes personal traits and somewhat downplays specialized instructional skills. Kraushaar (1972), who collected some of the first survey data on these teachers for his study of nonpublic schools, concluded that

> the profile of the independent school teacher . . . is that of the dedicated amateur—a man or woman broadly educated in the humanistic liberal arts tradition, not highly specialized, and but lightly burdened, if at all, with the pedagogical formalism of professional education. [p. 145]

The same image was nicely captured in 1956 by a former headmaster of the then all-male Phillips Academy: Andover's John Kemper wrote:

> At the heart of secondary education is the relationship of man and boy. . . . In his every contact with a boy a great teacher communicates what he is and stands for as a person; his love for things of the mind, his integrity, his moral values. From the example and encouragement of such a man, a boy sets his sights high and grows in self-reliance, self-control, and confidence. In the last analysis he will probably not learn in any other way. [quoted in Allis, 1979, p. 644]

Such a sentiment validates personal attention on grounds that go beyond "caring and love." If the good teacher teaches by modeling and exemplifying a total personality, then students are best served when teachers' associations with them are increased and distance is minimized.

Yet the day-to-day realities of personalization within independent schools are often more problematic than the discussion so far might suggest. The expectation of close faculty/student relations may exhaust teachers, if family expectations for out-of-class help of all kinds become excessive. Conversely, some students may rebel from environments where adults know too much about them. They may feel under surveillance and seek some small measure of defensive anonymity.

At the same time, the expectation places an unusual premium on mutual respect between teachers and students. Some shared and understood purpose is crucial. It makes a great difference for teachers to know that students, at least to some degree, have chosen to attend the school and broadly accept their responsibilities. Despite this, tensions may arise. In Kane's (1986) study, a slightly higher fraction of the New Jersey independent school teachers found their students to be a problem than the public school teachers, not because of their motivation but because of their values. Another study (Cookson & Persell, 1985) has pointed to the "structural discrepancy" between the wealth and privilege of independent students and most of their teachers. Teachers can become frustrated if they are perceived as "akin to the family retainer—unobtrusive, hardworking, and ultimately expendable" (p. 93). The frustration is exacerbated when the expected norm is a close and caring relationship. (Also see Coles, 1977.)

Finally, the varied conditions, practices, and beliefs we have called "personalization" appear to affect life outside classrooms far more than classroom instruction itself. Teachers with very small classes are just as likely to lecture to them as teachers with larger classes, and they are just as likely to confuse Socratic method with a question-and-answer format. The enabling conditions of small scale and commitment to personal attention have not made classroom pedagogy different in independent schools. It is notable how resistant teaching itself is to change in these schools. Perhaps the main reason is that pedagogy and personalization are seen as opposing rather than as complementary forces; that is, exemplary instructional skill may seem less important than exposure to an exemplary individual. Herein lies the continuing tension in private schools over whether teaching is considered a calling/vocation or a contemporary American profession (Powell et al., 1985).

TEACHER AUTHORITY

The nature of teachers' authority is an important condition of teachers' work, but it is a controversial issue within the school reform movement. Many states and districts have mandated tests and courses to upgrade student performance. Their top-down requirements often presume that teachers are a major part of the national educational problem. External standards of various kinds have been established, not only to provide incentives for students to achieve but to guarantee that teachers are held accountable to precise public objectives. Teachers often perceive such standards as reducing their already marginal educational authority and diminishing the quality of their work life. The erosion of their authority seems a demeaning workplace condition (McNeil, 1987).

But other reform initiatives have moved in a quite different direction. They advocate "empowering" teachers by increasing their authority over in-class decision making and school policy in general. Spearheaded by the national teacher unions, the Carnegie Corporation, and individual reformers, these bottom-up strategies assume that top-down reform schemes can never succeed because they discourage teachers from becoming involved in and committed to the reforms. They also assume that teaching cannot recruit and retain high-quality personnel unless it becomes a more professionally autonomous vocation (Grant, 1988).

To complicate matters further, the idea of teacher empowerment sometimes can conflict with the idea of strengthened administrative leadership at the school site. Strong (and wise) principals have long been an important component of most approaches to making schools effective and have been given a further boost by bottom-up ideas such as school-site management. Yet it is not clear on what basis empowered teachers and strong school-site managers can peacefully and usefully coexist.

In these muddled circumstances, the nature and problems of teachers' authority in independent schools offer an instructive contrast. By definition, independent school authority is concentrated at the school site. Independent school teachers have not worked under a relentless cloud of public, political, and academic criticism about their work or its results. They are much freer from external mandates set by political authority far from the school. They are also freer from bureaucratic rules, regulations, and procedures established by strangers in distant central offices. Their authority is neither eroded nor enhanced by collective negotiations between organized management and organized teachers. Unions are exceedingly rare in independent schools. In all these ways, the issue of teachers' authority in independent schools is distinctly a within-school issue.

But it is still a very important issue. Within the school setting, how do authority relations affect the conditions of teachers' work? Are teachers "empowered" by virtue of their relative freedom from external requirements? Or is powerlessness a condition of their work lives?

Perhaps the best introduction to these questions is to explore the role of the head of an independent school. School heads (in most cases the word *principal* is actively avoided) are expected by most boards of trustees to be powerful figures. They feel comfortable with business-derived descriptions such as "chief executive officer." Although the typical school size is smaller than most public schools, and the student bodies more homogeneous and less resistant to engagement in the schools' academic agendas, heads often compare themselves to superintendents rather than principals, because the scope of their authority is so wide.

That boards expect heads to exercise wide authority is best seen by examining school salary policies. It is well known that independent school teachers' salaries, on average, are substantially lower than public school salaries. Independent school teachers cite remuneration as the least satisfactory condition of their work (Kane, 1986). In the.1987–1988 school year, for example, the average teacher salary in independent day schools was $22,755, compared with an average public school salary of $28,085, a national gap of more than 23% (NAIS, 1988b). Of course, the more affluent, suburban public schools that are the most appropriate reference group for independent education pay their teachers more than the national public school average.

But the situation is very different when independent school heads' salaries are compared to those of public high school principals.[9] According to NAIS (1987a) figures, the median cash salary of independent school heads in 1987–1988 was $57,000. In addition, nearly 46% of these heads had their housing provided fully by their schools, and another 10% received partial housing as a benefit. (These statistics include elementary and secondary schools, as well as schools spanning both grade levels.) The mean salary of public school principals for the same year, according to the National Association of Secondary School Principals (NASSP, 1988) was about $47,000. If only public schools with the highest per-pupil expenditure of $5,000 or more are included, the median principals' salary was roughly $53,000 to $54,000. Few of these individuals received any housing benefits.

The general direction of these differences is striking. The comparative disadvantage of independent school teachers does not exist for heads. On average, heads are compensated at least as well as—and, when housing is included, substantially better than—public school principals. Further, the salary gap between teachers and heads in independent schools is much greater than the salary gap between public school teachers and principals. Independent schools make a very significant and unique investment in their heads. They expect them to be powerful leaders and personify school purposes to an extent that is unusual in most public schools. These large expectations for heads inevitably shape important aspects of teachers' work lives. Heads are expected to build competent faculties. Most are centrally involved in faculty appointments, and even those who choose not to be have veto power. Teacher contracts are usually given on an annual basis, and formal tenure is rare. In general, teachers know that reappointment (plus career references) depend on satisfying the head (Baird, 1977).

Yet the substantial authority of the head is typically not exercised in an authoritarian way. The incentives for heads to succeed and hold their jobs, especially since heads lack tenure as well as teachers, usually encourage other administrative styles. Chubb and Moe (1985) argue that private schools tend to operate on a more democratic than authoritarian organizational model. "Relative to public schools," they conclude, "private schools appear to delegate significant discretion to their teachers, and to involve them sufficiently in school level policy decisions to make them feel efficacious" (p. 37). They attribute administrative trust in teachers mainly to the heads' power over who gets hired and who gets reappointed. "The leaders are able to staff the school the way that they wish. It is safe, therefore, for them to involve teachers integrally in decision-making processes" (p. 38).

Heads tend to support and trust teachers rather than supervise and evaluate them, for reasons that go beyond their authority over appointments. Their attitude is partly a function of the scale of the schools. In small institutions that are not part of a larger system, bureaucratic regulation and supervision are less necessary to monitor expectations and keep track of what is going on.

Excessive authoritarianism is also held in check by the sometimes overlooked reality that independent school heads need good and satisfied teachers perhaps more than do many public school principals. The faculty is always perceived as one of the most marketable features of the school. Marketing the school well—getting enough students and the right students to attend—is one of the bottom-line ways by which boards judge heads. Supporting a faculty in every possible way—through expressions of personal appreciation, gentle evaluations, involvement in a variety of school duties, providing attractive physical facilities, and improving compensation—is near the top of heads' priorities.

Professional development programs of various types are an increasingly important method of faculty support. Independent schools have little tradition of in-service education, in part because schools are not components of systems and in part because appointment and advancement have not depended on accumulating credits in professional courses. What has evolved is a quite varied notion of what professional development entails.

Nearly 20% of the independent schools, for example, support an internship program to help train beginning teachers (Powell, 1986). About 30% of independent secondary schools have sabbatical programs in which schools pay for teachers' travel to other countries, graduate study in their fields or in education, short-term workshops, visits to other schools, and solitary independent study (Powell, 1988a). Characteristically, these programs place the burden for designing an appropriate experience on the individual teacher. Teachers are not told what to do.

Though most heads have learned that supportive management is in their own best interests, one cannot underestimate the variety of leadership styles or different school traditions in which heads' power is exercised. At one extreme, some independent schools remain a last bastion of paternalistic, patronizing one-person rule. (Many such schools were literally created by their heads, sometimes with their own money.) At times, as Lightfoot (1983) observes, the "unquestionable dominance and benign power" of the head only underscores the faculty's "relative powerlessness and reinforces the childlike impulses" (p. 341). In such schools, the teachers could seem the "least powerful, most disenfranchised group" (p. 238), regardless of the plethora of supportive benefits, such as sabbatical opportunities, open to them. (Also see Cookson & Persell, 1985.)

Yet, in other schools, equally powerful heads treat teachers as adult colleagues. The collegial model makes these schools seem more like serious colleges. Teachers are regarded as akin to professors: They are assumed to be learned women and men, "thinkers." Within one such faculty, Lightfoot (1983) writes, "there are striking differences in teacher style, an unusual concern for the philosophical issues that shape educational matters, and an expressed need for intellectual invigoration" (pp. 337–338). Sometimes a school faculty thinks of itself enough like a college faculty to make many important decisions on its own. Each school, Lightfoot concludes, interprets teacher rewards differently, but all "search for a balance between the expression of teacher autonomy, initiative, and adulthood on the one hand, and the requirements of conformity, discipline, and commitments to school life on the other" (p. 341).

Despite these environmental differences, the authority of independent school teachers seems relatively straightforward. Classroom freedom, for example, is not a major problem; it is a well-established condition of teachers' work. In New Jersey, 70% of independent school teachers cited "autonomy" as the single factor they liked best about working in their schools, compared with 34% of the public school teachers sampled (Kane, 1986). The former cited the "freedom to choose texts," "freedom to construct curriculum," and "freedom to teach the way I want within the structure" as the chief advantages of working in their schools. Moreover, public school teachers pointed to administrative practices, especially to frustration with principals and supervisors, as the factor they liked least about their schools. Twenty-eight percent mentioned this, compared with 19% of the independent day school teachers and 10% of the boarding school teachers. Eighty-eight percent of the public teachers in that state had to turn in lesson plans for approval, compared with 20% of the independent teachers. (Also see Baird, 1977; Chubb & Moe, 1985.)

Classroom freedom, of course, is not absolute. Some independent secondary teachers complain, for example, about the subtle curricular power of the Advanced Placement (AP) examinations of the College Board. Originally designed to make college-level work and college credits available to able high school students, AP courses often function instead to make students' transcripts more impressive to selective colleges. The AP tests thus exert pressure on the independent school curriculum similar to that of state-mandated testing in public schools (Dillon, 1988).

Beyond the classroom, independent school teachers often have substantial influence over school educational policies. Trustees and heads often delegate considerable authority over these matters to faculty committees and faculties as a whole. Indeed, faculty meetings occur frequently at independent schools. Policies are often debated and voted on, rather than just announced. Most schools have a senior administrative position for an academic dean, director of studies, or dean of faculty, a position with no ordinary equivalent in most public schools. One important responsibility is to involve teachers in curricular policy making (Kane, 1986).

These procedures attempt to establish within the faculty a sense of shared authority and responsibility for the school as a community, as distinct from simply a sense of individual authority over each teacher's own classroom. Freedom within the classroom, in these schools, tends to be less a goal to be worked toward than a reality that is somewhat problematic. It is easier for teachers to agree to let each other alone in the classroom than to strive for more cooperative approaches to instruction itself, such as cooperative teaching, team teaching, and joint planning. Although cooperative approaches to schoolwide policy making are common, collaboration in teaching itself is less frequent.[10]

CONCLUSION: NOTES ON DIGNITY AND EFFECTIVENESS

This tentative mapping of the territory concerning workplace conditions in one type of school may illuminate two policy questions faced by all schools. First, how can teachers' work become more dignified and appealing so that teaching attracts and retains its fair share of able young Americans? Second, what conditions of teachers' work seem most closely associated with the fundamental goal of improving student learning and development? These are classic questions with no ready answers. The prestige, status, and desirability of the teaching vocation has long been problematic, especially in the United States. The impact of workplace circumstances on the effectiveness of schooling (as distinct from the impact of instructional and curricular strategies) is a newer and perhaps more subtle concern. But it is rooted firmly in the tradition of examining how structural arrangements and school climate affect both faculty and student behavior.

Our discussion suggests that working conditions at independent schools have many ingredients that reinforce the notion that teaching is attractive and dignified work. In a market-driven "industry" in which most schools must constantly sell themselves to potential clients, teachers are a major marketing tool. In many ways, including participation in educational policy making, they are constantly reminded by their schools how important they are and how good they are. In a society where criticism of teachers is often the norm, such positive market visibility is refreshing. The impact of being advertised as important at the local level should not be underestimated as one source of vocational self-esteem.

Another source of dignity is that the conditions of work in these schools tend to put teaching and learning near the center of institutional concern, rather than on the periphery. One problem with the teaching career in general is not that teaching itself is unappealing or undignified to many young adults, but that teaching is hard to do in many schools. Too many other things, for one reason or another, get in the way. Each of the themes we have examined give support to the teaching role; they do not detract from it. They are enabling conditions that make it easier to teach, rather than harder. This, of course, is not the same thing as saying that good or imaginative teaching will in fact occur. But if it does not, many traditional culprits cannot be blamed. One cannot blame, for example, a fragmented sense of school purpose where policies must accommodate active resistance to learning. Nor can one blame policies where large teaching and counseling loads provide valid excuses for not knowing students and their work.

A third source of dignity is that affluent and educated independent school families tend to demand conditions of work for their children that spill over into teacher workplace conditions. The schools do not look like or feel like large processing plants. If they did, students would not come. Facilities in general are by no means lavish, but they are maintained and rarely appear shabby and neglected. Bathrooms are usable and generally free from graffiti. Student behavior is relatively civil. Visitors often find such schools inviting rather than impersonal. Such features are not merely the inevitable (and therefore dismissable) results of money and social class. They express a commitment to create a decent living environment for all. They express respect for the students, and for the teachers. To stay afloat these schools must convey such signs of respect.

On some other dimensions, however, independent teachers' workplace conditions do not promote the idea of teaching as dignified and appealing work. In the New Jersey study, for example, a higher fraction of independent day teachers believed teaching to lack prestige as a career than did public school teachers (Kane, 1986). Part of this problem may arise from how prestige is viewed by different populations. Many independent school teachers attended independent schools themselves and attended selective colleges populated by students drawn to the highest-status careers in the society. It is perhaps harder to make a commitment to schoolteaching when one's peers routinely enter such occupations as medicine, law, business administration, and Ph.D. programs in academic disciplines. Likewise, it may be harder to feel comfortable in the role (and perhaps with one's students) when the students are bound for the same kinds of selective colleges and the same types of high-status careers. A more prosaic but still powerful explanation may be teacher compensation policies. Low pay is what independent school teachers like least about their work, and in America low pay is closely associated with low prestige. It is by no means clear that the schools know how to change this crucial condition in the near future.[11]

How do these conditions of teachers' work affect students? Is there sufficient "payoff" for *all* schools to emphasize policies that would forge more purposeful communities, more personalization, and more teacher authority? What are the educational limits of such policies? From an educational perspective, one that focuses on students rather than teachers, the general thrust of these policies is somewhat different from those typical of public schools. The latter have tended to respond to the realities of student diversity and the commitment to include and retain all students in school, by offering more educational opportunities (courses, programs, etc.). More recently, proponents of equity have come to realize that providing opportunities is useful but insufficient. All students, not just a few, should have genuine access to those opportunities.

The conditions of work we have discussed bear directly on the issue of access. Their intention is not necessarily to expand curricular and other programs from which students may or may not choose; rather, it is to push, press, and otherwise engage students in whatever learning opportunities are available. The central educational strategy is seen as engagement, not the expansion of curricular opportunity.

Purposeful communities, for example, establish deeply imbedded expectations for participation in learning. Engagement at some level becomes a school norm. Personalization undercuts student anonymity and the preferences of many to remain unengaged, to pass quietly through, accumulating credits and not much more. It is harder to negotiate high school this way if one is known.

So these conditions seem to have important benefits for students as well as for teachers. Yet they also contain certain educational limitations. A central one is that they support cautious and traditional conceptions of educational engagement just as much as they do more fundamental "restructuring" of the educational objectives and pedagogies of schools. They are not neutral about the importance of engagement in school, but they are solidly neutral about the forms engagement can take. There is nothing about these conditions, for example, that calls into question engagement defined as memorizing facts in order to do well on tests. There is nothing about them that weighs the practice of lecturing to small groups of students, or that challenges students to think things through more on their own. Consequently, these conditions of work do not exert much specific impact on how teachers teach in classrooms, or on how they work together, or on what conceptions of learning their students take away.

Thoughts about restructuring education in these fundamental ways are usually far from the minds of independent school clients. In most of the schools there is little market demand for basic changes in classroom pedagogy or in conceptions of what students should know and be able to do after school is over. Nor do most independent school teachers seem dissatisfied by extant classroom practices and student expectations. It is hard enough work—for both students and teachers—to "cover" the curriculum as it is currently defined, without their spending time imagining alternatives. This is especially true when parents are often satisfied if students work hard and achieve decent grades and scores. In these schools there is little sense of educational failure; in fact, the conditions of teachers' work may well encourage complacency.[12]

NOTES

1. Estimates of the number of independent schools and student enrollments include not only National Association of Independent Schools (NAIS) member schools (roughly 900 schools, enrolling 353,000 students) but nonmember schools who generally meet NAIS eligibility requirements. Since paying NAIS dues seems the major deterrent to seeking NAIS membership for most otherwise eligible schools, it seems fair to conclude that NAIS schools constitute the most financially privileged of the independent schools.

2. For a comparison of independent secondary schools to affluent suburban public schools, in which educational similarities outweighed educational differences, see Baird (1977), Chapter 8.

3. NAIS has made a school's commitment to diversification, especially racial nondiscrimination, a criterion for membership. By collecting and publishing statistics about financial aid and gender equity, and endorsing multicultural curricula, NAIS has attempted to redefine independent schools in ways that supplement technical matters of governance and finance with ethical concerns.

These include a school's commitment to free and open educational inquiry. In this sense, to the limited extent that a voluntary member association can articulate principles for a diverse community of schools, the definition of an independent school has gradually incorporated social meanings that were neither present nor explicit a generation ago.

4. It is very difficult to obtain reliable data on family income within independent schools. One annual effort is the Student Descriptive Questionnaire, a voluntary survey completed by most students taking the Scholastic Aptitude Test. Analysis of the 1986–1987 data from independent school test takers suggests that nearly half of independent school seniors had family incomes of more than $70,000 and that two-thirds had family incomes of $50,000 or more. This contrasts, respectively, with 12% and 28% for SAT test takers from other schools (Powell, 1987). It should be noted, however, that upper-income adolescents may be unlikely to know family income with much precision, in part because it often derives from sources in addition to salaries and wages. These data certainly underestimate independent school faculty income.

5. St. Paul's wealth and sense of distinctive educational purpose enabled it to finance, for *Daedalus* magazine, a collection of scholarly essays on American public and private education. Lightfoot's (1983) essay on the school, and Grant's (1988) awareness of it as a contrast to Hamilton, grew from their participation in this project. For more evidence of how the school's "revolution" seemed finished by 1980, see Jackson's (1981) laudatory treatment of St. Paul's. Although the late 1960s transformed few independent schools in the manner of Hamilton High, many experienced severe strain. At Andover, for example, the library's card catalog was vandalized and a warning shot was fired during a break-in attempt (see Allis, 1979, pp. 636–682). The most comprehensive account of how independent schools experienced the late 1960s is in Blackmer (1970).

6. Major surveys involving independent school teachers start with Kraushaar (1972), whose work rests in part on a survey returned by some 844 private school teachers, of whom 275 were from "independent" private schools. An early and primitive federal survey (Abramowitz & Stackhouse, 1980) polled 600 private school heads, not teachers, and made no effort to break out different types of private schools. The large-scale High School and Beyond project funded by the Department of Education included an Administrator and Teacher Survey that was one of the largest private school teacher surveys to that time. But only a very small number of independent school teachers were included. The survey results are reported in Chubb & Moe (1985).

During the 1980s, the Department of Education itself began to collect more detailed data on private schools, including teacher surveys. The most recent published material was collected during the 1985–1986 school year, in a survey of 5,295 private school teachers, of which about 23% taught in "nonsectarian" private schools, as distinct from "Catholic" and "other religious" schools. These data are summarized in NCES (1987).

None of the post–Kraushaar (1972) teacher surveys breaks out "independent" schools from "other private" schools, although this is a clear intention of the

1988 Schools and Staffing Survey (SASS) of the National Center for Education Statistics, and also of the federally sponsored NELS:88 longitudinal study in which more than 60 independent schools participated. First reports from these studies will appear in 1990.

For the purposes of this chapter, the most suggestive survey data on independent school teachers comes from Kane (1986). Kane created a representative sample of 130 public secondary and 113 private secondary teachers from 60 New Jersey schools, and collected data through 243 structured interviews in 1985. Since Kane's work is cited throughout this chapter, it should be emphasized that it is one small study within one state. Its results are suggestive, but nothing more.

7. The organization is called Boarding Schools. In addition, certain girls' boarding schools have engaged in cooperative marketing research.

8. Twenty percent of NAIS-member schools are also affiliated with associations representing Episcopal, Roman Catholic, and Friends' schools.

9. For purposes of this analysis I have compared school heads' salaries to principals', not superintendents'. The focus of this section is on authority relations within schools. Further, my experience is that the comparison with principals is not inappropriate, even though the roles differ in important respects.

10. The academic department is probably the most important high school setting for shaping teacher attitudes about independence and collaboration. It would normally be the place to debate, for example, the merits of having the required junior-year American history curriculum taught as a single course by several teachers but experienced in roughly similar ways by students because of similar materials, pacing, and joint experiences. Another proposal might be to make it a series of quite distinct courses operating under the same name but with different purposes, materials, examinations, and so forth, mirroring the preferences of the instructors. The choices schools make on this issue determine whether courses will have regular staff meetings associated with them, and these are often the only setting where teachers ever interact on substance, as distinct from logistics. Unfortunately, there is very little literature on this aspect of teachers' work lives, and less still on the situation in independent schools.

11. It is not easy to bring about substantial, across-the-board increases in faculty compensation within independent schools. Virtually all their income comes from a small base of tuition-paying families. Only a tiny number of schools, mainly boarding schools, have endowments yielding significant income. No public assistance is available for student financial aid. In these circumstances, few policy options for generating additional funds for major salary increases have seemed attractive. In a market-sensitive world, few schools have opted for substantial increases in school size, or reductions in faculty size, or dramatic increases in tuition. For examples of creative attempts to raise salaries despite these constraints, see Goldman (1988).

12. Evidence for these last assertions is found in the field notes for the national inquiry called "A Study of High Schools" (1981–1985) and in my own experiences to date with members of the Coalition of Essential Schools, Brown University.

REFERENCES

Abramowitz, S., & Stackhouse, E. A. (1980). *The private high school today.* Washington, DC: U.S. Department of Education.

Allis, F. S., Jr. (1979). *Youth from every quarter: A bicentennial history of Phillips Academy, Andover.* Hanover, NH: University Press of New England.

Anson, R. S. (1987). *Best intentions: The education and killing of Edmund Perry.* New York: Random House.

Baird, L. L. (1977). *The elite schools: A profile of prestigious independent schools.* Lexington, MA: Lexington Books.

Blackmer, A. R. (1970). *An inquiry into student unrest in independent secondary schools.* Boston: National Association of Independent Schools.

Boarding Schools. (1987). *The new marketing handbook for independent schools.* Boston: Author.

Chubb, J. E., & Moe, T. M. (1985, August). *Politics, markets and the organization of schools.* Paper presented at the Annual Meeting of the American Political Science Association, New Orleans, LA.

Coleman, J. S., & Hoffer, T. (1987). *Public and private high schools: The impact of communities.* New York: Basic Books.

Coles, R. (1977). *Children of privilege.* Boston: Little, Brown.

The competitive state of private-independent schools. (1989). *Ideas & Perspectives, 13*(2), 53–56.

Cookson, P. W. Jr., & Persell, C. H. (1985). *Preparing for power: America's elite boarding schools.* New York: Basic Books.

Dillon, D. H. (1988). The AP effect. *Independent School, 47*(3), 34–35.

Finn, C. E. Jr. (1989). Are public and private schools converging? *Independent School, 48*(2), 45–55.

Goldman, R. P. (1988). *Profession at risk: Eight schools face the faculty compensation issue.* Boston: National Association of Independent Schools.

Grant, G. (1988). *The world we created at Hamilton High.* Cambridge, MA: Harvard University Press.

Graubard, S. R. (1981). Introduction. *Daedalus, 110,* xi.

Griffith, T. (1987). *The audiovisual marketing handbook for independent schools.* Boston: Boarding Schools.

Heckscher, A. (1980). *St. Paul's. The life of a New England school.* New York: Charles Scribner's Sons.

Jackson, P. W. (1981). Secondary schools for the privileged few: A report on a visit to a New England boardingschool. *Daedalus, 110,* 117–130.

Kane, P. R. (1986). *Teachers in public and independent schools: A comparative study.* New York: Columbia University, Teachers College, Klingenstein Center.

Kraushaar, O. F. (1972). *American nonpublic schools: Patterns of diversity.* Baltimore and London: Johns Hopkins University Press.

Lightfoot, S. L. (1983). *The good high school: Portraits of character and culture.* New York: Basic Books.

Lloyd, S. M. (1987). *The Putney School*. New Haven: Yale University Press.

McNeil, L. M. (1987). Exit, voice and community: Magnet teachers' responses to standardization. *Educational Policy, 1,* 93–113.

National Association of Independent Schools (NAIS). (1985). *NAIS fall 1985 statistics*. Boston: Author.

National Association of Independent Schools (NAIS). (1987). *NAIS fall 1987 statistics*. Boston: Author.

National Association of Independent Schools (NAIS). (1988a). *NAIS spring 1988 statistics*. Boston: Author.

National Association of Independent Schools (NAIS). (1988b). *NAIS fall 1988 statistics*. Boston: Author.

National Association of Independent Schools (NAIS). (1989). *Student attrition in NAIS member schools*. Boston: Author.

National Association of Secondary School Principals (NASSP). (1988). *Salaries paid principals and assistant principals, 1987–88 school year*. Reston, VA: Author.

National Center for Education Statistics (NCES). (1987). *Private schools and private school teachers: Final report of the 1985–86 private school study*. Washington, DC: Author.

Powell, A. G. (1980). *The uncertain profession: Harvard and the search for educational authority*. Cambridge, MA: Harvard University Press.

Powell, A. G. (1986). [Preliminary tabulation of intern-beginning teacher survey]. Unpublished report, Commission on Educational Issues, Boston.

Powell, A. G. (1987). *1986–87 independent school family income distribution*. Boston: National Association of Independent Schools.

Powell, A. G. (1988a). [Survey data on independent school professional development programs]. Unpublished raw data.

Powell, A. G. (1988b). Author's analysis of NAIS data.

Powell, A. G., Farrar, E., & Cohen, D. K. (1985). *The shopping mall high school: Winners and losers in the educational marketplace*. Boston: Houghton Mifflin.

Roeser, S. (1987). School selection factors: What research tells us. In Boarding Schools, *The new marketing handbook for independent schools* (pp. 24–26). Boston: Boarding Schools.

Rutter, M., Maughan, B., Mortimore, P., Ouston, J., & Smith, A. (1979). *Fifteen thousand hours: Secondary schools and their effects on children*. Cambridge, MA: Harvard University Press.

5

Schoolwork: Perspectives on Workplace Reform in Public Schools

THOMAS B. CORCORAN

The working conditions in public schools and the effects these conditions have on teacher work performance are important factors that must be addressed in efforts to reform public education. Comparing actual workplace conditions described by teachers to those identified by researchers as optimal focuses attention on issues that must be addressed by reformers. Such a comparative analysis is undertaken here to help reformers achieve their dual goals of making teaching a more attractive profession and improving the performance of the public schools. In addition, to provide a framework for a critical examination of current reforms in the schools, the analysis produces agendas for both researchers and policy makers.

A descriptive summary of recent surveys of teachers' opinions about their working conditions is followed by a brief review of the findings from research on effective schools. Next, the conclusions from a recent study of the effects of varying working conditions on urban teachers are presented and compared with the survey data. Arguments for increasing teacher participation in school decision making are then examined, followed by a discussion of the congruence between the workplace issues identified as critical by teachers and researchers and those being addressed by reformers. Finally, implications are drawn for efforts directed at improving workplace conditions in the schools and at "professionalizing" teaching.

This chapter was commissioned by the Center for Research on the Context of Secondary School Teaching, supported by funds from the U.S. Department of Education Office of Educational Research and Improvement (Grant No. G0087C0235). The analyses and conclusions do not necessarily reflect the views or policies of this organization.

TEACHERS' VIEWS OF THE SCHOOL AS A WORKPLACE

When asked about their concerns about working conditions, do teachers identify the same issues as those identified in the effective-schools literature? Four surveys of teacher opinions about working conditions are reviewed here:

1. The Conditions and Resources of Teaching study (CART), a national survey conducted for the National Education Association (NEA) (Bacharach, Bauer, & Shedd, 1986)
2. The Metropolitan Life (1986) survey
3. An Eagleton Poll survey of New Jersey teachers (Center for Public Interest Polling, 1986)
4. The 1986 survey of California teachers conducted by Policy Analysis for California Education (PACE) (Koppich, Gerritz, & Guthrie, 1986)

In this section, when discussing these four surveys, I will refer to them by shortened title only (i.e., CART, Metropolitan Life, Eagleton, and PACE), dispensing with the formal citations listed here.

Analysis of the results of these surveys yields 11 workplace conditions of critical concern to public school teachers. Although the conceptual frameworks and the questions used in the four surveys differed somewhat, there was considerable overlap in the issues covered. Due to these differences in the surveys, however, the 11 conditions discussed here are not always supported by findings from all four surveys.

Condition 1: Salaries and opportunities for advancement are often inadequate. Studies of job performance have repeatedly found that adequate compensation is critical to employee satisfaction (Lawler, 1987; Yankelovich & Immerwahr, 1983). The CART survey did not ask respondents about salaries, but teachers responding to the Metropolitan Life survey felt that raising teacher salaries was the most important single reform to fund. Fifty-three percent of New Jersey teachers responding to the Eagleton survey expressed dissatisfaction with their salaries, and 43% of those who planned to leave the profession within 5 years cited low salaries as their primary reason. Furthermore, 94% of all Eagleton respondents agreed that low salaries were a major reason that good teachers left classroom work in public education. Similarly, in the PACE survey, 100 of 800 California teachers, responding to an open-ended question, said that increased salaries would be the one change that could most improve their jobs. While this may not at first seem like a strong response, it should be noted that some surveys may overestimate the importance of salary and other workplace factors because they allow for "ideal" responses, whereas data from open-ended questions may reflect more accurately the actual concerns and expectations of respondents.

Additional evidence about the inadequacy of teacher salaries comes from the number of teachers holding second jobs. In the Eagleton sample, 29% reported holding a second job during the year (50% of the men, compared with 20% of the women), and 42% worked in the summer (66% of the men, compared with 29% of the women). The PACE survey found that 4 in 10 of all California teachers and half of the secondary teachers held second jobs.

Experienced teachers cannot easily improve their salaries or positions by moving from one district to another, due to barriers in the labor market. Loss of salary, tenure, and professional status among their peers act as constraints against seeking jobs in other districts. The Metropolitan Life survey reported that 30% of teachers had been negatively affected by such restrictions on teacher mobility between school districts. This may be one reason why 80% of the California respondents favored career ladders and 50% of the New Jersey respondents said they would apply for master teacher positions if they had the opportunity. The Metropolitan Life survey found that teachers familiar with career ladders (only 39%) were split equally for and against the proposal.

Condition 2: Many teachers spend significant amounts of time beyond regular working hours on their work, and employers take this extra effort for granted. One of the characteristics of a good work environment is that people are given adequate time to do the work (Bacharach, Bauer, & Shedd, 1986). The two state polls by Eagleton and PACE asked teachers how many hours they spent on schoolwork. One out of every four New Jersey teachers reported working 55 hours a week or more on schoolwork. Nearly half of the California teachers reported spending 11 hours a week or more beyond the regular workday on grading, planning, and talking to parents.

Heavy workloads, the time spent on paperwork and other nonteaching duties, and ambiguous expectations about responsibilities compound the time problems faced by teachers. Lack of time to prepare was often mentioned as a source of job dissatisfaction by New Jersey teachers (28%), and over a third of the California teachers in the PACE poll reported putting in at least 11 hours weekly in clerical work and record-keeping unrelated to instruction. Over a third of the California teachers reported they had no planning time during the workday, and almost two-thirds of the elementary teachers in the California sample also had none.

While the CART survey did not address the issue of preparation time directly, teachers did report that they had problems finding time for counseling students (57%), grading (55%), and planning (48%). The other surveys did not address this issue.

Condition 3: Many teachers face too many children each day. A primary factor in job performance is that the employees must believe that the assigned work is feasible. Teachers' views about the feasibility of their assignments are influenced by the number of students they must teach on a daily or weekly basis. For many teachers, especially those in secondary schools, the numbers are too large to provide the degree of personal attention that teachers and researchers feel is necessary (Stedman, 1985).

In New Jersey, a high-expenditure state, public school teachers by and large expressed satisfaction with their class sizes; only 20% were dissatisfied. However, this figure rose to 32% for urban teachers, whose classes were generally larger. In the PACE survey, however, much higher numbers of teachers reported that their classes were too large. Seventy-four percent of the elementary teachers faced 26 to 50 children a day. Twenty-six percent of secondary teachers had over 150 students a day, and 40% had between 100 and 150. The Metropolitan Life results were similar to those from California; 68% of the teachers said that their class sizes were too large and the median number of students faced was 25 per class. The CART survey did not ask about class size.

Condition 4: Teachers have too few opportunities for interaction with their colleagues. Studies of effective schools show collegiality and opportunities for staff interaction to be related to job satisfaction and organizational effectiveness (Little, 1982; Purkey & Smith, 1983). The CART survey did not ask about collegiality, but the Metropolitan Life survey reported that 71% of teachers favored formal structures such as teacher centers where they could get help from other teachers, 69% wanted other teachers to help them with difficult students, 61% supported more structured time for talking about professional matters, 59% wanted more support from the noneducational professionals in their systems, and 56% thought opportunities to observe other teachers would help them improve their performance.

PACE also found that teachers believed that they could improve their teaching by working with their colleagues, but most reported that they had only limited contact. Fewer than 14% of the respondents said that their school administrations scheduled time when teachers could talk to one another about professional matters, while 93% said they wanted such time. Data on opportunities for observation of colleagues are equally striking: While 97% said that this would help them improve their teaching, only 6% reported opportunities to do so on a regular basis. Similarly, 92% said they would like help with student and parent problems, but only 33% reported that they got such help. In contrast, almost 80% of Eagleton's New Jersey teachers expressed satisfaction with the opportunities they had for collegial interaction. This may be the result of smaller class sizes and workloads in New Jersey, or it may simply be an artifact of the survey design.

Condition 5: A significant minority of teachers lack the material resources needed to carry out their jobs. To be optimally productive, employees must have the resources needed to do their jobs (Kanter, 1983; Stein, 1983). The CART survey defined the critical material resources for teachers as time, space, equipment, supplies, and teaching materials. As discussed earlier, time is a particularly scarce resource for teachers. The CART survey also reported that 15% of the teachers sampled ran into frequent problems with supplies and workbooks. PACE found that 25% lacked sufficient books and materials. On the other hand, the Eagleton survey found teachers were generally satisfied with the supplies available to them, the exception again being urban teachers, of whom 28% expressed dissatisfaction.

Condition 6: Teachers have few opportunities to bring their professional expertise to bear on school decisions. Employees' participation in decisions affecting their work increases their job satisfaction and may increase their productivity (Corcoran, 1987; Kanter, 1983; Shedd, 1987). The CART survey examined five categories of school decisions: organizational policies, student policies, teacher development and evaluation, work allocation, and teaching processes. Teachers reported limited opportunities to influence workplace decisions, with the exception of those concerning what and how to teach and selection of texts and materials. Some of the results were surprising. The percentages of teachers who said they seldom or only occasionally had input into the following areas are as shown: discipline codes, 61%; grading policies, 61%; staff-development planning, 60%; school assignments, 54%; and what to teach, 38%.

The Metropolitan Life survey found almost universal support among teachers for team management (97%), but only half of the teachers reported that they currently shared in decisions. The vast majority of teachers wanted, and administrators agreed they should have, a bigger role in decisions affecting academics, pedagogy, and students. They were less interested in influence over administrative decisions such as scheduling or setting budgets. In the Eagleton poll, only one in seven of the teachers surveyed was satisfied with their policy input. All four polls reported great discrepancies between the influence teachers actually had over school policies and what they felt was appropriate.

Condition 7: Teachers feel that school administrators are not supportive of their efforts. Kanter (1983) describes support (endorsement, backing, approval, and legitimacy) as one of the three basic sources of power in an organization. Teachers often feel a lack of such support from their supervisors. Communication between teachers and building-level administrators is less frequent than desired and seldom focuses on instruction. Over half of the teacher respondents to the CART survey spoke to administrators only a few times a week or less. Two-thirds said they seldom spoke to administrators about their performance, educational ideas, course content, or instructional problems. Only half of the teachers indicated administrators showed any appreciation for their work.

The Eagleton survey found problems with administrators to be one of the most frequent sources of teacher dissatisfaction; in fact, 18% of all respondents cited it. One-quarter said that more contact with administrators would make their jobs easier. Teachers wanted more support with discipline, dealing with parents, and handling paperwork. Inaccessibility or lack of interest was cited by 29% as a problem with administrators.

In California, most teachers said their school administrators offered insufficient professional support. Only 15% reported formal systems for helping new teachers, and only 58% reported principals assisting with student and parent problems. One-fifth of the PACE respondents (22%) reported lack of access to specialists who could help with specific students.

Condition 8: Many experienced teachers find evaluation and supervision practices to be unhelpful. One of the primary purposes of teacher evaluation systems is the improvement of the individual's craft (Wise, Darling-Hammond, McLaughlin, & Bernstein, 1984). Analysis of the data from the CART survey found supportive supervisory behavior correlated with job satisfaction; conversely, critical and formal supervisory behavior was related to dissatisfaction. Supportive behavior was defined as complimenting good performance, encouraging participation in decisions, and setting clear expectations. Fewer than half of the respondents attributed these behaviors to their supervisors. PACE found that only 54% of teachers felt that their supervision process was fair, and only 52% felt that the evaluators knew teachers' specific strengths and weaknesses. Less than half reported receiving useful feedback. The Eagleton survey found that 38% of New Jersey's teachers felt their most recent evaluation was unhelpful; only 27% said it was very helpful. Teachers with more experience were more likely to find evaluations unhelpful.

Condition 9: Recognition of good work, extra effort, or special achievements is infrequent, and there are few rewards for good performance. Being rewarded or recognized for good performance is one of the aspects of work that enhances individual productivity; it is both a motivator and a source of job satisfaction (Stein, 1983; Yankelovich & Immerwahr, 1983). While neither the Metropolitan Life nor PACE surveys asked teachers about rewards or recognition of their work efforts, the Eagleton survey of New Jersey teachers reported that 65% of the respondents said that lack of rewards for good performance in the classroom was a major reason that people left teaching. The same survey, however, found over half of the respondents opposed to any form of recognition pay. Teachers opposed it because they questioned the fairness of criteria used to evaluate teaching and because they feared that classroom performance would not determine recognition pay decisions. The CART survey found that positive supervisory behavior, including compliments about good performance, correlated with job satisfaction, but not with career commitment.

Condition 10: Teachers do not view the professional development opportunities available to them as particularly useful. Development of new skills and abilities is a major source of motivation in the workplace (Yankelovich & Immerwahr, 1983). The CART survey found that teachers regard personal experience and contact with other teachers as the most effective sources of additional knowledge. In-service training ranked last; only 12% of the respondents considered it to be effective. University graduate courses were more highly rated, with almost 40% finding them to be effective. The Metropolitan Life survey asked no direct questions about professional development, but did find strong support for "teacher centers." The two state surveys did not ask respondents to assess the quality of in-service programs or professional development opportunities, but both surveys found strong support for collegial interaction, indirect evidence for the proposition that teachers feel they learn more, or learn more efficiently, from their peers.

Condition 11: Teachers do not always receive respectful treatment from administrators, students, or parents. Working with people who respect you is one of the most widely valued characteristics of a good workplace (Yankelovich & Immerwahr, 1983). For teachers, this means respect from students, parents, administrators, school staff, and other teachers. The

Eagleton poll asked teachers about the problems of uninterested students and unsupportive parents. Over three-quarters (78%) of the respondents said that uninterested students were a somewhat or very serious problem; 75% responded similarly about unsupportive parents. In addition, more than half of these New Jersey teachers said that lack of student respect and discipline were serious problems, and 11% listed lack of respect as the most important reason for leaving teaching. The other surveys did not deal directly with this issue.

The findings from the four surveys paint a bleak picture of the conditions of teaching in the public schools. It is clear from the survey results that the work environments experienced by most teachers are inadequate. According to the surveys, a majority of teachers believe that their salaries are too low, and majorities also report a lack of respect at work, low levels of influence over decisions affecting their work, limited opportunities for collegiality, and little support or recognition from their supervisors. Large numbers of public school teachers also feel that their workloads are too heavy, their classes too large, their instructional resources inadequate, their supervision unfair and unhelpful, and their opportunities for professional development ineffective.

Clearly, these conditions will not attract talented young people into teaching, nor will they inspire people who enter teaching to remain in the profession. Finally, such conditions do not encourage teachers to give their best efforts on the job and to work to improve their effectiveness. Improving the schools and strengthening the profession require that these conditions be changed.

RESEARCH ON EFFECTIVE SCHOOLS AND WORKING CONDITIONS

Studies of effective schools have examined many of the same issues raised by the teacher surveys. These studies also have raised, but have not satisfactorily answered, questions about the linkages between teacher working conditions and student achievement. This literature has directed the attention of policy makers to the importance of staff collegiality and collaboration and to the effects that professional cultures in schools have on overall effectiveness.

Two recent reanalyses of effective-schools studies, one by Rosenholtz (1985) and another by Stedman (1985), have concluded that the schools identified in the studies as the most effective were more successful at recruiting and holding talented teachers. Rosenholtz (1985) concluded that principals in these schools created conditions under which

teachers received more support and encouragement from their colleagues and supervisors and, as a consequence, felt more confident about
their eventual success with their students. These conditions contributed
to actual success with students, bringing greater psychic rewards for
the teachers, who were thus motivated to work even harder. Rosenholtz found that the most important factors in effective schools are
leaders who create good conditions for teaching; the recruitment of
talented teaching staffs; and the effort, commitment, and involvement of
those staffs.

Other reviews of the effective-schools literature have reached similar
conclusions about the importance of good teachers and the role of good
working conditions in their recruitment and retention. Analysts have
recommended increasing the influence of teachers over school policy
(Bird & Little, 1986; Purkey & Smith, 1983), giving teachers more control
and discretion over matters affecting their work (Corcoran, 1987), providing more opportunities for teachers to interact with their professional
peers (Little, 1982), lowering child/adult ratios (Stedman, 1985), and
increasing teachers' involvement in planning and delivering staff development (Purkey & Smith, 1983).

The effective-schools literature also describes some of the characteristics of the work environment in which teachers are likely to be most
effective (Purkey & Smith, 1983; Stedman, 1985). These include

1. Shared goals and high expectations of success
2. Respectful and dignified treatment as professionals, by superiors, parents, and students
3. An orderly school climate in which discipline is a by-product of
   school organization
4. Strong and supportive instructional leadership and supervision
5. Adequate and protected instructional time
6. Participation by teachers in the decisions affecting their work
7. Regular opportunities for collegial interaction and sharing that
   promote skill development and professional support
8. Recognition and rewards for efforts and achievement
9. Opportunities for professional growth
10. Decent and safe physical working conditions

These 10 conditions appear to have significant impact on the skills,
behavior, and attitudes of teachers and contribute to higher levels of
teacher performance, positively affecting teacher attendance, level of
effort, commitment to the school, sense of efficacy, and job satisfaction
(Corcoran, 1987; Firestone, 1986; Rosenholtz, 1985). Viewed as a gestalt,

they provide a framework for the design of good professional teaching environments. They also set the agenda for the reform of the school as a workplace.

A STUDY OF URBAN SCHOOLS BY THE INSTITUTE
OF EDUCATIONAL LEADERSHIP

The findings drawn from the effective-schools research are corroborated by a qualitative study of working conditions in urban public schools conducted by the Institute of Educational Leadership (IEL), reported by Corcoran, White, & Walker (1988). The IEL data draw upon 400 in-depth interviews with teachers and administrators from 31 schools in five urban districts, providing a detailed description of working conditions in urban settings and documenting the variations in working conditions across schools and districts. The study provides insights into the effects of working conditions on the attitudes and job performance of urban teachers and the factors that account for variations in these effects across school sites.

The IEL (Corcoran, White, & Walker, 1988) findings are summarized as follows:

- *Physical conditions.* Twenty-two of the 31 school facilities were adequate, but many were dreary and suffered from delayed repairs and lack of space. The 9 inadequate schools suffered from severe problems of overcrowding, neglect, decay, and lack of security.
- *Resources.* Twenty-five schools had serious shortages of staff and supplies. The most common problems were lack of counselors, specialists, support staff, and basic supplies such as paper.
- *Workload.* Class sizes averaged over 25 in 18 schools and over 30 in 8 schools. Teachers averaged 8 to 10 extra hours on schoolwork per week.
- *Autonomy.* There was a loss of teacher influence over curricula due to testing and monitoring programs, but most schools gave teachers considerable autonomy over how they taught.
- *Influence.* A high level of influence was accorded to teachers in setting goals, selecting materials, and defining student rules, but their influence was low in most other areas of decision making. More input was desired on student assignments, time allocation, enforcement of rules, teaching assignments, and class size. Teaming and elected faculty councils affected staff influence positively.
- *Supervision.* The staff at most schools assessed supervision as inadequate. In spite of the introduction of new "clinical" supervision proce-

dures in 20 of the schools, supervision was seen as unhelpful and pro forma in most of them.

- *Professional growth.* Opportunities were viewed as inadequate in 18 of the schools. They were viewed more positively where there were building-level programs and staff input into planning.
- *Rewards.* In 27 of the schools, little or nothing was done to reward or recognize teachers. Informal appreciation was rare in most of the schools.
- *Leadership.* Administrators played critical roles in shaping school working conditions. Leadership was described as good in only 9 schools, while in 11 the administrators were seen as ineffective and incompetent.
- *Students.* The behavior and performance of students affected teacher attitudes and performance, but the ethnic and social background of the students did not. Student discipline, attendance, and commitment to school tasks had powerful effects on teacher morale and sense of efficacy.

In summary, then, dreary physical conditions, inadequate human and material resources, heavy workloads, low levels of teacher input and influence over school policy, weak supervision and professional development, lack of recognition, and weak or mediocre administrative leadership were characteristic of the urban schools studied. Working conditions were worse in the high schools, and there was considerable variation within as well as across the districts. The conditions were more severe than those reported in the teacher surveys discussed previously, but this would be expected, given that this study focused exclusively on schools in urban settings where the social and economic circumstances are more extreme. The overall pattern of working conditions described in the IEL study (Corcoran, White, & Walker, 1988) substantiates the problems identified by teachers in the other surveys.

Working Conditions and Teacher Behavior

Most of the teachers interviewed by IEL (Corcoran, White, & Walker, 1988) felt that the working conditions in their schools had significant effects, both positive and negative, on their colleagues. The most commonly mentioned positive effects were enthusiasm, high morale, cooperation, and acceptance of responsibility. The most frequently cited negative effects were absenteeism, reduced level of effort, lowered effectiveness in the classroom, low morale, and reduced job satisfaction.

By comparing teacher perceptions of working conditions and staff attitudes and behavior from pairs of schools serving the same grade levels in each of the five districts, IEL found strong support for the contention that working conditions in schools affect teachers' attitudes and behaviors. Of 15 pairs, 14 were comprised of schools whose working conditions, as perceived by their staffs, differed. In 12 of these 14 sets, there were positive correlations between working conditions and teacher attitudes and behaviors. The two exceptions involved pairs of schools that included turnaround schools in which strong positive leadership, orderly climates, and high staff collegiality appeared to be compensating for poor physical conditions and resource inadequacies. Teacher attitudes in these schools were as positive as those in the matched schools with better overall working conditions.

Good Work Sites

Data on 10 dimensions of working conditions in the 31 schools were compiled into an index, and the schools were ranked in terms of their overall working conditions. The 10 dimensions examined were physical plant, resources, teaching load, teacher influence in the classroom, staff collegiality, teacher participation in school decisions, professional development, rewards, supervision, and administrative leadership. Of the top 5 schools, 3 were elementary schools. Elementary schools are smaller and have a less-differentiated workforce, higher goal consensus, and more frequent contact between teachers and administrators (Firestone & Herriott, 1982). These factors undoubtedly contributed to the positive teacher assessments of conditions in these schools.

The student populations in the five schools with the best overall conditions did not differ significantly from those in the other schools studied. The social and ethnic backgrounds of their students and the size of their enrollments varied widely. The proportion of minority students ranged from 60% to 90%. One school's clientele were 85% low-income children, and all schools enrolled one-third or more low-SES children. The teachers, however, reported having fewer disciplinary problems and receiving more parental support than teachers in the other schools in this sample. As a consequence, teachers in these schools felt more positive about their students.

When other working conditions were examined, there were some significant similarities across the five sites. All were described positively with regard to their physical conditions, staff collegiality, staff participation in decision making, and administrative leadership. All had mechanisms for staff participation in decision making: Three had team planning, and three had councils for faculty participation in decision making. Four of the five also received positive ratings on the amount of influence teachers exercised over curriculum and instruction. Finally, staff assessments of rewards and recognition in these schools, while not always positive, were still higher than those in the other schools in the sample. Staff assessments of the other four dimensions of school work life examined by IEL varied considerably, however.

These positive overall working conditions seemed to contribute to similarly positive patterns of staff behavior. Staff working in the schools with better working conditions generally reported that they and their colleagues had more positive attitudes and felt more effective. Morale was said to be higher. There was less staff absenteeism, and more hours were being devoted to schoolwork outside of the normal workday.

Poor Work Sites

The schools with the worst overall working conditions were examined in a similar manner. These schools were characterized by their staffs as having poor resources, low collegiality, poor professional development opportunities, low levels of teacher influence over school decisions, little recognition and few rewards, and poor leadership. Teacher effort, classroom effectiveness, morale, and job satisfaction were all negatively affected in the 10 schools with the worst overall working conditions.

The schools given the most negative evaluations by staff had four common characteristics: poor resources, low collegiality, low rewards, and low levels of teacher influence on school decisions. Six of the 10 had poor administrative leadership; in 3 of the other 4 cases, the principals were new to the school and were rated as adequate by their staffs, who appeared prepared to grant them time to prove themselves.

None of the remaining schools in the IEL sample had the combination of conditions characterizing either the "best" or the "worst" sites. Some of them had good leadership but had terrible resource deficiencies or extremely difficult student populations, or lacked good collegial relations due to conflicts among the staff. Others had high levels of collegiality and teacher influence but lacked good leadership or had terrible physical working conditions. The point is that, if they did not have the entire gestalt of positive factors found in the "best" sites, teachers described them as less than adequate workplaces and their attitudes and behaviors were affected accordingly. In these schools, teachers coped but were unable or unwilling to sustain their best efforts.

Interpretation of Data

The IEL data support the hypothesis that working conditions affect teacher attitudes and behavior, specifically their level of effort, attendance, effectiveness in the classroom, morale, and job satisfaction. The data also suggest that some dimensions of working conditions have more powerful effects than others on teachers. Adequate physical conditions, moderate to high levels of teacher influence in their classrooms and in the school, high levels of collegiality, some recognition, well-behaved students, and good leadership appear to be the critical factors. Factors such as access to professional development, amount of workload, and the quality of supervision appear to be less important, perhaps because the range of variation in these areas was found to be lower. These findings are consistent with the findings from the effective-schools research: When teachers feel sufficiently positive about their work, they are willing to give extra effort. They also are more likely to have higher rates of attendance and feel more effective in their classrooms.

In the worst cases, none of the conditions associated with high teacher work effort were positive and, in addition, resources were terribly inadequate. Under such conditions, teachers became frustrated and discouraged. Their morale sank to low levels, and it affected their work effort and attendance. They felt ineffective in their classrooms as a consequence of conditions in the school.

The data suggest that, when resources are adequate and some other work conditions are positive, teachers will cope and keep a school functioning. To get the best out of teachers and make a school function well, however, a particular combination of positive factors is required.

If teacher commitment to task (as evidenced by level of effort and attendance) and sense of efficacy are important to school effectiveness, then creating the gestalt of conditions found in the "best" sites among the IEL sample must be part of any reform agenda. The data clearly suggest that the entire gestalt must be present to produce the desired effects on teachers. Improvements in supervision and staff development, for example, are less likely to produce significant positive changes in teachers' attitudes and behavior if these other conditions are not present.

SUMMARY OF FINDINGS ON WORKING CONDITIONS

Table 5.1 summarizes the working-conditions issues raised by the teacher surveys discussed earlier, various studies of effective schools, and

TABLE 5.1. Summary of Variables Identified as Significant Problems in Various
Studies of Teacher Working Conditions

Dimension	Teacher Surveys	Effective Schools	IEL
Salaries	Yes	ND[1]	ND
Class size	Yes	No	Yes
Workload	Yes	No	Yes
Prep time	Yes	ND	Yes
Instructional resources	Yes	Yes	Yes
Physical conditions	ND	Yes	Yes
Leadership	Yes	Yes	Yes
Supervision	Yes	Yes	No
Shared goals	ND	Yes	ND
Teacher influence in decisions	Yes	Yes	Yes
Collegiality	Yes	Yes	Yes
Teacher autonomy	No	Yes	Yes
Recognition and rewards	Yes	Yes	Yes
Respectful treatment	Yes	Yes	Yes
Professional growth	Yes	Yes	No
Student behavior/attitudes	Yes	Yes	Yes

[1]ND = no data.

the IEL study (Corcoran, White, & Walker, 1988). The similarities in the three sets of findings are more significant than their differences. The survey data make it clear that the work situations of significant numbers of teachers do not measure up on factors identified by all three as critical. Negative evaluations on the dimensions of leadership, respect, influence over policy, opportunities for collegiality, instructional resources, support and recognition, and student behavior are identified as serious problems in all three lists. Deficits in these conditions seem to be more the norm than the exception in public education. All represent deficiencies in the professional cultures of schools. Given these conditions, it is not surprising that many schools are less effective than the public expects them to be, nor is it surprising that it is difficult to recruit and retain teachers.

The data from these sources also suggest that resource problems must be addressed if teaching is to become an attractive profession. Among the areas that one or more of these sources named as problematic are salaries, workloads, class sizes, and instructional materials. The survey data and the IEL findings point to adequate resources as a base from which to build quality schools. These findings expand the agenda for workplace reform suggested by the effective-schools studies. Remedying these resource problems should help improve school effectiveness in the long run, because it will attract better teachers and is likely to improve the performance of all teachers.

Good supervision and professional development are stressed in the effective-schools literature and receive considerable attention from those seeking to improve the schools. The teacher surveys identify both as areas of serious deficiency. The IEL findings suggest, however, that improvements in these areas may not be the first order of business. This is not to say that better supervision and creative professional development cannot make positive contributions to school success; obviously they can and do. They may, however, have limited impact on teachers if other, more critical working-conditions problems are not addressed. It may not be cost effective to spend money on expensive professional development programs or expand the number of teacher observations, for example, when little or no time is provided for teachers to work together or when instructional materials are inadequate. Simpler, less costly forms of professional development that bring teachers together to share techniques and build a common professional culture may be better choices than staff academies or effective-schools programs.

THE SPECIAL CASE OF TEACHER INFLUENCE

One dimension of working conditions—increasing teacher influence through structured participation in school decision making—receives such strong endorsement from so many quarters that it deserves special attention. This factor is seen by its advocates as an especially powerful method of attracting talent into teaching, increasing the motivation and work effort of the teaching force, and making better use of the skills and experience of teachers.

Increasing influence over decisions affecting their work is seen as particularly significant for professionals, such as teachers, who work in bureaucratic settings like the public schools and who often complain that they are neither respected nor consulted. Teachers, however, report that their influence over decisions outside of their classrooms is severely limited (Bacharach, Bauer, & Shedd, 1986). Centralization of decision making in school districts has reduced the autonomy of classroom teachers and reduced their influence over curriculum, textbooks, sequence and pacing, and even instructional methods (Cuban, 1984; Talbert, 1980). Professional control over educational matters has given ground to administrative rules and regulations, and to testing programs.

Moreover, when teachers participate in decisions, they do not always exercise significant influence (Corcoran, Hansen, & Shidlowski, 1988; Duke, Showers, & Imber, 1980). So reforms emphasizing employee participation in decision making appear to be especially appropriate and timely for teachers in public education and appear to offer great potential for improving the schools.

As has been noted already, there is some evidence of a positive relationship between staff participation and effectiveness in schools and other organizations (Brookover & Lezotte, 1977; Corcoran, White, & Walker, 1988; Locke, Schweiger, & Latham, 1986). Teacher participation in decisions has been shown to be related to lower levels of staff conflict (Belasco & Alutto, 1972), higher morale and more positive feelings about school leaders (Conway, 1984), greater commitment to new policies and programs (Berman, 1981; Fullan, 1982), and more effective enforcement of discipline (U.S. Dept. of Health, Education and Welfare, 1978). There is some evidence that participation reduces absenteeism (Dawson, 1985). Lack of opportunity for participation may increase teacher stress and burn-out (Bacharach, Bauer, & Conley, 1986).

In addition, some of the most successful school improvement programs (e.g., the California School Improvement Program, the IGE program developed by the Kettering Foundation, and many of the effective-schools programs) provide for staff participation in planning (Purkey & Smith, 1985). Unfortunately, there is no clear, definitive answer to the question of whether higher levels of teacher influence affect educational outcomes, because most of the research on influence has looked at its effects on teachers rather than the effects on student achievement (Corcoran, 1987; Shedd, 1987). If, however, the level of influence over school policies and programs affects teacher variables such as attendance, level of effort, adherence to rules, acceptance of policies, and turnover, there may be some positive effect on educational outcomes.

While evidence of the benefits of increased teacher influence is fragmentary, reformers are assuming that there is a causal relationship between staff influence and school effectiveness. Some studies of school-based improvement programs emphasizing staff participation in decision making, however, have found that the staff were willing to initiate noninstructional changes but tended to avoid issues dealing with instruction or teacher responsibilities (David & Peterson, 1984; Dawson, 1985). These data suggest that increasing teacher influence may enhance staff satisfaction without necessarily altering the technical core of the school or the educational outcomes; moreover, it may not be a sufficient intervention to ensure school improvement.

The findings from the teacher surveys and related research discussed earlier show that increased teacher influence is important, but they also indicate that it is only one part of the agenda for workplace reform. Providing a greater voice for teachers without, for example, providing them with the basic resources they need, does not seem like a formula for success. The evidence in favor of greater influence is strong enough, however, to justify continued experimentation with participation mechanisms and additional research on the issue, but it does not support the popular contention that teacher empowerment by itself will lead to more effective schools.

THE AGENDA FOR REFORM OF WORKING CONDITIONS

During the latter half of the 1980s, educational reformers in the United States shifted their focus from raising academic standards and tightening up accountability systems to improving the quality and productivity of public school teachers. Policy makers belatedly came to the realization that good teachers and good teaching were the essence of effective schools. Often collectively criticized by the public and the media as less than competent, lacking in commitment, or being responsible in one way or another for the inadequate achievement of American students, public school teachers suddenly were seen as the engines for progress in public education—or at least they would be if they accepted the proposed new professional standards and responded positively to the incentives and changes in the workplace being advocated by reformers.

The 1983 report of the National Commission on Excellence in Education and later reform reports expressed concern that too few academically able students were being attracted to teaching. These early reports called for higher entry standards, higher salaries, better working conditions, and new opportunities for advancement for teachers. The initial thrust of the reform movement in the states responding to these reports was to raise salaries for beginning teachers, raise the standards for entry into the profession, and improve teacher education. There were isolated, although well publicized, attempts to introduce new incentive structures, such as merit pay and master teacher programs, but, by and large, other workplace issues were ignored.

By the early 1980s, there was mounting evidence that talented teachers were leaving the profession, and particularly leaving the public schools, because of poor working conditions as well as inadequate salaries (Schlecty & Vance, 1983; Sykes, 1983). To launch the second wave of the reform movement, the Carnegie Foundation for the Advancement of Teaching (1986) issued a dramatic call for the creation of a profession of well-educated teachers prepared to assume new powers and responsibilities in redesigning the public schools. The report recommended restructuring schools to provide more professional work environments for teaching and freeing teachers to determine collectively how best to meet the needs of their students and fulfill state and local goals, while holding them accountable for student progress. The report also recommended the creation of career ladders in teaching, higher salaries, incentives for good performance, and, of course, changes in teacher preparation and licensing. The education report of the National Governors Association (1986) echoed these recommendations, citing better work environments, higher salaries, more policy influence, and career ladders as needed reforms in teaching. Both reports argued that better working conditions would attract and hold better people and that teachers would be more effective if their conditions of work were changed.

While the recommendations in these reports and the experiments they have stimulated are responsive to the desires of teachers for increased participation in school decision making, more frequent interaction with their colleagues, more respect and support, and, of course, higher salaries, the reforms are dependent upon a wholesale restructuring of the public schools that few teachers can envision and many may not want. There appears to be no incremental game plan in these reports for addressing the pressing needs of the schools as they are now organized. Problems that frustrate teachers on a daily basis—poor facilities, shortages of materials, increases in paperwork, heavy workloads, and disrespectful students—are being neglected as reformers focus on the big issues of restructuring schools and empowering the profession.

TEACHERS' UNIONS AND REFORM

Leaders of teachers' unions have long recognized the need for work reform in schools. Up until recently, however, they have emphasized workplace improvements that materially benefited all union members by reducing workloads or restricting the scope of teachers' responsibilities. Unlike the reformers, they have sought to remedy the resource issues described in the teacher surveys discussed earlier and the IEL study (Corcoran, White, & Walker, 1988) by bargaining and lobbying for better salaries and benefits, smaller classes, reduced workloads, and stronger grievance procedures. Until recently, however, they have opposed merit pay, career ladders, differentiated staffing, and even teacher participation in decisions traditionally made by management. They have used work rules to define jobs and protect the rights of their members and have been rather inflexible about altering those rules to meet the needs within particular schools or to reduce costs.

These union positions are changing in the 1980s, under pressure from the public, the reform movement, and union members themselves, and in response to leaders who understand that structural reforms are necessary to preserve the public schools. National and local union leaders have advocated increased teacher influence in school decision making and debated different approaches to making teaching a more attractive professional career. Local unions have taken the initiative to collaborate with local boards of education on designing restructuring experiments in a number of districts across the country.

There is growing recognition among union leaders that the industrial union model of collective bargaining does not mesh well with work processes or staff norms in professional organizations. Concern over work rules competes with professional norms governing teacher behavior. Teachers want to be treated as professionals. They have a stake in making schools work; their careers and job satisfaction are affected by school success and public support. Teaching also requires personal commitment; successful teachers go well beyond the minimums defined by work rules.

The revolution now under way in management/labor relations is based on the premise that an enterprise functions best if all stakeholders participate in decisions affecting their work. The "school-team" model of staff organization is manifestly different from the classic labor/management model, yet some feel that it might be made compatible with unionism (Kerchner & Mitchell, 1986). Purkey and Smith (1985), after reviewing studies of effective schools and school improvement and their implications for school district policy and practice, call for cooperation between district administrations and local associations in mounting school improvement programs. Without such cooperation, the experiments with collaborative planning and shared decision making at the building level will be undermined by criticisms that they are simply efforts to weaken the unions and the collective bargaining process and to give increased responsibilities to teachers without additional compensation.

It is critical that those who study working conditions or recommend changes in school structure understand and respect the union perspective. In some districts, unions have initiated significant reforms in the organization of schools and in the roles and responsibilities of teachers, but other union leaders remain skeptical. They fear that such changes may only be inexpensive palliatives to divert attention away from the more costly improvements that their members have been demanding and may require to be successful. They also fear these changes will reduce teacher reliance on their associations, weaken teacher organizations, and, therefore, eventually weaken the bargaining position of public school teachers. They are skeptical about career ladders and changes in staffing patterns and need reassurance, even guarantees, that such changes will not simply mean increased responsibility and accountability for teachers already working under adverse conditions. They are open to structural reform, but they want the resource deficiencies addressed as well. They also want to be sure that the changes are compatible with collective bargaining and strong teacher organizations.

The fears of union leaders are not entirely unfounded. Some of the recent reform proposals may have been efforts to undermine bargaining and weaken the teacher organizations. It is critical that reformers be sensitive to the bargaining implications of proposals such as school-site management, merit pay, differentiated staffing, or career ladders. Even school-site management can be implemented in a manner that requires extra effort without extra pay. It also can make teachers and their unions more accountable for educational outcomes without providing the human and material resources needed to do a better job.

SUMMARY AND CONCLUSIONS

There is considerable overlap between the working-conditions issues that concern teachers and those identified by researchers as critical to high levels of teacher performance and school success. The message here is obvious: Policy makers need to listen carefully to what teachers are saying about their working conditions. The problems that teachers have been complaining about not only affect their job satisfaction and the ability of the public schools to recruit good teachers, but they also affect students. Workplace reform in schools is not only in the teachers' interests, but in the public interest as well.

While it is important to call attention to the inadequate, often horrendous working conditions faced by many teachers, it is also necessary to retain a healthy skepticism about the efficacy of popular proposals for structural workplace reform, such as school-site management and career ladders. The data reviewed in this chapter suggest a broader agenda for workplace reform that addresses resource and workload problems as well as changing teacher roles and influence. It is questionable whether structural reforms, even if fully implemented, can produce the results that their advocates claim unless the full range of workplace problems is addressed. Only a comprehensive approach is likely to produce the teacher attitudes and behaviors that are associated with school success and also attract new talent into the profession. This demands a reform agenda that includes increased teacher influence and control over educational matters, and perhaps career ladders, but also more time to share with colleagues, smaller classes, lighter workloads, better physical conditions, and better instructional resources.

Implementing this agenda will be more costly than merely granting teachers more influence over school decisions. Providing better facilities and equipment, smaller classes, more preparatory and discretionary time, and, of course, higher salaries will require additional public funds, which means higher state and local taxes to support the public schools. It is not surprising, therefore, that most state and local policy makers find it easier to support experiments with school restructuring or career ladders, because these mean offering higher salaries and new responsibilities to only small groups of teachers. Even these reforms are likely to have unanticipated costs, as teachers are required to spend more time on noninstructional duties and as more of them qualify for higher steps on career ladders. There simply are no cheap ways to achieve the two goals of recruiting better teachers and making schools more effective, especially in the urban areas.

The pricetag for comprehensive workplace reform willl be politically unacceptable unless other changes in school organization and instruction produce offsetting reductions in the costs of operating the public schools. This issue has received little attention in the current debate over school reform, but it must be addressed. Year-round schooling, increased user fees, increased use of paraprofessionals, more effective use of instructional technology, and elimination of marginal programs and services are among the options that should be examined.

Both short- and long-range strategies for the reform of the school as a workplace should be considered. Teacher organizations must be active partners in both processes of reform. The short-range plan needs to address the immediate needs described here and would include improvements in workload, time allocation and scheduling, physical conditions, administrative leadership, and the influence of teachers within the framework of the existing school organization. The aim would be to insure adequate working conditions in all school districts. Special priority, however, must be given to the needs of urban teachers, many of whom must cope with unacceptable circumstances. The immediate material needs of urban teachers must be met. Grand designs for teacher empowerment will achieve little if we are not willing to meet the basic needs of teachers, such as adequate supplies of paper, access to copy machines, or time at work to cooperate with colleagues.

The long-range strategy needs to encourage more radical, more experimental approaches to school reform, such as those advocated in the Carnegie (1986) report and currently being implemented in a small number of districts. These experiments would explore the benefits of alternative forms of schooling. Local initiatives to empower teachers and alter their roles and responsibilities could be encouraged, but they also should be carefully evaluated. Their effect on teachers, students, and parents should be analyzed and their costs monitored. These initiatives should not be treated as successes simply because they receive positive media attention, nor should widespread adoption be promoted prior to careful assessment of their effects. School-site management, career ladders, peer review, and mentoring are all policies worthy of consideration. It would be unfortunate, even disastrous, if these initiatives were allowed to become educational fads and doomed to an early death by premature media attention and dissemination.

REFERENCES

Bacharach, S. M., Bauer, S. C., & Conley, S. C. (1986). Organizational analysis of stress: The case of secondary and elementary schools. *Journal of Work and Occupations, 13,* 7–32.

Bacharach, S. B., Bauer, S. C., & Shedd, J. B. (1986). *The learning workplace: The conditions and resources of teaching.* Ithaca, NY: Organizational Analysis and Practice.

Belasco, J. A., & Alutto, J. A. (1972). Decisional participation and teacher satisfaction. *Educational Administration Quarterly, 8,* 44–58.

Berman, P. W. (1981). Educational change: An implementation paradigm. In R. Lehming & M. Kane (Eds.), *Improving schools* (pp. 253–286). Beverly Hills, CA: Sage.

Bird, T., & Little, J. W. (1986). How schools organize the teaching occupation. *The Elementary Journal, 86,* 493–512.

Brookover, W. B., & Lezotte, L. W. (1977). *Changes in school characteristics coincident with changes in student achievement.* East Lansing: College of Urban Development, Michigan State University.

Carnegie Foundation for the Advancement of Teaching. (1986). *A nation prepared: Teachers for the 21st century.* New York: Author.

Center for Public Interest Polling. (1986). *The New Jersey school teacher: A view of the profession.* New Brunswick, NJ: Eagleton Institute.

Conway, J. A. (1984). The myth, mystery, and mastery of participative decision making in education. *Educational Administration Quarterly, 20*(3), 11–40.

Corcoran, T. B. (1987, February). *Teacher participation in public school decision making: A discussion paper.* Paper presented at a seminar conducted by the Work in America Institute, Washington, DC.

Corcoran, T. B., Hansen, B. J., & Shidlowski, A. M. (1988). *Who makes decisions: The role of New Jersey teachers in school decision making.* Trenton, NJ: New Jersey School Boards Association.

Corcoran, T. B., White, J. L., & Walker, L. (1988). *Working in urban schools.* Washington, DC: The Institute for Educational Leadership.

Cuban, L. (1984). Transforming the frog into a prince: Effective schools research, policy, and practices at the district level. *Harvard Educational Review, 54*(2), 129-151.

David, J. L., & Peterson, S. M. (1984). *Can schools reform themselves? A study of school-based improvement programs.* Palo Alto, CA: Bay Area Research Group.

Dawson, J. A. (1985). *School improvement programs in thirteen urban schools: A report of a four year documentation study.* Philadelphia, PA: Research for Better Schools.

Duke, D. L., Showers, B. K., & Imber, M. (1980). Teachers and shared decision making: The costs and benefits of involvement. *Educational Administration Quarterly, 16*(1), 93-106.

Finn, C. E. (1985). Teacher unions and school quality: Potential allies or inevitable foes? *Phi Delta Kappan, 66,* 331-338.

Firestone, W. A. (1986). *The commitments of teachers: Implications for research, policy, and administration.* Philadelphia, PA: Research for Better Schools.

Firestone, W. A., & Herriott, R. E. (1982). Prescriptions for elementary schools don't fit secondary schools. *Educational Leadership, 40*(3), 51-53.

Fullan, M. (1982). *The meaning of educational change.* New York: Teachers College Press.

Kanter, R. M. (1983). *The change masters.* New York: Simon & Schuster.

Kerchner, C. T., & Mitchell, D. (1986). Teaching reform and union reform. *The Elementary School Journal, 86,* 449-470.

Koppich, J., Gerritz, W., & Guthrie, J. W. (1986). *A view from the classroom: California teachers' opinions on working conditions and school reform proposals.* Palo Alto, CA: Policy Analysis for California Education.

Lawler, E. E. (1987). The design of effective reward systems. In J. Lorsch (Ed.), *The handbook of organizational behavior* (pp. 234-279). Englewood Cliffs, NJ: Prentice-Hall.

Little, J. W. (1982). Norms of collegiality and experimentation: Workplace conditions of school success. *American Educational Research Journal, 19,* 325-340.

Locke, E. A., Schweiger, D. A., & Latham, G. P. (1986). Participation in decision making: When should it be used? *Organizational Dynamics, 15*(3), 65-79.

Metropolitan Life Insurance Company. (1986). *The American teacher, 1986: Restructuring the profession.* New York: Author.

National Commission on Excellence in Education. (1983). *A Nation at Risk.* Washington, DC: U.S. Government Printing Office.

National Governors Association. (1986). *Time for results*. Washington, DC: Author.

Purkey, S. C., & Smith, M. S. (1983). Effective schools: A review. *The Elementary School Journal, 83*, 427–452.

Purkey, S. C., & Smith, M. S. (1985). School reform: The district policy implications of the effective schools literature. *The Elementary School Journal, 85*, 353–388.

Rosenholtz, S. J. (1985). Effective schools: Interpreting the evidence. *The American Journal of Education, 93*, 352–388.

Schlecty, P. C., & Vance, V. S. (1983). Recruitment, selection, and retention: The shape of the teaching force. *The Elementary School Journal, 83*, 469–487.

Schwartz, H., Olson, G., Bennett, A., & Ginsberg, R. (1983). *Schools as a workplace: The realities of stress* (Vol. 1). Washington, DC: American Federation of Teachers.

Shedd, J. B. (1987). *Involving teachers in school and district decision making: A review of research and summary of issues*. Ithaca, NY: Organizational Analysis and Practice.

Stedman, L. C. (1985). A new look at the effective schools movement. *Urban Education, 20*, 295–326.

Stedman, L. C. (1987). It's time we changed the effective schools formula. *Phi Delta Kappan, 69*, 215–224.

Stein, B. (1983). *Quality of worklife in action: Managing for effectiveness*. New York: American Management Association.

Stein, B., & Kanter, R. M. (1980). Building the parallel organization: Towards mechanisms for permanent quality of worklife. *Journal of Applied Behavior Science, 16*, 371–388.

Sykes, G. (1983). Public policy and the problems of teacher quality: The need for screens and magnets. In L. Schulman & G. Sykes (Eds.), *Handbook of research on teaching and policy* (pp. 97–125). New York: Longmans.

Talbert, J. E. (1980). *School organization and institutional change: Exchange and power in loosely-coupled systems*. Palo Alto, CA: Institute for Research on Education, Finance, and Governance.

U.S. Department of Health, Education and Welfare. (1978). *Violent schools—safe schools* (Vol. I). Washington, DC: Author.

Wise, A. E., Darling-Hammond, L., McLaughlin, M. W., & Bernstein, H. (1984). *Teacher evaluation: A study of effective practices*. Santa Monica, CA: Rand Corporation.

Yankelovich, D., & Immerwahr, J. (1983). *Putting the work ethic to work*. New York: Public Agenda Foundation.

6

The Primacy and Potential of High School Departments

SUSAN MOORE JOHNSON

Seven years after the National Commission on Excellence in Education (1983) warned the public that the nation was at risk, controversy persists about what is wrong with the public schools and what should be done to fix them. Some would mandate curriculum and monitor students' progress; others would increase teachers' autonomy and encourage the professionals to set the standards. Some would increase certification requirements, while others would eliminate them. Some would reinforce the role of universities in training teachers; others would move teacher training to the schools. Some would raze what they regard as irreparable structures and build anew from the ground up; others would renovate the schools that we have, reinforcing their strengths and improving them with new features.

Those who set out to improve high schools confront organizations that are larger and considerably more complex than the elementary schools that were the primary focus of most research on effective schools. Whereas elementary schools are typically homogeneous institutions composed of separate but similar classrooms headed by teachers who are generalists, high schools classify teachers by subject specialties and group them spatially and organizationally within departments, such as English, art, or physical education. Whereas elementary school teachers' primary reference group is the school—or, in some buildings, the grade or cluster—high school teachers usually regard themselves as members of departments, their interests and identities resting primarily with colleagues who share similar academic interests and training.

Departments have endured over time in a wide range of settings and thus are not likely to be dismantled and replaced in short order. Although,

This chapter was commissioned by the Center for Research on the Context of Secondary Teaching, supported by funds from the U.S. Department of Education Office of Educational Research and Improvement (Grant No. G0087C0235). The analyses and conclusions do not necessarily reflect the views or policies of these organizations.

ultimately, they may not prove to be ideal structures for organizing teachers' work, they are the ones that persist. Wilson and Herriott (1989) recently found that 78% of the 81 junior and senior high schools they surveyed had subject-matter departments. Departments deserve close scrutiny so that researchers might accurately describe how they function and policy makers might suggest how they could promote high school reform.

Recent developments in educational policy increase the likelihood that reformers will not dismiss high school departments as obsolete structures and discard them. First, subject-matter knowledge has become the centerpiece of influential reform efforts. Lee S. Shulman, who heads Stanford's Teacher Assessment Project, designed to provide research support for the proposed National Board for Professional Teaching Standards (Olson, 1988), argues that content knowledge is the "first source for the [teaching] knowledge base," the basis of teachers' claim to professional status (Shulman, 1987, p. 8). Second, members of blue-ribbon commissions such as the Holmes Group (1986) and the Carnegie Forum's Task Force on Teaching as a Profession (1986) advocate teachers' exercising increased professional control of their schools through differentiated roles. High schools already offer some teachers the opportunity for advancement as department heads, roles that span the domains of teaching and administration. This dual focus by policy makers on subject-matter expertise and differentiated staffing must ultimately lead reformers to examine the potential of high school departments to become centers for change.

Unfortunately, little empirical research is yet available to inform those seeking to understand high school teachers' work better. Wilson and Herriott (1989) note that "very little is known about the structure or power of formal subunits in American public schools" (p. 2) and advocate that those who make policy come to a better understanding of the potential importance of subunits such as high school departments. This chapter focuses on the role of departments in high schools as they are experienced by a sample of high school teachers from eastern Massachusetts, outlining how departments work, suggesting what they mean to teachers, and recommending productive lines for further inquiry. The discussion draws on interview data I collected from a sample of 39 high school teachers, all of whom were recommended by their principals as "very good" teachers, who were respected by their colleagues, and whose contribution to education would be missed if they were to leave teaching. These valued teachers were chosen because it is they who, under current working conditions, are most likely to leave teaching after several years. It is these teachers for whom new roles are being designed. It is they who are most likely to reform their schools from within.[1]

Twenty-five of these respondents taught in public schools, 9 in independent schools, and 5 in Catholic schools. Twenty were women, 19 men. Six were department heads. They had taught school for an average of slightly more than 14 years. All 39 respondents worked in different departments.[2] The 25 public school teachers worked in 21 schools located in a diverse array of communities;[3] independent schools included boarding and day schools; Catholic schools included diocesan and nondiocesan institutions. Although there are obvious constraints on generalizing from this small, geographically limited, purposive sample, these data offer useful guidance in drawing up plans for further study.

Respondents from both the private and public sectors indicated that departments were their key professional reference groups. High school teachers' most frequent professional interactions and regular collegial relationships were said to be with departmental peers rather than with colleagues from other disciplines. As institutional units, departments exercise considerable influence over practices that are central to the instructional enterprise—the selection, supervision, and evaluation of staff; course definition and sequencing; tracking; curriculum development; textbook selection; and assignment of teachers to courses and students to classes.

Departments varied in size and in their practices regarding curriculum, tracking, testing, and student assignment, even within the same school and district. Those differences appeared to result from several factors, including the different styles and perspectives of department heads, the organizational and political context of the school or district, and the particular subject being taught and the priorities of those who chose to teach it.

CONDITIONS OF WORK IN HIGH SCHOOL DEPARTMENTS

How Departments Are Structured

Apart from size, there was little reported difference in the structure of high school departments in public, independent, or church-related schools. Teachers were grouped by discipline and regularly identified themselves as members of particular departments, even when alternative house or cluster structures were also present in their schools: "I'm in math"; "I'm in the social studies department"; "I teach English."

The schools represented in this sample all had departments in English, social studies, science, mathematics, and foreign languages. Notably, some of those major departments were more heterogeneous in composition than others. For example, mathematics departments were said to be fairly homogeneous, with staff having had similar training and being prepared to teach the full range of courses offered by the department. By contrast, the members of the science department were usually a varied lot, both in training and subject-matter specialty. Earth sciences teachers might never teach physics but were always departmental colleagues with those who did. Similarly, Latin teachers were no more likely to teach Russian than social studies, but they were routinely grouped with foreign language teachers. Despite such heterogeneous composition, these major academic departments were similarly defined from school to school. They were neither consolidated into interdisciplinary units nor divided into subspecialties such as physical sciences or life sciences.

It is not obvious why these departmental boundaries persist as they do. Teachers' certification requirements do not adequately explain their prevalence, for, although social studies teachers receive a general certificate applicable for all courses in the department, science teachers were required to have more specialized certificates in, for example, biology or physics. Graduation requirements also corresponded to the departmental structures; that is, students were required to study 4 years of English or 3 years of social studies. It was not clear, however, whether those requirements served to shore up the departmental boundaries, or if the departmental structures were driving the graduation requirements.

Although academic departments were similarly defined across public and private schools, nonacademic departments, such as industrial arts, home economics, art, business, physical education, special education, and bilingual education, were grouped in various ways. The consistency and structural integrity of these departments were less predictable than were those of the major academic departments. One home economics teacher was a member of a career department including business and industrial arts teachers. An art teacher who was part of a unified arts department had colleagues there who taught drama, dance, and culinary arts. The major academic departments, whose boundaries remained intact, were said to have more status and influence in the school than the minor departments, which could be redefined and regrouped in response to changes in enrollment or curriculum.

What Departments Do

Throughout this sample, departments were active to varying degrees in introducing and sequencing courses, writing and amending curricula, and selecting textbooks. There is no state-mandated curriculum in Massachuetts, so local districts independently adopt instructional programs. A few teachers reported that they were simply expected to execute the plans of a districtwide curriculum over which the department had little control. One urban teacher whose history curriculum was specified in detail by the central office, said that she felt like a "robot . . . [on] an assembly line. . . . Everything is set up for you." More commonly, however, teachers were active within departments, developing and coordinating their course offerings with little or no oversight from principals or central office administrators. A mathematics teacher said that he and his colleagues had "laid out the curriculum for algebra II and trig on the honors level, and said, 'This is what we will do here, here, and here.' And it was implemented." One social studies department head described a decision by her department to include 1½ years of U.S. history so that the classes would "get to 1986. That was a major decision on the part of that teacher as well as our whole department. . . . We've done that together."

Yet, for other departments, the only curricular function was to coordinate loosely the various courses developed independently by members of the staff. An English teacher in one such department said that she had never been told what to teach: "It's open-ended, even though a curriculum guide exists."

Textbook selection varied as well. In a few instances, individual teachers were free to adopt virtually any textbook for their classes. One suburban English teacher said, "We basically choose what we want, within reason. . . . I've yet to see anybody get turned down on anything that's reasonable." However, most respondents said that the members of their departments had jointly selected the texts from which teachers could choose. A social studies teacher explained that her department had "autonomy in choosing the texts, but we have a whole criteria procedure that we go through." A few teachers reported that, although the state did not regulate textbook selection, their departments' choice of texts was constrained by a districtwide list of acceptable books.

Some department heads in the public sector were active in selecting new staff, a responsibility that was standard practice for both teachers and department heads in independent schools. In virtually all public schools, the department heads conducted formal teacher evaluations and recommended the reappointment, dismissal, or tenure of junior staff. Many were also active in supervising the work of veteran teachers, through periodic classroom visits and subsequent verbal and written reviews of their performance. It must be noted that these respondents all were valued teachers and therefore not necessarily typical of all department heads. Independent school teachers were far less likely to be observed in their teaching, but department heads were prominent in assessing their performance indirectly on the basis of reputation and comments by students and teachers.

Assigning teachers to courses was a major responsibility of most departments. Some department heads could make final decisions about teachers' programs, while others recommended a roster to the principal, who had the final say. Department heads assessed teachers' qualifications for taking on particular assignments and then allocated courses among staff. In some departments, the teachers' seniority determined their chances of teaching advanced classes, with junior teachers routinely assigned to the bottom tracks. In others, all teachers were given a balanced schedule of advanced and basic classes. As one department head explained, "Usually a teacher gets a smattering of everything." Most department heads encouraged teachers to state their preferences for teaching assignments and then proceeded to build a schedule that maximized those preferences, using either the locally employed criterion of seniority that produced "tracked teachers" or the deliberate distribution of ability groupings among staff.

How Teachers Experience Departments

Teachers were not only attentive to the formal functions of departments in setting the curriculum or making course assignments, but they also regarded their departments as organizations to which they belonged. Lortie (1975) and others have observed that teachers are more concerned with matters that directly affect their classrooms than with those that affect the school organization as a whole. That priority will be apparent in the teachers' involvement in their departments, which assemble colleagues whose primary professional interest is a subject and how to teach it. Doing a good job as a high school teacher means successfully teaching history or art or Spanish. The interviews indicated that these high school teachers' satisfaction with their work often depended on their experiences as members of departments. One English teacher said that his department head's leadership and practices were "90% of why I like it here." By contrast, a foreign language teacher spoke of withdrawing from collegial interactions in a new assignment because "the chemistry is really not there. There's not that kind of collegiality. There's not the kind of warmth and relaxed atmosphere that there was in [my former assignment]."

Teachers reported that, at their best, departments provided socialization and training for new members; ongoing personal encouragement and recognition; support for the maintenance of standards; the opportunity to be creative and influential; and the chance to improve their practice through joint planning, peer observation, coteaching, and staff development.

For fledgling teachers, work with experienced peers in a particular field may well provide the direction and support that preservice training failed to give. If they learn to teach in isolation, they will inevitably rely on their wits and their recollections of their own teachers' practice. If they learn to teach among colleagues who offer a variety of pedagogical models and lead them through the uncertainties and hazards of the first few years, their work will likely be more satisfying and satisfactory. An experienced English teacher at a large technical/vocational high school said that veteran teachers assisted new recruits there primarily out of sympathy: "Most new teachers were so totally thrown by the whole system, and everybody knew what that felt like, so everybody went to their rescue." This senior teacher "would spend hours with [the new teacher], showing shortcuts for things and giving her everything that [she] had."

Few teachers reported that their departments offered any such sustained support or organized inculcation of norms and values. Often departmental colleagues also were said to provide encouragement and recognition in work that was plagued with uncertainties. Peers who themselves had experienced the successes and inevitable disappointments of teaching and could encourage the celebration of a good class or a good day enabled teachers to carry on.

Departments also supported individual teachers in setting and maintaining standards for their own performance as well as that of their students. Because the teaching profession itself has not settled on the tenets of good practice and because public schools are so varied, the standards for good work must be determined school by school and department by department. However, Paule (1986), who studied decision making in four departments (English, mathematics, science, and social studies) of three high schools in one northwest district, found that, in departments such as mathematics, where subject matter is sequential and faculty must rely on their peers to prepare students for their courses, collegial attention to standards is more explicit than in departments with less sequential subject matter, such as social studies and English.

Departments also served as units through which teachers could initiate change, both inside and outside their classrooms. For example, one Latin teacher spoke enthusiastically about his success in developing a new course in mythology after having gone to his department head and asked, "Will you just let me give this a try?" A history teacher organized members of his department to petition the school board to reduce the teaching load of senior teachers who served as advisors for students' senior projects.

To the extent that high school teachers worked together on improving their practice, it was primarily within departments that they did so, although teachers were also said to group informally by subject specialties within departments; that is, history and sociology teachers might work in separate subgroups within the social studies department. Many teachers reported that they jointly planned lessons or shared ideas and materials with one or two other staff members. Members of an English department who had attended a workshop on learning differences decided to "cowrite lesson plans and to spend more time observing each others' classes—making comments about how the format approach is actually implemented."

When they occurred, departmental meetings centered primarily on curriculum and pedagogy rather than on schoolwide matters such as discipline or student services. Some teachers said that they kept current in their fields through interactions with departmental colleagues. For example, a foreign language teacher said that she and her colleagues tried "to keep abreast of new methodology" by discussing what they learned at professional workshops. Although most in-service training is currently sponsored by the school or district rather than the department, teachers made it clear that they valued talking with colleagues who teach their subjects rather than hearing from outside experts about general principles of pedagogy or noninstructional issues such as drugs or adolescent development.

There was considerable evidence throughout these interviews that departments could provide the context for valued support, the opportunity for influence, and the encouragement and direction for improved practice. In these teachers' views, however, few departments functioned as effectively as they might have.

Variation Among Departments

The interviews suggest that practices among departments vary widely within the same school, and that, in many ways, working in different departments is like working in different organizations. In one department, class observations may occur only when required by law or local policy, while in another, teachers and the department head may move freely in and out of each others' classes. Course offerings in one department may remain virtually unchanged over time, while those in another vary from year to year.

Departments varied in the extent to which they coordinated or regulated teachers' practice. Some were simply loose associations of autonomous individuals. For example, one independent school teacher

said that departmental meetings were rare: "There's just a general open-
ing meeting at the beginning of the year [where he says,] 'Just remember
what we have to do and let's correct the tests on time . . . so that they can
see their progress,' and so forth." Some departments in public schools
were similarly unregimented, while others were expected to function as
components of larger hierarchies, implementing prescribed practices. A
foreign language teacher said that her department head got direction
"from meeting with the principals and the superintendent of schools. . . .
You kind of feel the effect throughout." Yet other departments were said
to function democratically and cooperatively, setting their own standards
and practices and, in some cases, serving as the base for gaining influence
in the larger organization. An English teacher said that he and his colleagues "all have input. We don't even have a need for formalized . . .
meetings because we're constantly meeting and talking and coming up
with ideas and new courses."

SOURCES OF VARIATION IN DEPARTMENTAL CONDITIONS OF WORK

The variation in practices within schools appeared to result primarily
from three factors: the style and preferences of the department head, the
organizational and political context of the school and district, and the
distinct character of those who taught a particular subject.

Department Heads

Department heads can provide internal leadership and external ad-
vocacy on behalf of their departments. They formally represent departmental interests in the larger organization of the school, where they lobby
to garner scarce resources such as course sections in the master schedule,
priority in student scheduling, funds for special projects, office equipment, and clerical or support services.

Generally, department heads are appointed or, occasionally, elected
from the ranks of teachers in the school or district, rather than being hired
from outside as other administrators often are. Sometimes they serve for
specified terms so that the position rotates among colleagues, although
many hold their positions for as long as they remain in their schools. Some
department heads are officially classified as administrators for purposes
of collective bargaining. Department heads may be compensated financially for their work with a fixed stipend or percentage increase in their
salary, or they may receive nothing more than the regular teacher's wage.
However, since virtually all department heads teach less than the stan-

dard load and have greater influence outside the classroom than other teachers, respondents generally viewed the position as a promotion, even when financial compensation was slim or nonexistent.

Teachers described their department heads as having different conceptions of their roles. Some heads were said to function as authoritative or authoritarian agents of administrative expectations and to assume a top-down approach to their work. For example, one department head said that she and her counterparts were to be "links to the teachers" in implementing a new districtwide curriculum on critical thinking. There were also department heads who set policy on their own, without reference to the preferences of either the district's upper echelon or teachers in their departments. One teacher described meetings at which her department head would "give us our objectives for grammar, or for writing, or for listening."

By contrast, heads of other departments were said to act more as representatives and facilitators than as authorities. For example, one teacher said of his department head, "When it comes to the actual relationship with the teachers in the department, I think he sees himself more as one of us as opposed to The Leader." Another said that his department head "breaks his back to try and satisfy us. . . . He's extremely supportive and extremely helpful. If you need anything, within budgetary constraints, he'll get it for you." Yet another teacher praised his department head for "asking people what they prefer to do and then trying to help them out."

Teachers widely believed that department heads' styles of administration resulted primarily from their personal strengths, weaknesses, preferences, and prejudices. For example, one teacher said that her department head was "fabulous—a great curriculum writer." Another spoke of his own "enlightened department chairman" and said, "The evaluations are helpful because he is the guy he is." All respondents were not so laudatory. One mathematics teacher said that his department head was "probably the world's worst teacher and maybe the second worst department head. . . . He just doesn't show any leadership whatsoever." Another was critical of his department head for promoting competition among staff: "I think he sees anxiety and tension as a motivating factor for people. He's willing to let that feed into what people do."

Although personal style was certainly important in determining how department heads did their jobs, there was also evidence that they were influenced in their approach to administering the department by the organizational context of their work. One teacher from an independent school described his setting as one that permitted considerable room for variation:

It's one of those places where you can do as much as you want as a department chairman. I mean, there are some department chairmen who sign book slips and don't do much else, and there are others who get very much involved in what's going on.

By contrast, a public school department head saw changes in the district organization alter her responsibilities so that the role became more distinctly administrative. "Instead of just being a 'gofer,' a budget maker, a schedule setter, or a clerk, that job has changed. . . . We now evaluate. We're now part of the administrative decision-making team." Although this individual clearly welcomed the change, a social studies teacher in another school lamented such a shift in his district:

> The department chair's job should have been the best job in that school system. And it was for a long time. They had a good deal of control and a good deal of support from their staff. Often they had been partly selected by their staffs and they were considered to be the best qualified, the most academically knowledgeable. Since then, they've become administrators more than they have head teachers.

The fact that the position of department head is part teacher and part administrator contributes to its unique significance and creates what can be a productive tension in the school organization. The extent to which the individuals who hold these positions emphasize either the teaching or administrative components of the role affects their subsequent working relationships with teachers. Those who saw themselves primarily as teachers tended to work more as peers with colleagues and to regard the department as a democratic organization that could be a base for building influence in the larger organization. Those who saw themselves primarily as administrators were more inclined to oversee teachers' work closely and to expect staff to implement their superiors' decisions.

The ambiguity that results from this dual allegiance of the department head may well be at once the most promising and most challenging aspect of the position. Those department heads who regard themselves as peers may feel awkward about overseeing the work of their colleagues. One English teacher said that he would prefer to be evaluated by a principal or assistant principal who would "be a little bit more honest with you, where the head of the department is a lot closer with you." However, a foreign language teacher argued that she would prefer to be supervised by her department head, "because the principal is too removed." Department heads may well be the ablest administrators to assess performance and provide assistance, because they know the daily challenges of teaching and may have earned the respect of colleagues for success in the classroom. One teacher praised his department head's effectiveness as a teacher: "He's probably the most competent teacher I've ever come across. His greatest characteristic as a teacher is that he can actually personalize every lesson to the students. So there begins the respect for him."

The Organizational and Political Environment

Departments also differed in response to the organizational and political environment in which they operated. Neufeld (1984) studied how teachers in eight high schools from a national sample of districts influenced the assignment of courses and students. She found that, when confronting enrollment declines, high school principals consulted less with department heads about course assignments than they did during periods of stability or growth. Interviews for the present study also suggested that, during periods of teacher layoffs and transfers, department heads could say little about who was assigned to teach with them. One science department head in a large urban district undergoing cutbacks argued that he could not influence the school department's decisions about teacher assignments:

> I've always thought that, as a department head, I'd like to have more input on which teachers I get. They just send us a teacher. . . . This is a decision that is made by the central administration, by the person who is in charge of personnel. Of course, a lot of this is controlled by contract and by seniority.

One might also expect that principals would exert direct influence on how departments work. Curiously, the role of the high school principal in regulating departmental practices was virtually unmentioned by respondents in this study. This may be a consequence of the study design, which did not explicitly pursue the issue; or it may reveal the limited perspectives of teachers who were not aware of the principals' influence in their departments; or it may be attributable to regional peculiarities that promote departmental autonomy; or it may be a meaningful finding suggesting that nondepartmental administrators have little direct impact on curriculum and instruction. Teachers believed that principals made good teaching possible by maintaining discipline, tending to the facility, and securing resources from the central office, but they did not suggest that principals routinely influenced departmental practices. Similarly, Paule (1986) suggests that the curriculum vice-principals in her four schools generally intervened at the margins of instruction, determining the number of course offerings, dividing the supplies budget, and deciding when to replace large sets of books.

The prevailing educational expectations of a local community also influence the practices of department heads and departments. Neufeld (1984) found that principals allocated greater resources to English and mathematics departments when test scores in these subjects were publicly scrutinized. Data from my study support that finding and further document how parents with high academic aspirations for their children prevail upon school officials when decisions are to be made about the size, course prerequisites, and teacher assignments for accelerated classes—all factors that influence teachers' work in departments.

Subject Specialty

Finally, departments also appear to vary within schools as a consequence of their subject specialties and the training and socialization of those who teach in them. Some departments, such as science or mathematics, represent fields that have high status in society and are therefore more influential in the schools. Other departments, such as English or social studies, offer required courses and therefore command more resources and attention within the schools simply by virtue of their size (Neufeld, 1984).

Paule (1986) found differences among academic departments that seemed to result from the character of the subject matter itself. Interestingly, there appears to be more similarity among the mathematics departments of several schools than there is between the mathematics and social studies departments in any single school. Mathematics departments typically offered the same sequence of courses and adhered to a durable set of standards by which to judge students' performance. Paule concluded, "Mathematics teachers depend on each other to pave the way while social studies teachers carve out their own little niches and chart their own separate paths" (p. 138). Data from my study supported her findings. A mathematics teacher who claimed, "I can do anything that I want," also observed that

> the nature of the subject makes the curriculum prescribed. . . . So do we have a chance to implement what we like? Yes, we can talk about it, but then, once it's set, you're pretty much expected to follow it. And it should be that way. It has to be in mathematics.

By contrast, Paule (1986) found that social studies departments seemed to promote continuous debate about their priorities and practices and were likely to respond more to political pressure and changes in the organizational environment in setting their curriculum. Similarly, a social studies teacher in this study emphasized that, in her department, courses are often redesigned and the "curriculum is not dead on the shelf."

The differences in these approaches reflect differences in the subjects themselves. Mathematics is based on permanent and predictable relationships that can be expressed in principles and rules, while the stuff of social studies—politics, conflicting interests, and the reconciliation of opposing positions—is far more fluid. Paule (1986) notes that, even at the national level, there is little consensus about what ought to be taught in social studies. The staff of a mathematics department is also likely to be a fairly homogeneous group with similar training, compared to the social studies staff, which typically draws from the diverse disciplines of history, economics, sociology, and political science. As a result, the mathematics department may more readily reach consensus about what matters, exhibit greater respect for formal policy, and experience less flux in routine practices; while the social studies department can be expected to debate about priorities, challenge the formal authority of the school hierarchy, organize for initiating change in the larger organization, and regard their current practices as temporary and subject to review. Paule found that, in heterogeneous departments such as science, "departmental leadership plays a significant role in unifying the groups or in maintaining the ready-made fragmentation" (p. 89).

IMPLICATIONS FOR RESEARCH AND REFORM

If high school departments are to be examined, what deserves research attention? First, in order systematically to sort out the factors that account for variation within schools, within districts, and across districts, we need to explore each of these issues just discussed, but with larger, more diverse groups of teachers working in more geographically diverse schools and districts. We must ask, How do departments function, and to what extent are they shaped by departmental leadership? How much are their practices determined by organizational and political context? To what extent do similarities and differences derive from differences in subject specialties? The extant research on departments (Neufeld, 1984; Paule, 1986) looks almost exclusively at major academic departments, although nonacademic departments are often as important in students' total experience. It is important to compare the structure and practices of the two.

In exploring the dimensions of departmental difference, it is necessary to identify the departments' various sources of autonomy and influence. Which of their powers have been formally granted, and which have been derived politically? How much of their practice is responsive to the organizational context of the school or district, and how much of that practice appears to operate independently of that context?

We need to understand better the objective indicators of departmental strength (enrollments, course offerings, released time positions, scheduling priority, allocations for supplies) and to explore whether teachers do, in fact, report enjoying their work as teachers more in departments that are strong according to these measures. We should investigate whether teachers assess departmental strength using different, more subjective, standards such as status of the subject matter, reputation of the department head, extent of collegial interaction, history of innovative practices, or record of curricular continuity. By better understanding what it is that matters to teachers, we can consider the extent to which those conditions that promote teacher satisfaction are consistent with those that support good teaching practice.

Given that department heads are so central to teachers' experiences, it is important to study how widely their roles vary and what effects variations in their roles have on both the experiences of current departmental members and the career choices of prospective department heads. Important questions include

- What difference does it make whether the position is temporary or permanent, elected or appointed, and compensated handsomely or modestly?
- Do differences in selection practices influence the quality of the department heads who are selected?
- What are the consequences of department heads' having more or less released time?
- Under what circumstances do department heads come to see themselves as primarily teachers or primarily administrators, and does this attitude follow from who they are or how the position is structured?
- How do teachers respond to this difference in emphasis?
- How do department heads, themselves, deal with the inherent tensions in the role?

Finally, it is important to explore the ways in which high schools seek to balance the competing interests of departments. To understand the complexity of interdepartmental relations, it will be necessary to map the actions and interactions of all departments within several schools and to explore whether departmental strength and influence is, in fact, a zero-sum game. Little is yet known about the interaction of principals and department heads, but one might expect that individuals in those positions would promote different and perhaps competing sets of priorities—one set being schoolwide, the other department specific. In what ways do department heads collaborate and coordinate their efforts?

Throughout this inquiry, it will be important to document exemplary practices in those schools where departments are believed to serve both students and teachers well, to seek to account for the factors that make them successful in satisfying teachers and promoting effective teaching, and to consider whether such practices could be duplicated in other settings. There is some evidence from the present study that teachers working in strong departments enjoy a greater sense of influence and efficacy than do those whose departments are low in status and resources. Given this, one might readily conclude that departments should be strengthened by augmenting the number of decisions made there about such issues as hiring and curriculum, by increasing the amount of released time and compensation for the department head, or by redirecting staff development funds from the district or school to the department. Such changes might well enhance teachers' identities as subject-matter specialists; focus attention and resources on instruction in subject areas; respond to teachers' expressed interests for in-service training in their fields; reinforce expectations for coherent collegial standards and values; and provide forums for governance close to the classroom, where teachers can best influence their work and are, therefore, willing to commit their energy and time. There is evidence that departments can serve teachers well, so perhaps schools should be reorganized to enable and encourage them to do that better.

My data also suggest, however, that reformers should proceed cautiously in strengthening departments, for two reasons. First, it appears that the allocation of resources within a high school may be something of a zero-sum game, with the parochial interests of one group being enhanced only at the expense of another. There may well be limits to the number of dollars, faculty members, and slots in the master schedule. What English gets, business loses. Inequities may increase among departments of different size and status or among those having more or less politically astute department heads. Given scarce resources and the political character of schools, it may not be possible for all teachers to enjoy the benefits of working in strong departments.

A related concern is that, if departments become not only the primary, but also the exclusive, reference group for teachers, it is likely that decisions about curriculum and staffing will be driven solely by departmental interests and will result from political struggles rather than from some balanced understanding of schoolwide needs. If departments are to be strengthened, schools must also plan carefully how the specialized concerns will be coordinated and reconciled in the best interests of the school as a whole. Ironically, a collection of strong, competing departments might require stronger principals to insure that all are dealt with equitably.

A second reason for caution is that any department attends to only part of a student's academic and social experience, so strengthening departments might further fragment students' total schooling experience. By contrast, successful interdisciplinary teams in middle schools and experimental high schools put the student rather than the subject at the center of their efforts. In most departmentalized high schools, no one but an overworked guidance counselor is expected to oversee the student's total program. If departments are to be strengthened, educators must consider how students' educational experience is to be integrated. Those who would reform schools by reforming workplaces must attend carefully to the likely effects of their proposed changes on students, whose interests are presumably at the center of the whole educational enterprise.

NOTES

1. While this analysis draws on data and findings relevant to high school departments, the complete findings of the study, which includes elementary and middle school teachers as well, are reported in my book, *Teachers at Work* (Basic Books, 1990).

2. The departments represented in this sample and the number of teachers in them, include English (9), mathematics (4), social studies (9), science (6), foreign languages (7), home economics (1), counseling (1), music (1), art (1), business (1), bilingual (1).

3. Six taught in schools with more than 25% of their students living below the poverty line; 8 taught where 5% to 25% lived in poverty; 10 taught in schools where fewer than 5% of their students were classified as poor (Market Data Retrieval, 1986).

REFERENCES

Carnegie Forum's Task Force on Teaching as a Profession. (1986). *A nation prepared: Teachers for the 21st century.* New York: Carnegie Corporation.

Holmes Group. (1986). *Tomorrow's teachers.* East Lansing, MI: Author.

Lortie, D. C. (1975). *Schoolteacher: A sociological study.* Chicago: University of Chicago Press.

Market Data Retrieval. (1986). *Curriculum Information Center's school directory, school year 1986/1987.* Shelton, CT: Author.

National Commission on Excellence in Education. (1983). *A nation at risk: The imperative for educational reform.* Washington, DC: U.S. Government Printing Office.

Neufeld, B. (1984). *Inside organizations: High school teachers' efforts to influence their work.* Unpublished doctoral dissertation, Harvard University, Cambridge, MA.

Olson, L. (1988, June 8). Capturing teaching's essence: Stanford team tests new methods. *Education Week, 7*(37), 1, 20.

Paule, L. (1986). *The curriculum decision environment of high school English, mathematics, science and social studies departments.* Unpublished doctoral dissertation, University of Oregon, Eugene.

Shulman, L. S. (1987). Knowledge and teaching: Foundations of the new reform. *Harvard Educational Review, 57*(1), 1-22.

Wilson, B. L., & Herriott, R. E. (1989). *Formal subunits within American public schools: Their structure, power, and consequences* (mimeograph). Philadelphia, PA: Research for Better Schools.

PART III

Analyses of Change in Embedded Teaching Contexts

7

Conditions of Professional Development in Secondary Schools

JUDITH WARREN LITTLE

The last decade has produced no fewer than six major studies of the American comprehensive high school. All of them devote considerable attention to the quality of teaching and the attitudes of teachers toward their work.[1] All of them chronicle, in greater or lesser detail, the teaching circumstances that appear to affect teachers' performance and commitment. This chapter attempts an analysis of those working conditions that directly and indirectly affect secondary school teachers' professional development, promoting or impeding their professional growth over time. The chapter is organized in two major sections. The first explores the ways in which teachers' motivations to develop professionally may be shaped by the intellectual and social demands of teaching and by circumstances that support or hinder teachers in making use of what they know. The second section describes teachers' access to formal and informal professional development opportunities, assessing the likelihood that such experiences will affect teachers' success and satisfaction in the classroom, their contributions to the school at large, and their commitment to teaching.

The analysis is informed by a broadened conception of professional development that encompasses the individual's professional experience both in and out of the classroom. Professional development opportunities might be expected to affect—and to reflect—at least three dimensions of a teacher's life: as classroom instructor, as colleague or member of a faculty, and as a participant in a broader occupational community. Such a conception is a departure from the bulk of professional development literature, with its nearly exclusive emphasis on the first of these, that is, on the teachers' classroom-specific knowledge and skills, teachers' participation in skill training, rates of classroom implementation or skill transfer, and performance outcomes.

The analysis is further informed by a concern for life in the ordinary secondary school and for the career of the mainstream secondary school teacher. That is, the chapter attends less to the evidence or theorizing regarding unusually effective schools (Lightfoot, 1983) than to the available descriptions of the typical high school. It devotes less space to celebrating the design and accomplishments of innovative professional development programs (Stevenson, 1987) than to characterizing the routine, widespread configuration of opportunities available to teachers at large. Such an approach moves us to take seriously in our research agendas and policy deliberations the prevailing conditions that necessarily affect both the supply and the quality of the teacher workforce. It also places the conditions of daily work at the heart of a discussion of professional development, taking its point of departure from the structure and context of the work of teaching.

MOTIVATION FOR PROFESSIONAL DEVELOPMENT: TEACHING CONDITIONS IN SECONDARY SCHOOLS

Independent of the cognitive abilities and personal dispositions of individuals, certain realities of teaching affect teachers' competence, commitment, and career decisions (Huberman, 1986; Rosenholtz, 1989; Sikes, 1984; Smylie, 1988). Conditions that motivate teachers or discourage them may do so both for the moment—affecting the ebb and flow of energy and engagement teachers bring to their daily work—and for the long term, bolstering or eroding their overall investment in teaching. In affecting the orientation that individual teachers hold toward their work, such pervasive realities also enhance or sap the collective capacity of a school to educate its students. Thus, the conditions of teaching that motivate or discourage professional development have both individual meaning and wider institutional or societal significance.

Certain features of social organization bear upon teachers' engagement in their work and, by inference, upon their motivation for professional development. The argument here rests in part on the proposition that "motivation to learn" and "motivation to work" are closely linked and that both reflect teachers' response to four aspects of secondary school teaching: (1) the degree to which the multiple goals characteristic of secondary schools give direction and meaning to teachers' professional activity; (2) the manner in which the age, number, and future prospects of students affect the relations between teacher and student, and in turn the investment that teachers make in their work; (3) the nature and consequences of affiliation among teachers, and the collective norms of performance and improvement that teachers share; and (4) the significance of departmental structures and teachers' traditional allegiance to subject-matter disciplines.

These are not the only aspects of life in secondary schools that affect teachers' inclinations and choices, nor are they the only roots of teachers' motivation to learn. They are, however, prominent and persistent elements of life in secondary schools that have been linked to variations in teachers' classroom performance and workplace commitment. They distinguish secondary schools from elementary schools and, in crucial and quite particularistic ways, distinguish secondary schools from one another. And finally, as features of social organization, produced and reproduced by persons through their interactions with one another, they lend themselves to purposive attention and local intervention.

Multiple Goals and the Importance of Achievement

Advances in the study of workplace commitment suggest that motivation derives in large part from the value that individuals, groups, and institutions attach to the work at hand, the relative ease or difficulty of doing that work successfully, and the rewards or other sanctions associated with success or failure (Fuller, Wood, Rapoport, & Dornbusch, 1982; Kerr & Slocum, 1981). By this argument, persons are spurred to do a task well and to improve over time when they and others around them find the task important and challenging—and find the necessary resources and rewards forthcoming.

If we are to judge by the available portraits of life in secondary schools, the sheer magnitude of the teaching task is immense. Public expectations for secondary schools have multiplied in number and escalated in intensity throughout the twentieth century. The scale of the task is in large part a societal dilemma, not merely an organizational one (Powell, Farrar, & Cohen, 1985). Objectively, the demands are large and difficult to satisy—more so in some schools and some communities than others. The multiplicity of intended outcomes, the diversity of the student population, and the range and complexity of curriculum all may affect teachers' sense of what is important to achieve.

The range of public expectations is mirrored in the array of goals—academic, vocational, socioemotional, moral, and political—to which secondary schools typically aspire. Secondary schools have been asked to be nearly all things to all students; goal ambiguity and goal overload are facts of life for many secondary teachers and administrators. These administrators and teachers must be prepared to succeed on several fronts, of which academic achievement is only one. One recent study argues that high schools provide four distinct curricula, each placing demands on the knowledge, skill, and energies of teachers:

> The official, adult-provided program . . . contains four elements. The most familiar is the horizontal curriculum, which consists of the various subjects taught for credit. . . . But some courses with virtually identical titles are offered at various levels of difficulty. These form a crucial but often less visible vertical curriculum. A third element embraces clubs, activities, and sports, which together form the extracurriculum . . . usually viewed as educationally indispensable by teachers and students alike. Finally, the different kinds of psychological and social services offered by schools make up a distinct services curriculum. [Powell et al., 1985, pp. 12–13]

The satisfactory achievement of multiple goals, each of them ambitious, is demonstrably a complex undertaking. By one view, this poses a challenge that stimulates teachers' creativity, initiative, and persistence, and wins for them the accolades of their students and the public. Seen in this light, the scale and importance of the teaching task may lead teachers to rise to a challenge, deriving their motivation from the need to satisfy a range of academic, social, and emotional demands (Fuller et al., 1982). To the degree that the various goals appear to be irretrievably in conflict or to be beyond reach, however, the motivational consequences may be quite different. The prospect of perpetual failure may defeat and discourage capable teachers who find that the challenges always seem to outstrip institutional resources and personal rewards (Beynon, 1985).

To sustain their enthusiasm for professional development, teachers must typically withstand two countervailing features of life in secondary schools. They must find sources of engagement and motivation in the face of (1) a multiplicity of goals, with a corresponding ambiguity regarding valued directions and outcomes; and (2) a relative devaluing of academic achievement in competition with other priorities. A closer examination of the internal dynamics of school life suggests how one might account for higher-than-anticipated levels of motivation and commitment in some schools or among some teachers.

First, the motivation potential of a school may be assessed by attending less to the nominal range of school goals and by accounting more precisely for the relative ordering of goals as perceived by administrators, teachers, students, and parents (Lightfoot, 1983). In particular, motivational consequences are likely to vary with the relative priority granted to those academic and vocational goals that most directly affect students' futures, and with the direction and intensity of norms of achievement for students and teachers. Where in the array of goals are those that link most closely students' and teachers' futures, identities, and mutual stake in schoolwork?

Second, teachers may exploit the array of purposes to find a satisfying personal niche in the organization. The very multiplicity of goals provides numerous grounds for commitment and engagement—a range of motivational "hooks" that permit teachers to forge idiosyncratic and entrepreneurial attachments to the school program. Such individually crafted connections between school and teacher may be of quite variable strength and substance. In his study of the faculties in two high schools, Cusick (1982) uncovered an astonishing collection of arrangements by which teachers pursued their personal interests while nominally satisfying their obligations to the school. Cusick observes that "teachers . . . were free to develop the pattern of accommodation and the approach to the curriculum that suited them" (p. 12). Writing in a similar vein about goal consensus in elementary schools, Rosenholtz (1989) has observed that, "If . . . schools are organized in ways that allow multiple performance dimensions, multiple bases from which to define teaching goals and values will also exist. Varied standards of performance essentially grant teachers freedom to enhance their own self-esteem by selecting only those goals that suit them best" (p. 15).

By enumerating the many goals to which schools are obligated, observers may overestimate or wrongly construe the goal-related dilemmas experienced by teachers. In research conducted by Lampert and summarized by Feiman-Nemser and Floden (1986), teachers "over and over again . . . illustrate how they managed to teach without having to make the dichotomous choices social scientists associate with the teacher's role (e.g., to satisfy either personal goals or institutional requirements; to foster either human development or academic excellence)" (pp. 513–514). Lampert's work parallels the in-depth case description of the high school English teacher "Sarah," authored by Elbaz (1983); both display a "'complicated personal and practical process of accommodation' in which teachers express their responsibilities to both students and society" (Feiman-Nemser & Floden, 1986, p. 514).

Third, departments or other subgroups may engage teachers' interest by supplying the goal coherence and sense of task that the school as a whole cannot impart. Case studies of high schools and departmentalized junior highs are filled with accounts of the "personalities" that distinguish one department, team, or group from another. Within comprehensive high schools, departments are marked by characteristic views of students and their capacity to succeed, and by dispositions toward "conservatism" or "experimentation" in matters of curriculum and instruction (Hargreaves, 1986; Lipsitz, 1984; Metz, 1978). Similarly, teachers' affiliations with persons, groups, or organizations external to the school may affect their interpretation of the school's purposes, their engagement in the school's work, and their motivation to pursue their own professional development or support that of others. Meaningful reference groups inside or outside the school act to reinforce or to attenuate teachers' attachments to teaching.

The goals for which teachers strive with students may be ambitious or modest. The ease or difficulty of achieving them derives not only from the absolute character of the goals themselves, but also from the capacity of the teachers who attempt them, the characteristics of the students with whom they work, and the resources on which both are able to draw. All other factors being equal, one might predict that the more demanding the goals, the greater will be teachers' motivation to seek assistance and the greater their actual rates of participation in professional development activities (Glidewell, Tucker, Todt, & Cox, 1983).

The Teacher/Student Relationship

The teacher/student relationship is perhaps the most profound and consequential of "working conditions" for teachers, the one that most directly affects their commitment to work and their motivation to learn. At all levels of schooling, teachers' own sense of efficacy is bound closely to the success and satisfaction they are able to find with their students (Smylie, 1988; also see Metz, Chapter 3 of this book). Consistent themes are sounded in two related bodies of literature on high schools. The first characterizes adolescents' experience as students (Oakes, 1985) and as members of peer groups (Eckert, 1989; Hargreaves, 1967). From this body of work, one can extrapolate to some of the challenges facing teachers. A second body of work concentrates more directly on teachers' own work with students of various backgrounds (Metz, Chapter 3 of this book) or on teachers' accommodations to student norms (Cusick, 1983; Metz, 1978; Powell et al., 1985; Sedlak, Wheeler, Pullin, & Cusick, 1986; Sizer, 1984; Swidler, 1979). Together, these portraits of life in high schools demonstrate the ways in which secondary teachers, unlike most of their elementary school counterparts, face a substantial challenge in establishing and sustaining a productive bond with students. The problem is intensified by the age and status of the students: Ranging in age from 12 to 18, they are adolescents intent on making a transition to independent adulthood (Sizer, 1984). The dilemma is further intensified for those teachers whose students see little in the way of economic or educational futures, and thus little reason to engage in schoolwork (Ashton & Webb, 1986; Metz, Chapter 3 of this book).

The influence of a teacher on a student (or, put another way, the opportunity for teachers to achieve the primary goals of teaching) is born of close contact and intensive interchange. Unlike elementary teachers who spend all day in close interaction with a class of 25 or 30 students, secondary teachers are assigned a pupil load of 100 students or more with whom they have only sporadic and short-term contact. The composition of the class changes with each class period, and a teacher's entire student population may change with each quarter or semester. The academic curriculum vies with other attractive competitors for students' attentions and loyalties. Blocks of concentrated time that might otherwise have been reserved for study are splintered by the 50-minute class period, field trips, extracurricular school activities, and students' employment schedules (Powell et al., 1985). Not only is this teaching in a crowd, as Jackson (1968) first described it, but teaching in a crowd always on the run.

The relationship between students' expectations of the curriculum and teachers' orientation to professional development is relatively uncharted. Responsive students who seek academic honors may reinforce teachers' own regard for academic traditions and disciplinary integrity, and may spur teachers' own scholarship; these are the patterns suggested by observations of affluent suburban schools (Metz, Chapter 3 of this book) and elite independent schools (Lightfoot, 1983; also see Powell, Chapter 4 of this volume). Yet there are also teachers in such schools who rest secure (and complacent) in the knowledge that the students who attend such schools are likely to succeed regardless of how much or how little attention their teachers pay to new curriculum content or teaching methods. Conversely, "curriculum bargains" that weaken the intellectual content of courses permit students and teachers alike to adopt a passive stance toward academic achievement (Cusick, 1983; Hargreaves, 1967; Powell et al., 1985; Sedlak et al., 1986). Such bargains might be expected to compromise teachers' commitments to an academic discipline and erode their incentives for professional development. These are patterns characteristic of many urban schools, especially those in cities experiencing economic decline (Cusick, 1983). Teachers in some urban schools may find that their students' low economic status and dim future prospects only exacerbate a creeping "status panic" that has beset teaching generally (Webb, 1985); a low-status clientele does little to compensate the teacher's own "special but shadowed" status (Lortie, 1975, p. 10).

As teachers and students define "schoolwork" with and for one another, setting the limits and enlarging the possibilities for success in their joint endeavors, they jointly construct the meaning of commitment and engagement. The "bargains" and "treaties" struck between students and teachers both reflect and reproduce the expectations each group holds for the other's performance.

Autonomy, Affiliation, and Accountability

How much do colleagues count in shaping teachers' inclination to pursue professional development? Although the relationship between teacher and student is profoundly personal and looms large in one's sense of identity as "teacher," schoolteaching is nonetheless institutional work. In schools as in other organizations, staff members' orientation toward their work is affected by interactions with the larger work group (Cummings, 1981; Kerr & Slocum, 1981). Teachers interviewed about their professional lives have consistently granted peers an important role in accounting for their own greater or lesser degree of professional involvement. They describe peers who variously celebrate or denigrate classroom experimentation, university study, inservice workshops, or other routes to new ideas, new relationships, and new career opportunities. In one recent study of staff development participation (Little et al., 1987), teachers who were vigorously and enthusiastically involved in formal professional development activities also reported working in schools in which their colleagues and administrators valued participation, making continuous learning an integral part of the work life of the school. By contrast, teachers who were relentlessly critical of staff development and less involved in it also tended to describe a work environment in which professional development was treated with disinterest.

The motivational potential of schools is enhanced to the extent that teachers find in one another both pressure and support for performance. Teachers' obligations to and involvements with one another arise first out of the organization of the work itself. Mutual interdependence is presumably increased by shared responsibility for student success and by shared agreements about the curriculum; conversely, it is undermined when teachers bear no obligation for one another's success with students or for the overall quality and coherence of the curriculum. The conventional assignment of students to individual teachers communicates a message of mutual independence among teachers. The assignment of groups of students to groups of teachers—as groups—communicates a different relationship. At issue here is the degree to which the responsibilities of teaching create perceptions of independence or interdependence, and whether the very conduct of the work breeds isolation or interaction.

Secondary schools have been distinguished from one another by the degree to which they perpetuate long-standing traditions of teacher isolation or foster close collaboration and experimentation (Ball & Lacey, 1984; Bird & Little, 1985; Hargreaves, 1986; Metz, 1978). On the whole, however, the search for task-related faculty networks or work groups has been less fruitful in secondary schools than in elementary schools (Cusick, 1982). Collective intent and coordinated practice have been demonstrated to produce schoolwide effects, but the secondary school examples are few (Lipsitz, 1984; Rutter, Maughan, Mortimore, & Ouston, 1979). Instances of individual entrepreneurialism outnumber the instances of professionally cohesive faculty action. In the available portraits of schools, most descriptions accord with that offered by Cusick (1983), who observed that "neither for students nor for teachers were the schools in any sense normative or communal societies. There was no case I could find of teachers exercising any pressure on a colleague to alter his or her classroom behavior" (p. 58).

In some respects, the nature of the teaching task presents teachers with reason for close affiliation with their colleagues. It is a commonplace of organizational theory that nonroutine tasks tend to drive the formation of collaborative relations (Cohen, 1981), while routinized tasks that can be accomplished alone tend to fortify independence. Secondary school teaching confronts teachers with complex demands, uncertain technology, and indefinite rewards—conditions that benefit from close lateral relations. Despite the demonstrated complexities and ambiguities of the work, however, most teachers work in a kind of isolation that retards the ability of individuals and groups to make sense of teaching and to improve it (Glidewell et al., 1983).

Teachers' relations are further determined by the nature and extent of discretion they preserve in curriculum decision making. On average, secondary schools have not taken it as a collective problem to "make up a curriculum that everybody can do" (Powell et al., 1985, p. 1). The proliferation of electives serves both to limit interdependence (Cusick, 1983) and to introduce a measure of interpersonal competition among teachers as they vie for the most favored students (Finley, 1984). Teachers use the electives system to develop courses consistent with personal interests (Cusick, 1983) and to achieve a "good schedule" (Finley, 1984). In this manner, the work of teaching becomes a form of "idiosyncratic specialization" (Pellegrin, 1976) or "entrepreneurial teaching" (Cusick, 1983). Curricular and instructional choices rest primarily in the hands of individual teachers who are rarely called upon to justify the choices they have made.

The persistent autonomy of the self-contained classroom and the importance of the diverse "menu" of electives in most secondary schools serve to sustain teachers' independence from peers and to limit their sense of community. To the extent that the basic conditions of work bind teachers more closely to the immediacies of the classroom, they produce "not only a noncosmopolitan orientation with respect to the wider occupation but also a local orientation within the school itself" (Bishop, 1977,

p. 178; see also Lortie, 1975). Just as individual teachers construct the curriculum day by day and person by person (Cusick, 1982, 1983), so teachers in most schools pursue the improvements in their knowledge and skill on their own. Under such circumstances, most teachers not only teach what they choose, but also learn what they choose. To the extent that teaching remains an isolated and isolating enterprise, we can expect professional development to mirror the experience of teaching: Individual prerogative and privacy will prevail over collective priorities or public debate. Individual teachers decide what and how much new development they will do to meet the demands of the curriculum. Rates of participation in professional development are predictably variable for secondary teachers who have otherwise comparable teaching assignments and levels of experience. Consider these two profiles of professional development involvement by high school science teachers, each with less than 5 years' teaching experience:

A beginning high school biology teacher, characterized as an avid participant in continuing education, logged over 1600 hours in additional coursework, independent research, selected conferences and workshops, and school-based decision-making groups over a 3-year period; another beginning teacher, described as a reluctant participant, logged only 29 hours of continuing education in the same 3-year period. [Lanier & Little, 1986, p. 548]

An additional contributor to teachers' professional orientation is the department: Structurally, at least, the independence of the secondary teacher is modified by department membership. The near-universal use of subject-area departments as the organizing structure of secondary schools raises the possibility that department members owe mutual accountability for the choices each makes regarding curriculum depth and breadth. The focus on departments, however, probably overrepresents the degree to which subject-matter curriculum is collectively decided and organized. Although the literature contains examples of departments that operate as interdependent collegial groups (Lightfoot, 1983; Tyree, 1988; also see Johnson, Chapter 6 of this volume), these appear to be exceptions to a more common rule: Departments are more likely to serve as administrative conveniences than as instruments of curriculum policy (Cusick, 1982). In department meetings, teachers may demonstrate their "unwillingness to let any collective effort affect their individual teaching," while administrators' actions serve to support teachers' "private versions of the job" (Cusick, 1983, pp. 90, 98). In few schools would teachers claim that the formally assigned department heads, the informal opinion leaders, or even their closest colleagues exerted substantial influence on the content or methods they chose to use with their own students.

The subject-oriented curriculum of the secondary school may either relieve or exacerbate more generalized features of teacher isolation. Some small-scale case studies provide examples of cohesive "subject subcultures" whose members are bound by common orientation to subject paradigms and/or subject pedagogies (Ball & Lacey, 1984), or by common pursuit of innovations in curriculum or instruction (Bird & Little, 1985). Other case study research suggests that such instances of subject-oriented coherence are rare (Cusick, 1983; Tyree, 1988). At the same time, the departmental structure obscures other common ground among teachers; for example, teachers' assignments to classes of high-track, average, or remedial students might constitute a more powerful basis of interdependence or affiliation than departmental membership (Finley, 1984).

Finally, the practices of performance evaluation (or other mechanisms for feedback) have been found to affect teachers' own conceptions of their work and their colleagues. Consistent with the broader research on workplace motivation and performance evaluation (Dornbusch & Scott, 1975), teachers' motivation for professional development has been linked to the consequences they perceive for performance, and to the regularity of supervision in the work life of the school (Meyer & Cohen, 1971; Rosenholtz, 1989). On the whole, there are few clear rewards for continuous professional development, and virtually no penalties for failing to develop. The evaluation and supervision of teaching is a less substantive, more cursory business in secondary schools than in elementary schools; evaluators' credibility is harder to achieve, especially when authority for evaluation is restricted to administrators whose ability to judge appropriate treatment of content across the curriculum is limited (Little & Bird, 1987).

Predictably, secondary schools have been found to vary in the extent to which administrators expect and obtain accountability from teachers regarding their classroom choices. The extremes are evident in contrasting cases reported by Tyree (1988). In one school, administrators require from departments a "steady flow of communication" about departmental curriculum goals, teachers' plans for reaching them, and students' progress. In another, social camaraderie substitutes for collegiality of a sturdier sort; in that school, administrators tolerate a wide range of classroom idiosyncrasy in exchange for teachers' willingness to handle their own discipline problems and to limit the number of failing grades they give.

Teachers who work in schools where administrators invest large amounts of time directly in the classroom—and in classroom-related discussions with teachers—tend to applaud the forthright and public examination of teaching that such involvement generates. Such informal and labor-intensive arrangements, however, are vulnerable to other external and internal demands on administrators' time, and effects may be limited to those departments or teachers to whom administrators have devoted the most attention (Little & Bird, 1987). On the whole, teachers' professional development has been dissociated from teacher evaluation and from other personnel policies formulated at the district level (McLaughlin & Pfeifer, 1988; Schlechty et al., 1982).

In sum, teachers' relationships with one another—and thus the motivation that they might derive from membership in a meaningful collegial group—are affected by four variable features of secondary school life: (1) the level of joint responsibility teachers bear for student success, (2) individual and collective discretion or autonomy in defining curriculum, (3) the salience of subject-matter departments, and (4) the frequency and import of performance evaluation or other feedback that teachers receive about their work. Together, these form conditions surrounding teachers' professional life; in small or large measure they supply teachers with reason to learn anything new, learn from one another, learn together, or directly influence one another's work.

Subject Affiliation

Subject-area organization modeled on higher education is a long-standing feature of secondary schools that creates both possibilities and limitations for teachers' professional development. Subject-area departments form the taken-for-granted structure of the American secondary school. Some argue that departments are the most likely home for teachers' improvement efforts (see Johnson, Chapter 6 of this volume). Others maintain that departments form an administrative convenience but not an intellectual home (Cusick, 1982), or that teaching assignments linking teachers to particular academic tracks may have greater salience than departmental membership (Finley, 1984; Riseborough, 1984). More vociferous critics maintain that departmentalization is a conservative force that inhibits innovation by teachers and fragments students' experience of the curriculum (Hargreaves, 1987; Sizer, 1984). Nonetheless, departmentalization remains one of the fundamental facts of life in the work of most secondary teachers. Two aspects of subject-area organization have been examined for their potential effect on teachers' commitment to teaching and to professional development: recruitment, preparation, and socialization of subject specialists; and the nature of subject-area teaching assignments that teachers acquire.

Recruitment, preparation, and socialization. Secondary teachers (or at least high school teachers) are recruited into teaching, prepared for teaching, and socialized into teaching on the basis of subject-area enthusiasms. Career biographies of science and art teachers confirm that "the subject had been the major factor influencing all of [the] teachers' decisions to teach" and "most of what teachers say about their careers relates to their subject" (Sikes, Measor, & Woods, 1985, pp. 180, 181). Once hired, secondary teachers typically conduct their work as members of subject-area departments. It is the case that the subject specializations of high school teachers may lead us to overestimate the importance of the academic major and to underestimate the importance of the broad liberal arts education of which the major is one part. It is also the case that little attention has been devoted to the availability of professional development experiences that continue the traditions of undergraduate liberal arts education, enabling teachers to become models for students and for one another of "the well-educated person." In teachers' eyes, nonetheless, professional development achieves greater legitimacy to the degree that it is demonstrably linked to their primary subject-area identities.

Recruitment, preparation, and socialization are not processes that end when a teacher is hired. In the first year(s) of teaching, early conceptions and commitments are confirmed or altered by teachers' encounters with students and by their affiliation with colleagues inside and outside the school. As they tell the stories of their teaching careers, teachers recall incidents that have crystallized their own sense of identity over time (Measor, 1985). Early on, critical incidents with students loom large, marking a trajectory from clumsy to more polished performances in the classroom and from awkwardness to certainty in relations with students. Teachers align themselves with colleagues whose work they admire and distance themselves from others whose work they disparage. Commitments to professional development are plausibly related to the professional models that teachers witness and to the professional identities they assume.

To account for the development of secondary teachers' professional identities and inclinations requires that one acknowledge their origins within a disciplinary tradition, and that one attend simultaneously to teachers' preoccupations with teaching the subject. The commonplace distinction between elementary school teachers who "teach students" and secondary teachers who "teach subjects" appears a crude distinction in the light of recently developed case studies. In the intellectual biographies they have crafted of beginning teachers, Grossman and Richert (1986) reveal how student teachers' "actual contact with students forced them to re-examine their subject matter content from a new perspective"

(p. 13), breaking it into teachable pieces while retaining a grasp of the whole, uncovering and analyzing taken-for-granted concepts or skills, making accessible what they knew to those who did not know, trying to grasp students' misconceptions and confusions. In their struggle, novice teachers brought to bear their knowledge of broad subject paradigms and specific subject content; their knowledge of general learning principles and specific students' understandings; their knowledge of general pedagogy; and their increasing awareness of local preferences, standards, and histories. Experienced teachers speak with greater assurance, but reach for the same rich integration of subject matter with student, place, and time. The 20 teacher portraits constructed by Macrorie (1984) include 5 of high school teachers whose sense of student and sense of subject are so intertwined as to be separable only by violent artifice. Macrorie celebrates these teachers for their "practice of eliciting good works from students," good works that follow from the intimate encounters that teachers arrange between the hidden possibilities of subject materials and the understandings, curiosities, confusions, or doubts of students.

Over time, secondary teachers locate themselves both in relation to the intellectual traditions and priorities of a discipline and in relation to the lives of students and communities. Cognitively, teachers develop "pedagogical content knowledge, . . . an understanding of what it means to teach particular subject matter to students" (Grossman & Richert, 1986, p. 3) and, one might add, to these particular students. The combined sense of "subject and student" is evident in this description of the subject-matter knowledge held by Sarah, the Canadian high school teacher portrayed by Elbaz (1983):

> Sarah's view of English literature as a discipline to which she owes academic allegiance, and which imposes critical standards, is detailed but also subject to conflict . . . precisely because she must mediate between her academic conceptions and the need to engage students in literary activity. . . . Thus to work only within the view of English as discipline was unacceptable to Sarah. But she apparently found it entirely possible to hold simultaneously two diverse views of English literature, and to mediate between them only in practice, in terms of priorities determined by another dimension of her practical knowledge—for example, her conception of students and their needs. [pp. 56–57]

As teachers acquire an identity that serves them well or ill in their classroom work, they also acquire the values and norms of the institution at large—its expectations for the present achievement and future success of students and teachers. Among the messages communicated to teachers are those that conceive of teaching as either a complex, subtle task learned continuously throughout a career, or as a relatively routine matter mastered in a few short years through an accumulation of "tricks of the trade." Teachers come to understand whether the work of teaching and its improvement is viewed with enthusiasm, indifference, or disdain.

Teaching assignments. Teachers' affiliations with an academic discipline are influenced (for good or ill) by the instructional assignments they are able to secure in the formal curriculum. Ties to the subject discipline are strengthened or weakened by the meaning that "math teacher" or "English teacher"or "art teacher" comes to have in daily work (Ball & Lacey, 1984; Bennet, 1985; Sikes et al., 1985).

The widespread departmentalization of the high school may lead us to assume a close correspondence among teachers' professional preparation, their instructional assignments, and their academic orientation. The department would reasonably appear to present a home for "like-minded" persons who have been similarly prepared in their discipline and who are similarly disposed toward teaching it. On the basis of available evidence, such assumptions appear suspect, especially for the core academic disciplines. Teachers assigned to a department may or may not share common levels of academic preparation in the subject. They may teach part time or full time for the department. And they may vary substantially in the orientation they hold to the subject matter or the way in which they teach it. Teachers who have received similar preparation in a discipline may not be similarly disposed toward what to teach or how to teach it. In terms coined by Stephen Ball and Colin Lacey (1984), they may differ with regard to subject paradigms or subject pedagogy. "[A] subject perspective [is] by no means necessarily a collective view of content and pedagogy," according to Sikes et al. (1985, p. 181).

Patterns of actual instructional assignment may make good or poor use of teachers' professional preparation and in turn bolster or diminish teachers' subject identities and commitments. When teachers are secure in the material they are assigned to teach and when they are successful in negotiating a "good schedule" that assures them the specific levels and topics they want to teach (Finley, 1984, p. 237), then professional development can be expansive in character. That is, teachers can devote time to achieving greater curriculum depth, enlarging the supply of materials available for student work, refining instructional options, or even pursuing new topics quite outside the current instructional assignment. When teachers are well prepared for their assignments and positively disposed toward them, their lives and those of students arguably stand a better chance of being intellectually lively and emotionally rich.

But when teachers are assigned to teach one or more classes outside their major area of specialization, professional development takes on a whole new meaning. Teachers must scramble to stay one day ahead of their students in an unfamiliar area; at the same time, any efforts that teachers might have made to remain current in their own specialization must be placed on hold. When teachers are ill prepared for the subject they are assigned to teach, they may substitute affective and social goals for academic goals (Sedlak et al., 1986, pp. 100–101) or retreat to text-book-bound teaching (Ball & Lacey, 1984, p. 236). In departments populated by nonspecialists, curriculum policy is harder to achieve and instructional quality suffers: "The presence of non-specialist . . . teachers inhibits both the development of a formal instrument of [curriculum] 'policy' and the implementation of pedagogies like team teaching, leading instead to what is regarded as an unproductive over-dependence upon the use of textbooks" (p. 237).

It is not clear how many American secondary teachers are teaching in areas for which they are not qualified, but estimates range from 8% of secondary teachers (Guthrie et al., 1988) to more than 20% (NEA, 1987). Articles in the popular media sound the alarm that mathematics and science classrooms are staffed by the unqualified and incompetent. In one recent small-scale study (Gehrke & Sheffield, 1985), a district's policy of reassignment was described as "dismal," even before a 6-year period of repeated layoffs began in 1975.[2] Science classes in this study district were the hardest hit by misassignment; one-half of all general science and physics classes and one-fifth of the chemistry classes were taught by teachers lacking either a major or minor in the subject, even prior to the period of layoffs. The pattern of reassignment showed that the core academic departments—English, social studies, math, and science—were the most vulnerable to staffing manipulations that threatened curricular quality and integrity.

Similarly, departments weaken their capability to maintain a credible program for students when otherwise properly credentialed teachers fail to remain current in their field. One might argue that the problem is most severe in technical fields that advance rapidly (for example, the sciences or computer technology). In fact, the problem applies more broadly. It is difficult to imagine how one would teach English literature without a grasp of contemporary authors, or teach art uninformed by those artists who are now painting and sculpting, or attempt an unraveling of history without the tools of current economic and political theory. When teachers are poorly prepared at the outset to treat a subject in depth, or when their competence erodes as the field passes them by, academic goals are likely to suffer. The department's incentives and capability to sustain a well-conceived core curriculum are thereby diminished.

Departments, therefore, can be described in terms of the individual and collective competence of their members. How adequate is each individual's preparation, and what is the configuration of background, talent, and inclination represented by the group? A department's disciplinary strength, and its capacity to make advances in curriculum and instruction, can be assessed in terms of teachers' formal academic credentials, their familiarity with current developments and controversies in the discipline, and their instructional experience with all parts of the school's student population and the department's curriculum. For example, can the math department provide advanced placement classes in calculus or analytic geometry? Does the first-year math teacher understand what it will mean to teach ninth-grade general math, a subject she never took (having been placed in more advanced classes in high school), in a classroom populated by students who, unlike her, have difficulty in grasping mathematical concepts? Is anyone in the department familiar with recent developments in computer software that enable students to grasp the conceptual properties of algebraic functions? The demands on teachers' knowledge, skill, and confidence vary by subject, level, and the specific student composition of classes.

Whatever other influences may drive them closer to or further from their work, teachers' ordinary conditions of work are potent forces. Teachers' motivations to work and their motivations to improve are seen here as closely linked and as grounded in the situated combinations of purpose, students, fellow teachers, and subject matter that make up "teaching." Two major implications for teachers' professional development arise from these conditions. First, it is not categorically clear what intellectual pursuit would improve teachers' success and satisfaction in the classroom, bring them the esteem of public or peers, or enrich their career prospects. Where in this complex and diffuse array is a productive starting point for professional development? Second, the ambitious and ambiguous goals of secondary teaching, together with teachers' uncertain influence over students, may lead us to overestimate the advantages that professional development activity might yield. Certainly much of what has passed for professional development, if held to the standards of improved personal knowledge, innovation, or reform, would appear to be mere tinkering around the margins; the defining characteristics of classroom teaching have been remarkably durable (Cuban, 1985). Yet the magnitude of intellectual, social, and emotional demands entailed in secondary teaching suggest that schools face a considerable challenge in sustaining an adequate level of performance, or in preventing decline. Simply staving off compromise would seem to be a substantial accomplishment, and one that would go a long way toward preserving teachers' career satisfaction and commitment. This calls for a conception of professional development that is not confined to its conventional sense of advancing knowledge and practice, but that also anticipates its function in maintaining organizational stability and sustaining a consistent level of personal investment (Schlechty & Whitford, 1983).

SECONDARY TEACHERS' OPPORTUNITIES FOR PROFESSIONAL DEVELOPMENT

Where motivation is matched by opportunity, we might reasonably expect a steady increase in teachers' capacity to teach, their commitment to teaching as a career, and their worth as members of an organization and occupation. In the absence of opportunity to add to their professional competence and stature, teachers who are otherwise well-motivated to develop may experience frustration, alienation, an eventual decline in performance, and, for some, departure from the occupation (Berry, 1985; Beynon, 1985). Teachers' actual opportunities for professional development consist both in their participation in university coursework or other formal professional development activities and in the more informal "opportunity to learn" that inheres in the structure of time, task, and relationship in the salaried workday.

Participation in Formal Professional Development Activities

Teachers' opportunities for professional growth have been measured primarily in terms of their participation in formally designated activities, most prominently in university coursework, district-sponsored workshops, conferences hosted by professional associations, and sabbatical leaves. To this list, some surveys add participation in curriculum committees or other unspecified committees, educational television, and travel (NEA, 1987). Certain emerging patterns in teachers' participation have particular import for secondary teachers.

Declining participation in university coursework. University coursework has for decades held a privileged position in the professional development marketplace. Whatever criticisms have been levied regarding the

content and rigor of teachers' postbaccalaureate coursework, the university remains plausibly the center of continuing education for secondary teachers whose initial certification was premised on subject specialization and whose sustained worth rests partly on subject-matter depth. But the prominence of the university is diminishing.

In relative terms, participation in university coursework by secondary teachers has declined steadily for more than 15 years. Secondary teachers surveyed by the NEA in 1971 averaged 15 college credits during a 3-year period, slightly more than the 14 credits earned by their elementary counterparts (NEA, 1987). By 1981, secondary teachers averaged only 10 units during a comparable 3-year period (but still slightly more than elementary teachers). In 1986, the figure had declined to only 4 units for secondary and elementary teachers alike. More than half of all high school teachers (54%) earned no credits during the 3-year period ending in 1986.

Presumably, one attraction for university study comes in the form of the university's subject-specialist faculty. However, a small and declining percentage of secondary teachers surveyed by the NEA enroll in courses in subjects other than education. As recently as the 1983–1984 year, approximately 17% of secondary teachers enrolled in subject-matter courses during the school year (compared to 19% who enrolled in courses taught by school of education faculty); a still smaller percentage (11%) participated during the summer. By 1985–1986, the enrollment in courses outside education accounted for no more than 10% of secondary teachers during the school year, and 7% in the summer. (Because teachers who completed the NEA questionnaire could give multiple answers to this inventory of professional growth activities, the percentages are not additive; some unspecified proportion of the teachers is enrolled in both summer-school and school-year coursework.)

The causes of this campus desertion are unknown. It is possible that teachers have avoided coursework due to a growing disenchantment with what the university has to offer teachers. Certainly the"ivory tower" image persists, with its implication that knowledge originating in the university is of little immediate use in the secondary curriculum. But an explanation rooted in disappointment is not entirely persuasive. The university has also been home to some of the most highly regarded examples of professional development for secondary teachers. Beginning with the summer science and foreign language institutes that arose in the wake of Sputnik, universities have sponsored summer and school-year programs that enable teachers to work directly on the classroom applications of new subject-matter knowledge. Among the examples of programs available in the 1980s are the 15-year-old Bay Area Writing Project (the model for similar projects in 169 sites in 46 states) and the Math Collaboratives funded in 11 cities by the Ford Foundation. Arguably, such special institutes touch the lives of relatively few teachers, and even fewer schools and districts are well prepared to make good use of the teachers who do participate. A far greater number of teachers experience the university in the form of conventional coursework, at least some of which is justly criticized as part-time, fragmented, and substantively shallow; one can trace a rather continuous litany of criticism that extends over a 25-year period from Conant's *The Education of American Teachers* in 1963 to Lanier and Little's "Research on Teacher Education" in 1986. Even so, there is little evidence that teachers are more disappointed with coursework than with other forms of readily available professional development. On the whole, teachers who participate in coursework rate its impact at least as favorably as the impact of conferences and workshops (Little et al., 1987). Whatever room there may be for improvements in the quality of university-based in-service education, perceptions of quality are unlikely to account well for the 15-year slump in enrollments.

A more likely explanation, but one that has received little policy attention, stems from the financial incentive structure attached to university enrollment. The link between accumulated university credits and salary advances has been an established feature of district personnel policy for several decades; the extrinsic incentives for university study reside nearly exclusively in the salary schedule. As teachers acquire the semester units that move them to the ceiling on the salary schedule, a major incentive to participate in coursework is lost. In 1985–1986, more than 40% of secondary teachers surveyed by the NEA (1987) had worked 15 years or more—long enough to "top out" on the salary schedule in most states.

In recent years, even the course enrollment of less senior teachers has been undercut by the development of alternative routes to salary credit. Using the university model as a guide, districts have begun to award semester unit "equivalents" in place of stipends or release time. Teachers may now acquire salary credit for participation in district-sponsored workshops, curriculum development committees, or various special projects. These credits are not transferable across districts, nor has any district entirely supplanted the requirement for university credits. Nonetheless, this practice enables teachers to advance more quickly than they would be able to through university coursework alone. It serves a function for districts as well, enabling them to tie salary advances to locally controlled staff development that is at least nominally linked to district program priorities. For secondary teachers, the shift in practice may be especially consequential. District units require less investment of time and out-of-pocket expense than units acquired through university coursework, thus further eroding teachers' incentives to enroll in university courses that—at least in principle—promise greater subject-matter depth.

Finally, the lure of the university is dimmed by the prospect of substantial (and increasing) out-of-pocket expenses and the corresponding absence of direct financial subsidies for university study. Critics maintain that local governance boards do not support secondary teachers' continued study of their disciplines (Sizer, 1984, p. 190); rhetorical gestures, they say, go unmatched by direct monetary outlays. Less than one teacher in 100 enrolled for university coursework in 1985–1986 was supported by a paid sabbatical, and that number, too, represents a decline from previous levels (NEA, 1987).

The prominence of districts as "service providers." The decline in university study has been matched by a commensurate increase in teachers' participation in district-sponsored staff-development activities. More than two-thirds of secondary teachers surveyed by the NEA (1987) in 1985–1986 had participated in one or more district-sponsored events, up 14% in the 15-year period beginning in 1971. Also in 1985–1986, more than 90% of California's secondary teachers surveyed in a statewide study reported having attended at least one district-sponsored activity (though less than 40% were enrolled in coursework) (Little et al., 1987).

Over the past two decades staff development has become district business, conducted largely by specialists located in a district's central office. As a result, secondary teachers are more likely to choose from a menu of district-sponsored workshops than they are to receive release time or other individual subsidies to attend conferences hosted by subject-area associations or institutes sponsored by universities. They are more likely to attend presentations planned and led by district specialists or administrators than they are to join their colleagues in forging their own uses for noninstructional time reserved for staff development. And as Johnson reports in Chapter 6 of this volume, in-service activities are organized most often at the school or district level, and only rarely within the department (see also Little, 1989). Although teachers attend staff-development events together, they are only incidentally in one another's presence; rarely is collective participation in such an event part of a collective engagement in professional growth (Little, 1984).

The rise of generic pedagogy. In the wake of widely popularized "effective-teaching" research in the 1970s, locally sponsored staff development has been dominated by content-free, pedagogically centered skill-training workshops (Joyce & Showers, 1981; Little et al., 1987). At best, the research orientation has helped to bring teaching out of the realm of the intuitive and to foster discussion about central tenets of teaching. At worst, research findings have been reduced to rules and have contributed to a narrow, overly technical conception of teaching. Under the rubric of "applying research," professional development has tended toward greater procedural specification in teaching and in teacher evaluation; such a move represents an increase in bureaucratization that may serve to discourage professional investments by teachers (Hargreaves, 1987). Links to curriculum content have often been absent or superficial. The workshops and conferences that teachers attend within their districts are likely to introduce them to promising pedagogical techniques such as cooperative learning, but are less likely to engage them in the close study of the fit between those methods and specific subject curricula. Teachers would prefer that it were otherwise. As Johnson describes in Chapter 6 of this volume, teachers placed greater value on conferring with subject-matter colleagues than on attending presentations about general principles of pedagogy or adolescent development provided by outside experts.

Some established programs do meet teachers' expectations. The Bay Area Writing Project has attracted the participation of secondary teachers by combining subject-area expertise with pedagogical wisdom garnered directly from successful teachers (Gray & Caldwell, 1980). To participate in intensive summer institutes, teachers survive a two-stage nomination and interview process. They spend 5 weeks combining various dimensions of "learning to write," as writers themselves, as students and teachers of writing, and as prospective teachers of teachers in their own school and other schools.

The Bay Area Writing Project has earned a favorable reputation among teachers and has served as the model for similar ventures in other subject disciplines. Other initiatives achieve similar standards of substantive rigor combined with sensitivity to teachers' real-world classrooms; some, like the Bay Area Writing Project, emphasize collegial relationships between secondary teachers and university faculty. The EQUALS Program at the University of California's Lawrence Hall of Science involves teachers in finding ways to promote the involvement of girls and minority students in math and science (Kreinberg, 1980). Math collaboratives funded by the Ford Foundation in 11 cities bring secondary teachers and university professors together in a joint effort to improve mathematics teaching in inner-city schools. One example of such a collaborative, an intensive seminar on complex mathematics problems, "has renewed teachers' interest in mathematics itself as well as confidence in themselves as mathematicians and teachers" (Nelson, 1986, p. 51).

Such efforts exemplify experiences that contribute to specific knowledge and skill while engaging teachers with a larger professional community and enriching their own sense of career. It is not insignificant, however, that these special initiatives tend to operate independently of (and often in isolation from) mainstream district and university in-service educational opportunities. They are more likely to be supported by private than public funds. To the extent that they are studied and documented, they are treated as discrete entities. The examples of "best practice" remain outside the dominant patterns of professional development policy and practice.

The relative invisibility of a larger professional community.   To what extent do secondary teachers participate in a larger professional community that extends well beyond the classroom and the school? Associations between teachers and their higher-education colleagues or their nonteaching colleagues in industry or the arts might well serve to stretch teachers' intellectual grasp and their orientation toward subject matter. Career aspirations may be satisfied (or frustrated) in part by the nature of teachers' access to and collegial standing with professional reference groups outside the school (Bennet, 1985; Van Maanen & Barley, 1984).

Teachers' academic histories, present interests, and future aspirations may all serve to connect them with a wider professional community. The NEA (1987) reports that more than half of all secondary teachers belong to one or more subject-area associations, which organize national and regional conferences and distribute journals or other publications. Informally, teachers who are active consumers of professional development express their admiration for the National Council of Teachers of English, the National Council of Teachers of Mathematics, and other comparable organizations. We have, however, virtually no studies of teachers' involvement with subject-area professional associations or other elements of a large professional community. Unknown are the nature and extent of teachers' involvement in such organizations, the reasons for their involvement, the apparent influence on their classroom work or their commitments to teaching, or the influence on their commitments to the specific schools or districts that employ them. The actual or potential links between the activities of associations and those of universities or schools have gone unexamined.

Professional Development Opportunities
in the Salaried Workday

Most studies of professional development have concentrated on formal programs and activities, including coursework. Less attention has been given to investigating professional development obligations and opportunities in terms of the organization of time, task, and relationship within the salaried workday. Obligations and opportunities for professional development can be assessed by examining the nature and extent of teachers' workload, by examining the distribution of out-of-classroom time and responsibilities, and by examining how teachers are organized (or not) to benefit from one another's expertise.

When asked how they have learned to teach or how their work has developed over time, teachers emphasize "learning by experience," "learning on the job," and "trial and error." For some, learning on the job has been a lively, productive enterprise, well supported by the larger institution; these teachers find themselves in what Rosenholtz (1989, p. 80) has termed the "learning enriched" workplace. In such schools, the reasons to learn are expressed through explicit goal setting, frequent exchange among teachers, and teacher evaluation. The occasions for learning are many and varied, or what McLaughlin (n.d.) has termed a "rich soup of opportunities" (p. 19). For other teachers, by contrast, learning on the job has been a more desperate and disparate matter, personally frustrating and institutionally ill supported; these teachers labor in Rosenholtz's (1989, p. 81) "learning impoverished" schools. In such schools, institutional goals are more ambiguous, making it less clear to individuals (or less binding on them) what is important to achieve with students. Support for the daily round of teaching is meager.

Even under the best circumstances, opportunities for professional development must compete for time with the press of daily work. The day, week, and year are crowded with obligations that leave little time for scholarly development—or even reflection on everyday pragmatics. Like other professionals, secondary teachers experience crushing time demands that extend well beyond a 40-hour week. In *Horace's Compromise*, Sizer (1984) constructs a composite teacher—Horace Smith—from the assembled observations and in-depth interviews in 15 schools, a composite whose work demands and career perspectives are intended to typify those of American secondary teachers. Horace's week is a composite with the ring of truth: Before any student work is assigned or reviewed, 32 hours have been accounted for in instruction, administration, extracurricular duties, and other responsibilities. A single assignment completed by each of his 150 students will require another 13 hours of his week—or more, if he devotes more than a token 5 minutes to each student's piece. Horace's 45- or 50-hour week is not atypical. A study of public and private school teachers in New Jersey found public school teachers working an average 48-hour week, and teachers in nonresidential private schools contributing 55 hours (Kane, 1986). The NEA's (1987) summary (*The Status of the American Teacher 1985–86*) reports that high school teachers spent nearly 10 hours a week after school in instructional planning, preparation, and paper grading, in addition to the 34–37-hour work week in school and in addition to other noninstructional activities (coaching, student clubs, bus duty). The mean number of hours spent on all teaching duties by high school teachers exceeds 50 hours. We have here a cumulative picture of a workday (or week, or year, or career) that is not devoted to scholarship for students or for teachers, and in which even the times nominally reserved for intellectual endeavors are vulnerable to myriad interruptions.

Teacher workload. The workload creates pressures for development by giving teachers a reason to learn, but simultaneously places limitations on available time and energy. The greater the workload, the greater the need for fresh ideas but the more scarce the time that one might have to devote to assessing one's current approaches or considering alternatives. Professional development obligations and opportunities will be influenced by two aspects of teacher workload: teacher/student ratio, and the planning and preparation burden created by courseload.

Teachers' opportunity to read, think, talk, or plan on their own or with colleagues—as well as their inclination to do so—may be influenced by the number of students they must teach and by the time thereby required to evaluate student assignments, manage student paperwork, or simply pass the time of day with students. On average, secondary teachers are enjoying a respite from the heavy pupil loads of prior years. The mean pupil load in 1986 was 97, under 100 for the first time in 20 years and down 27% from 132 in 1966 (NEA, 1987). Even so, it is not uncommon for teachers in public high schools to carry a student load of more than 150 students, plus responsibility for extracurricular activities. More than one-third of the teachers surveyed for the 1987 NEA status report taught 125 or more students in 1986. In independent schools, the average load is typically below 100 students, but the demands on teachers' out-of-classroom time are more likely to include academic tutorials, academic advising, and nonacademic counseling (Kane, 1986; also see Powell, Chapter 4 of this volume).

Teachers' planning and preparation burdens can be expressed as the total number and range of preparations required by one's teaching assignments. The greater the amount of time required to prepare for daily work, the less time available to reflect on how that work is going or to pursue new ideas, materials, or methods. The burden is made heavier as the number of different preparations escalates (four is not uncommon, even for beginning teachers) and further intensified if teachers must teach some or all of their load outside their specialization or with a student population unfamiliar to them. Relief is felt in part through the availability of preparation time during the salaried workday, a matter in which secondary teachers routinely have the advantage over their elementary colleagues. In 1986, more than three-quarters of secondary teachers (77%) had five or more preparation periods a week during the school day—still an average of only 13 minutes of preparation time for each hour of instruction (NEA, 1987).

Out-of-class time. Time, according to teachers, is their most valued and least accessible resource. The actual patterned use of noninstructional time during the salaried workday and workyear has received little empirical attention, though nearly everyone agrees that more time would be better.

The ratio of in-class to out-of-class time during the workday is one measure of the time that is potentially available for professional development or program development. Secondary schools are typically differentiated from elementary schools by contractual provisions for preparation time, but the actual amount and use of out-of-classroom discretionary time varies across schools and within schools, and varies over time. The NEA collects information on the number of teachers' weekly preparation periods in its 5-year surveys, but evidence on the use of preparation time is anecdotal, scattered throughout the case-study literature (Cusick, 1982; Tyree, 1988).

Is out-of-class time organized in a way that constitutes a useful opportunity for individuals and groups to pursue professional development? The master schedule that appears on paper masks a set of program and policy choices regarding the professional opportunities for teachers. In many schools, the master schedule is constructed without reference to priorities associated with teachers' professional development or a school's program development. The schedule is designed with the singular aim of satisfying the largest possible number of student placement requirements; teachers may secure a preferred preparation time by lobbying administrators or department heads, who grant teachers their preferred schedule in exchange for other favors (Cusick, 1982; Finley, 1984). In some schools, however, the master schedule reflects a clear set of developmental aspirations for individuals, departments, and the school at large. In such schools,· the master schedule may give high priority to common planning time for teachers who have reason to profit from time together, or may ease the logistics surrounding classroom observation among peers (Bird & Little, 1985).

Schools vary with regard to the organizational demands they make on out-of-class time. In the course of collective bargaining, preparation time may be treated as a concession to teachers; once bargained, it is relegated to a list of individual rights and personal prerogatives and ceases to be a discretionary resource at the disposal of school leaders, departments, or faculties. Out-of-classroom time in such schools is often described as "free time," reflecting the latitude that individual teachers have to decide its use (Miller, 1980). But out-of-classroom time in some schools is not considered "free" (Bird & Little, 1985; Tyree, 1988; see Nias, Southworth, & Yeomans, 1989, for an elementary school example). Leaders of some secondary schools have succeeded in converting "free" or private time to public time; teachers in such schools are expected to devote a large proportion of out-of-class time to joint work with colleagues. In some instances, members of departments or interdisciplinary teams have applied powerful sanctions to group members who fail to pull their share of the collective weight. In one example, middle school faculty members reserved "calamity day" awards for team members who sloughed off their share of team assignments (Lipsitz, 1984).

Teachers' leadership opportunities. There are three reasons to make leadership opportunities *within teaching* an important component of teachers' professional development; two of the three reasons have specific import for secondary schools. First, one could reasonably argue that an expanded leadership structure is required by the sheer magnitude of the teaching and administrative tasks: ambitious and ambiguous goals, a curriculum requiring both depth and breadth, a large and diverse student population and faculty. Objective analysis of the goals and tasks of high school teaching would suggest that the complexity, anbiguity, and uncertainty of the work itself present ample grounds for teacher leadership.

Second, the demands of effective leadership cannot be satisfied by even the most energetic and well-organized administrative team. As a technical matter, administrators' own curriculum knowledge runs short of the depth required by a secondary school faculty. In managerial terms, the span of control is unacceptably large and the resources of supervision, support, and evaluation are slim. It is not uncommon for administrators to attempt the evaluation of 20 or 30 teachers in an academic year. It is no surprise that teachers do not count the resulting interaction as a form of professional development. Administrators who attempt to fashion a style of leadership based on direct classroom support and consultation are generally admired by teachers, but are unable to reach more than a small proportion of a faculty and are constantly vulnerable to pressures that draw them away from the classroom (Little & Bird, 1987). By broadening the structure of leadership to include teachers, secondary schools address these problems of scale while also concentrating both symbolic force and material resources in leaders who are close to the action, that is, directly knowledgeable about the subject area, the specific curriculum constraints and possibilities, the student population, and the faculty. The role of the administrator correspondingly shifts, in the fashion anticipated by Schlechty (n.d.), to a "leader of leaders."

Third, teachers' commitment to their work rests in part on a sense of belonging and influence that can be satisfied only in part by classroom work. Although teachers tend to downplay any interest in administrative posts, they are not inattentive to the intellectual and social opportunities that accompany other kinds of leadership opportunities. Asked about their career satisfactions and aspirations, teachers emphasize teaching assignments that make good use of what they know, stretch them intellectually, and satisfy them emotionally (McLaughlin & Yee, 1988). But as they mature personally and professionally, teachers also seek involvement and influence beyond the classroom (Bennet, 1985; Nias, 1989; Yee, 1986). Some teachers work in schools in which leadership by teachers is widely accepted and the benefits associated with teacher leadership are eminently clear (Lipsitz, 1984). Leaders themselves take pride in having their accumulated knowledge and skill recognized, and satisfaction in new learning. Their colleagues celebrate the accomplishments made possible by well-led departments, teams, or committees. Leadership opportunities within teaching thus can be seen to satisfy two components of a challenging career, as proposed by McLaughlin and Yee (1988): opportunity and capacity. Acknowledged leadership positions afford teachers the opportunity to use their accumulated expertise in arenas outside the classroom, thus yielding benefit to the larger institution. Teachers' professional capacity is enlarged by the discretionary resources that must accompany leadership responsibilities, and by the ability to influence institutional goals and directions.

The position of department head has been the most uniform response to the problems of school size and curriculum complexity. Although it has not been studied in depth, the role of department head deserves attention both because it is one of the few formal opportunities for teacher leadership within schools and because it is a relatively uniform structural feature of American secondary schools. The available studies are revealing for the variations, inconsistencies, and ambiguities they portray; that is, there appears to be no widely known and accepted role for the department head. The professional respect attached to the role varies substantially from district to district and school to school. In some schools, a teacher earns the right to lead a department by teaching well, developing state-of-the-art curriculum, and working productively with both colleagues and administrators; the professional development potential of the position—for its incumbent and for the department at large—seems reasonably high. In other schools, the role of department head is little more than an administrative burden shouldered in turn by each member of the department. In such schools, selection to the post has little to do with a teacher's substantive accomplishments, and fulfilling its responsibilities has little connection with the teacher's career aspirations or satisfactions. The potential of the position to contribute to professional development is correspondingly low.

What is acceptable practice by department heads in one school is taboo in another. For example, all department heads interviewed in one recent study (Johnson, Chapter 6 of this book) considered teacher evaluation a major part of their responsibilities; they did so in only two of the eight schools included in a study of "instructional leadership in secondary schools" by Bird & Little (1985), but in none of the three high schools studied in depth by Cusick (1982, 1983) or the eight high schools examined by Metz (Chapter 3, herein). Heads in Johnson's (Chapter 6) schools led departments where "teachers were active in jointly developing courses and writing curriculum" (p. 6). Teachers in the other studies were more likely to develop their courses independently, relying on the department head for administrative support (e.g., book orders) but not substantive guidance. What might we make of these anecdotal variations? It appears that the performance of department heads is most variable precisely in those areas that have greatest potential import for teachers' classroom performance.

Taken together, prevailing patterns of staff development might be thought to offer little to secondary teachers. Formal activities reveal an almost exclusive and often narrow concentration on teacher skills and on support for discrete reform initiatives. Less in evidence are initiatives that might be termed truly professional. It is rare to find teachers engaged either as colleagues or as independent scholars in the careful investigation of curricular and instructional alternatives. Few structured activities prepare teachers to evaluate their own teaching or to contribute in meaningful ways to a school's program or a departmental curriculum. Fewer still prepare teachers systematically for new roles and responsibilities. At best, only a small proportion of secondary teachers encounter a form of professional development that places a premium on the close study of subject matter, is respectful of the teacher's own knowledge and circumstances, and relies on teachers as colleagues. At the same time, the organization of the salaried workday militates against studied reflection of practice, mutual support among colleagues, or the exercise of leadership by those who have arguably earned the right to do so.

Certain innovative exceptions deserve closer study, but such exceptions achieve their significance in the context of broader patterns: the relative decline of the university as a source of intellectual development and career evolution; the concentration of formal staff-development resources and decision making at levels above the school; the dominance of generic pedagogy over subject disciplines in the content of staff development; the absence of attention to the structure of opportunity within the salaried workday; and the limited array of leadership roles that both motivate and reward teachers' learning.

CONCLUSION

Teachers' motivations and opportunities for professional development have been linked closely to certain fundamental conditions of teaching in secondary schools. On the whole, those conditions seem more likely to erode teachers' motivation than to bolster it, more likely to constrain than enrich their opportunity to learn. Secondary schools confront a wide array of purposes, of which academic achievement is only one. A meaningful focus for professional development is difficult to determine, and the benefits of professional development difficult to detect. Actual teaching assignments sometimes stimulate teachers to greater achievement, but also bore or defeat them. Subject departments are sometimes a productive intellectual center for teachers' lives, but such departments appear to be more the exception than the rule. Teachers' formal opportunities for professional development occur largely outside the school day and independent of current teaching assignments. They have been dominated in recent years by district-sponsored activities that rely heavily on generic instructional technique; teachers' participation in university coursework (and especially subject-specific coursework) shows a steady decline. Although a large proportion of secondary teachers maintain membership in subject-area associations, the significance of those associations to their daily work or career commitment is unknown. Meanwhile, informal learning-through-work is more typically hindered than supported by the way in which secondary schools organize workload, time, and teaching responsibilities.

The secondary school workforce, on average, does not form an enthusiastic constituency for formal staff development as it is currently organized. More often than not, local staff-development specialists find high school teachers a demanding or indifferent audience whose loyalties are to subjects, not students. The teachers, in turn, complain that it is difficult to derive benefit from workshops that are content-free or from university courses that are pedagogy-free. The ratio of supporters to critics in California's statewide staff-development policy study (Little et al., 1987) favored supporters by a 6 to 1 margin, but secondary teachers were more likely than elementary teachers to number among the critics. Elementary teachers were three times more likely than secondary teachers to participate in district workshops and were slightly more likely to enroll in coursework. Secondary teachers participated slightly less often in formal staff-development activities in the district and at the university. They were less likely to believe their peers valued professional development, less likely to say they were expected to use what they learned, and less likely to credit administrators with providing follow-up support for the professional development they did receive. Among secondary teachers, those teaching in middle and junior high schools were most dissatisfied with the quality and quantity of professional development opportunities.

Yet secondary teachers in the California study (Little et al., 1987) proved no less committed to professional development than their colleagues at the lower grade levels. Nearly three-quarters of high school teachers and two-thirds of middle-level teachers surveyed wanted more professional development opportunities; fewer than 10% wanted less involvement. Given an opportunity to highlight one "valuable" experience during a 1-year period, secondary teachers described events that ranged from 2-hour information sessions on drug abuse to intensive summer institutes in writing, literature, humanities, math, or science. There were more of the former than the latter; relatively few teachers reported having been involved in intensive activities that integrated curriculum content with pedagogy, were meaningfully connected to their instructional assignments, or lasted more than a few hours. By objective standards—and by comparison to the task that teachers confront daily— many of the activities that teachers label valuable are developmental only in name, meager in content, and passive in form. For many teachers, a single well-conducted information session may represent the best of a poor lot, and so be described as valuable. Other teachers—a far smaller number—are employed by schools or districts that routinely engage teachers as active partners in professional development activities that are both intellectually stimulating and well attuned to practical realities.

Under favorable circumstances, professional development experiences might deepen and broaden teachers' subject-matter knowledge and expand their repertoire of pedagogical options. They might equip secondary teachers to juggle successfully the intellectual, social, emotional, and other demands associated with educating adolescents. Over time, individuals could be expected to develop a sophisticated capacity for judging the merits of their own curricular and instructional choices. Faculties, collectively, could acquire the skill and the inclination needed to assess the cumulative effect of their choices; they could acquire the knowledge, imagination, and persistence needed to act on what they discovered. The grounds for leadership (and career advancement) among teachers would become widely known and accepted. Growth in teachers' capabilities, professional contributions, and occupational commitments would be closely linked. This scenario, now largely hypothetical, summarizes the case for integrating professional development more fully with teachers' work lives and with the institutional imperatives that schools confront. It also demands that research replace what is now largely speculation by establishing more precisely the import of the teaching context on teachers' motivations and opportunities for professional development, and by tracing the contributions that the professional development of teachers makes to the education of children.

NOTES

1. Analyses of teachers' competence, commitment, and working conditions have been a prominent part of the following studies: Boyer's (1983) report on the state of secondary education; Cusick's (1982, 1983) in-depth study of three midwestern high schools; a study of nearly 100 public and private high schools reported by Sizer (1984) and Powell, Farrar and Cohen (1985); Rutter, Maughan, Mortimore, and Ouston's (1979) account of differences between more-effective and less-effective secondary schools in London; Lightfoot's (1983) portraits of "the good high school"; and preliminary findings derived from Metz's (Chapter 3, herein; also see Tyree, 1988) study of urban and suburban high schools and from studies of urban high schools completed by Matthew Miles and Karen Seashore Louis (see Louis, Chapter 2 of this volume). On the whole, the analysis presented in this chapter is appropriate for high schools and for departmentally organized junior high schools. It does not take specific account of the conditions presented by middle schools organized around interdisciplinary teams (see Lipsitz, 1984).

2. Accurate projections are confounded by differences in the form of data collection; the two large-scale surveys reported by Guthrie et al. (1988) and NEA

(1987) tally the number of *teachers* who are assigned one or more classes outside their specialization. The Gehrke and Sheffield (1985) case study tallied the number of *classes* taught by teachers who were properly assigned or misassigned.

REFERENCES

Arends, R. (1983, April). *Teachers as learners: A descriptive study of professional development activities.* Paper presented at the annual meeting of the American Educational Research Association, Montreal.

Ashton, P. T., & Webb, R. (1986). *Making a difference: Teachers' sense of efficacy and student achievement.* New York: Longman.

Ball, S. J., & Lacey, C. (1984). Subject disciplines as the opportunity for group action: A measured critique of subject sub-cultures. In A. Hargreaves & P. Woods (Eds.), *Classrooms and staffrooms: The sociology of teachers and teaching* (pp. 232–244). Milton Keynes, England: Open University Press.

Bennet, C. (1985). Paints, pots, or promotion? Art teachers' attitudes toward their careers. In S. J. Ball & I. F. Goodson, *Teachers' lives and careers* (pp. 120–137). London: Falmer Press.

Berry, B. (1985). Why Miss Dove left and where she went: A case study of teacher attrition in a metropolitan school system in the southeast. *Occasional papers in educational policy analysis.* Research Triangle Park, NC: Southeastern Regional Council for Educational Improvement.

Beynon, J. (1985). Institutional change and career histories in a comprehensive school. In S. J. Ball & I. F. Goodson (Eds.), *Teachers' lives and careers* (pp. 158–179). London: Falmer Press.

Bird, T., & Little, J. W. (1985). *Instructional leadership in eight secondary schools.* Boulder, CO: Center for Action Research.

Bird, T., & Little, J. W. (1986). How schools organize the teaching occupation. *Elementary School Journal, 86*(4), 493–511.

Bishop, J. M. (1977). Organizational influences on the work orientations of elementary teachers. *Sociology of Work and Occupations, 4*(2), 171–208.

Boyer, E. L. (1983). *High school: A report on secondary education in America.* New York: Harper & Row.

Cohen, E. G. (1981). Sociology looks at team teaching. *Research in Sociology of Education and Socialization, 2,* 163–193.

Conant, J. B. (1963). *The education of American teachers.* New York: McGraw-Hill.

Cuban, L. (1985). *How teachers taught.* New York: Longman.

Cummings, T. G. (1981). Designing effective work groups. In P. C. Nystrom & W. H. Starbuck (Eds.), *Handbook of organizational design* (Vol. 2, pp. 250–271). London: Oxford University Press.

Cusick, P. A. (1982). *A study of networks among professional staffs of two secondary schools.* East Lansing: Michigan State University.

Cusick, P. A. (1983). *The egalitarian ideal and the American high school: Studies of three schools.* New York: Longman.

Dornbusch, S., & Scott, W. R. (1975). *Evaluation and the exercise of authority.* San Francisco: Jossey-Bass.

Eckert, P. (1989). *Jocks and burnouts: Social categories and identity in the high school.* New York: Teachers College Press.

Elbaz, F. (1983). *Teacher thinking: A study of practical knowledge.* London: Croom Helm.

Feiman-Nemser, S., & Floden, R. (1986). The cultures of teaching. In M. Wittrock (Ed.), *Handbook of research on teaching, third edition* (pp. 505–526). New York: Macmillan.

Finley, M. K. (1984). Teachers and tracking in a comprehensive high school. *Sociology of Education, 57,* 233–243.

Fuller, B., Wood, K., Rapoport, T., & Dornbusch, S. (1982). The organizational context of individual efficacy. *Review of Educational Research, 52*(1), 7–30.

Gehrke, N., & Sheffield, R. (1985). Are core subjects becoming a dumping ground for reassigned high school teachers? *Educational Leadership, 42*(8), 65–69.

Glidewell, J. C., Tucker, S., Todt, M., & Cox, S. (1983). Professional support systems: The teaching profession. In A. Nadler, J. D. Fisher, & B. M. DePaulo (Eds.), *New directions in helping* (Vol. 3, pp. 189–212). New York: Academic Press.

Gray, J., & Caldwell, K. (1980). The Bay Area Writing Project. *Journal of Staff Development, 1*(1), 31–39.

Grossman, P. L., & Richert, A. E. (1986). *Unacknowledged knowledge growth: A reexamination of the effects of teacher education.* Paper presented at the annual meeting of the American Educational Research Association, San Francisco.

Guthrie, J., Kirst, M. W., Hayward, G. C., Odden, A. R., Adams, J. E., Jr., Cagampang, H. H., Emmett, T. S., Evans, J. W., Gerianos, J., Koppich, J. E., & Merchant, B. M. (1988). *Conditions of education in California.* Berkeley: Policy Analysis for California Education (PACE), University of California.

Hargreaves, A. (1986). *Two cultures of schooling: The case of middle schools.* London: Falmer Press.

Hargreaves, A. (1987). *Curriculum policy and the culture of teaching.* Toronto: Ontario Institute for Studies in Education.

Hargreaves, D. H. (1967). *Secondary relations in a secondary school.* London: Routledge and Kegan Paul.

Huberman, M. (1986, April). *Some relationships between teachers' career trajectories and school improvement.* Paper presented at the annual meeting of the American Educational Research Association, San Francisco.

Jackson, P. (1968). *Life in classrooms.* New York: Holt, Rinehart & Winston.

Joyce, B., & Showers, B. (1981). *Teacher training research: Working hypotheses for program design and directions for further study.* Paper presented at the annual meeting of the American Educational Research Association, Los Angeles.

Kane, P. (1986). *The Teachers College New Jersey survey: A comparative study of public and independent school teachers.* New York: Teachers College, Columbia University.

Kerr, S., & Slocum, J. W., Jr. (1981). Controlling the performances of people in organizations. In P. C. Nystrom & W. H. Starbuck (Eds.), *Handbook of organizational design, 2* (pp. 116–134). Oxford: Oxford University Press.

Kreinberg, N. (1980). The EQUALS Program: Helping teachers to become researchers and problem solvers. *Journal of Staff Development, 1*(1), 19–30.

Lanier, J. E., with Little, J. W. (1986). Research on teacher education. In M. Wittrock (Ed.), *Handbook of research on teaching, third edition* (pp. 527–569). New York: Macmillan.

Lightfoot, S. L. (1983). *The good high school: Portraits of character and culture.* New York: Basic Books.

Lipsitz, J. (1984). *Successful schools for young adolescents.* New Brunswick, NJ: Transaction Press.

Little, J. W. (1984). Seductive images and organizational reality in professional development. *Teachers College Record, 86*(1), 84–102.

Little, J. W. (1987). Teachers as colleagues. In V. Richardson-Koehler (Ed.), *Educators' Handbook: A Research Perspective* (pp. 491–518). New York: Longman.

Little, J. W. (1989). District policy choices and teachers' professional development opportunities. *Educational Evaluation and Policy Analysis, 11*(2), 165–179.

Little, J. W., & Bird, T. D. (1987). Instructional leadership "close to the classroom" in secondary schools. In W. Greenfield (Ed.), *Instructional leadership: Issues, concepts, and controversies* (pp. 118–138). Boston: Allyn & Bacon.

Little, J. W., Gerritz, W., Stern, D., Guthrie, J. W., Kirst, M. W., & Marsh, D. D. (1987). *Staff development in California: Public and personal investments, program patterns, and policy choices.* Final report to the California Postsecondary Education Commission. San Francisco: Far West Laboratory for Educational Research and Development.

Lortie, D. (1975). *Schoolteacher.* Chicago: University of Chicago Press.

Macrorie, K. (1984). *Twenty teachers.* New York: Oxford University Press.

McLaughlin, M. W. (n.d.). *Institutional environments that support teachers' motivation and productivity.* Stanford: Center for Educational Research at Stanford (CERAS).

McLaughlin, M. W., & Pfeifer, R. S. (1988). *Teacher evaluation: Improvement, accountability, and effective learning.* New York: Teachers College Press.

McLaughlin, M. W., & Yee, S. M. (1988). School as a place to have a career. In A. Lieberman (Ed.), *Building a professional culture in schools* (pp. 23–44). New York: Teachers College Press.

Measor, L. (1985). Critical incidents in the classroom: Identities, choices, and careers. In S. Ball & I. Goodson (Eds.), *Teachers' lives and careers* (pp. 61–77). London: Falmer Press.

Metz, M. H. (1978). *Classrooms and corridors: The crisis of authority in desegregated secondary schools.* Berkeley: University of California Press.

Meyer, J., & Cohen, E., with Brunetti, F., Molnar, S., & Lueders-Salmon, E. (1971). *The impact of the open-space school upon teacher influence and autonomy: The effects of an organizational innovation.* Stanford, CA: Center for Research and Development in Teaching, Stanford University.

Miller, L. (1980). The high school and its teachers: Implications for staff development. *Journal of Staff Development, 1*(1), 5–18.

National Education Association. (1987). *Status of the American public school teacher 1985–86.* Washington, DC: Author.

Nelson, B. S. (1986). Collaboration for colleagueship: A program in support of teachers. *Educational Leadership, 43*(5), 50–52.

Nias, J. (1989). *Primary teachers talking: A study of teaching as work.* London: Routledge.

Nias, J., Southworth, G., & Yeomans, R. (1989). *Staff relationships in the primary school: A study of organizational cultures.* London: Cassell.

Oakes, J. (1985). *Keeping track: How schools structure inequality.* New Haven, CT: Yale University Press.

Pellegrin, R. (1976). Schools as work settings. In R. Dubin (Ed.), *Handbook of work, organizations, and society* (pp. 343–373). Chicago: Rand McNally.

Powell, A., Farrar, E., & Cohen, D. (1985). *The shopping mall high school: Winners and losers in the educational marketplace.* Boston: Houghton Mifflin.

Riseborough, G. (1984). Teacher careers and comprehensive schooling. In A. Hargreaves & P. Woods (Eds.), *Classrooms and staffrooms: The sociology of teachers and teaching* (pp. 245–257). Milton Keynes, England: Open University Press.

Rosenholtz, S. J. (1989). *Teachers' workplace: The social organization of schools.* New York: Longman.

Rutter, M., Maughan, B., Mortimore, P., & Ouston, J. (1979). *Fifteen thousand hours: Secondary schools and their effects on children.* Cambridge: Harvard University Press.

Schlechty, P. C. (n.d.). *Schools for the 21st century: The conditions for invention.* Louisville, KY: Gheens Professional Development Academy.

Schlechty, P. C., Crowell, D., Whitford, B. L., Joslin, A. W., Vance, V. S., Noblit, G. W., & Burke, W. I. (1982). *The organization and management of staff development in a large city school system: A case study.* Chapel Hill, NC: University of North Carolina at Chapel Hill.

Schlechty, P. C., & Whitford, B. L. (1983). The organizational context of school systems and the functions of staff development. In G. Griffin (Ed.), *Staff development: Eighty-second yearbook of the National Society for the Study of Education* (pp. 62–91). Chicago: University of Chicago Press.

Sedlak, M. W., Wheeler, C. W., Pullin, D. C., & Cusick, P. A. (1986). *Selling students short: Classroom bargains and academic reform in the American high school.* New York: Teachers College Press.

Sikes, P. J. (1984). Teacher careers in the comprehensive school. In S. Ball (Ed.), *Comprehensive schooling: A reader* (pp. 247–271). London: Falmer Press.

Sikes, P. J., Measor, L., & Woods, P. (1985). *Teacher careers: Crises and continuities.* London: Falmer Press.

Sizer, T. (1984). *Horace's compromise: The dilemma of the American high school.* Boston: Houghton Mifflin.

Smylie, M. A. (1988). The enhancement function of staff development: Organizational and psychological antecedents to individual teacher change. *American Educational Research Journal, 25*(1), 1–30.

Sprinthall, N., & Thies-Sprinthall, L. (1983). The teacher as adult learner: A cognitive-developmental view. In G. Griffin (Ed.), *Staff development: Eighty-second yearbook of the National Society for Studies in Education* (pp. 13–35). Chicago: University of Chicago Press.

Stevenson, R. B. (1987). Staff development for effective secondary schools: A synthesis of research. *Teaching and Teacher Education, 3*(3), 233–248.

Swidler, A. (1979). *Organization without authority: Dilemmas of social control in free schools.* Cambridge: Harvard University Press.

Sykes, G. (1983). Public policy and the problem of teacher quality: The need for screens and magnets. In L. Shulman & G. Sykes (Eds.), *Handbook for teaching and policy* (pp. 97–125). New York: Longman.

Tyree, A. K., Jr. (1988). Belonging and work control in two suburban public high schools and their effects on teacher engagement. In M. H. Metz (Ed.), *Final report, field study on teachers' engagement, project on the effects of the school as a workplace on teachers' engagement—Phase one* (chapter 5). Madison: National Center on Effective Secondary Schools, University of Wisconsin.

Van Maanen, J., & Barley, S. R. (1984). Occupational communities: Culture and control in organizations. *Research in Organizational Behavior, 6,* 287–365.

Webb, R. (1985). Teacher status panic: Moving up the down escalator. In S. J. Ball & I. F. Goodson (Eds.), *Teachers' lives and careers* (pp. 78–88). London: Falmer Press.

Yee, S. M. (1986). *Teaching as a career: Promotion versus development.* Stanford, CA: Stanford University School of Education.

8
Change Processes in Secondary Schools: Toward a More Fundamental Agenda

MICHAEL G. FULLAN

This chapter will examine what we know and, just as important, what we do not know about change processes within secondary schools. The focus will be on the school. Some reference will be made to those factors in the school context (that is, the district) that have most direct relevance to school change, but no attempt will be made to review contextual factors systematically. The school itself is our main interest.

First I will give a description and critical appraisal of knowledge about the characteristics and processes of change in effective secondary schools. Ten recent studies of secondary schools will be analyzed. In addition to identifying key characteristics of effective schools, three critical "process" questions will be asked: To what extent do the studies inform us about how an effective school currently functions? What do the studies tell us about how the school got that way? To what extent do the studies provide insights and guidelines for how to achieve success in new situations?

Then I will concentrate on key issues that have emerged in the context of other literature on effective change processes. The idea is to describe insights with respect to effective change processes and to identify gaps in knowledge.

CHARACTERISTICS OF EFFECTIVE SECONDARY SCHOOLS: A CRITICAL APPRAISAL

We do not need another review of characteristics of effective schools, although, as others have pointed out, secondary schools have been neglected until recently in much of the literature. Rather, I will take

I would like to thank Matt Miles, Dennis Thiessen, and the three anonymous reviewers for helpful suggestions for revising the first draft.

several of the more recent studies and analyze them from two perspectives: What do they tell us about key factors or characteristics related to success? What do they say or imply about the three process issues just mentioned?

The studies I will discuss were selected using two main criteria. First, I was interested in the most recent studies, the better to identify the latest themes and trends. Many of the studies were unpublished or in press at the time of the review. Second, and combined with recency, I was seeking research studies that deliberately focused on factors and processes associated with school improvement. I was not interested in projects that advocated secondary school reform without formulating and examining how reform occurs. I make no claim to be engaged in a comprehensive review. The 10 studies selected, however, are representative of current issues in the examination of the process of secondary school reform.

An outline of the 10 studies reviewed is provided in Table 8.1. They are presented in the order in which they are reviewed. In general, the latter studies in the table pay more attention to the process of change.

Bamburg and Andrews (1988)

Bamburg and Andrews (1988) begin their report by acknowledging a critique of the effective-schools research, which is that they tell us something about the characteristics of effective schools, but "less . . . about the change processes in their implementation" (p. 1). Presumably their study is intended to address this aspect. The sample is two high schools (Grades 9 through 12) in two separate small- to medium-size rural districts in the state of Washington. School A has 890 students; school B has 460. School B has 20% Native American population and 30% who qualify for free or reduced-price lunch; school A has few minority students and 15% who qualify for free or reduced-price lunch. A staff assessment questionnaire (SAQ) of 94 Likert-type items was used to measure nine effective-school factors:

1. Strong leadership
2. Staff dedication
3. Staff expectations of students
4. Identification of learning difficulties
5. Multicultural education
6. Sex equality
7. Curriculum continuity
8. Learning climate
9. Frequency of monitoring students

TABLE 8.1. Studies of Effective Schools, by Focus, Sample, and Illustrative Key Variables.

Study	Focus	Sample	Illustrative Key Variables
Bamburg & Andrews (1988)	Effective change in rural secondary schools	2 rural high schools	•Strong leadership •Staff dedication •Equity
Matthes (in press)	To identify characteristics of exemplary rural schools	4 nationally recognized rural high schools	•Integration with community •Teacher and student recognition •Teacher empowerment
Leithwood (1987)	Review of research on characteristics of exemplary secondary schools	20 studies	•Goals •Teachers •Culture •Student commitment
Stevenson (1987b)	Review of research on staff development and secondary schools	9 studies	•Governance •Collaboration •Technical assistance
Firestone & Rosenblum (1988)	Factors related to alienation and commitment	10 inner-city high schools	•Relevance •Affiliation •Support •Student and teacher commitment
Pink (1988)	Critical evaluation of process of change in an alternative program of at-risk students	4 schools in a pilot program; 16 schools district-wide	•School-within-a-school •Team teaching •University/central office/school coordination
Wilson & Corcoran (1988)	Major analysis of school conditions and processes that promote school improvement	571 nationally recognized exemplary high schools	•Active leadership •Work environment •Learning environment
Fullan & Newton (1988)	Role of secondary school principals and change processes in large urban schools	3 large urban high schools	•Active principal leadership •Curriculum change •Change cycles
Odden & Marsh (1988) Marsh (1988)	Study of the impact of comprehensive state reform legislation on secondary schools	17 California high schools, and their districts, selected as having made progress in implementing Bill 813	•District and school vision •Implementation management •Curriculum development •Ongoing leadership
Miles (1987) Miles et al. (1988)	Examining the implementation process in effective urban high schools engaged in major reform	5 urban high schools engaged in school improvement reforms	•Vision •Evolutionary planning •Initiative taking •Assistance •Problem coping

The first three and last three factors are recognizable from most effective-schools research. The middle three are unusual (not to say inappropriate) because they refer mostly to policy content in relation to various aspects of equity.

Other forms of data were also utilized, such as interviews and school documents. The design of the study involved gathering data using the SAQ in 1986, giving feedback (with no particular intervention), and readministering the SAQ in 1987. Bamburg and Andrews (1988) examine changes in the nine factors between 1986 and 1987, within each school.

The quantitative analysis shows that both schools increased significantly with respect to staff perception of strong leadership, dedicated staff, and positive learning climate. In addition, school B showed gains in dealing with early identification, multicultural education, and sex equity. No significant change was found relative to high expectations, frequent monitoring, and curriculum continuity.

The qualitative snapshots of each school provide additional knowledge. The authors summarize the situation at school A, at the time of the 1986 survey, as follows: "The staff was frustrated, the administration was ineffective and the students were out of control" (p. 10). The key question for our purpose, however, is, What does the study tell us about the process of change from 1986 to 1987? First, we find out that the decision to administer the SAQ reflected a districtwide effort to gather data in all schools. There was little or no consultation with principals or staff. In other words, it was arbitrarily introduced with no accompanying improvement plan. Second, it appears that the main reason for the change was that the principal was "devastated" by the results of the 1986 survey and set out to do something about it, with no outside assistance and only general support from the superintendent. (Bamburg and Andrews describe some of the actions taken by the principal, in their paper.)

What lessons about the change process can be derived from school A? First, we cannot conclude that the change was particularly substantial. We have data covering only the first year, and only a few of the more obvious dimensions changed. Second, we do get some insight into the importance and actions of the principal in a situation that is bad to begin with. Put another way, if there is a good deal of frustration and alienation, the principal, just by taking action to become more visible and involved, can improve the perception of leadership and in turn influence the learning climate and staff commitment. This is no simple accomplishment, but we have no reason to believe that it represents substantial or lasting change, either.

The circumstances at school B were different. Recall that gains on more dimensions (six of the nine), including content changes, were accomplished. The state had just issued regulations that each school would be required to conduct a self-study program and develop a school-improvement plan. The district administrator, in consultation with the school principals, decided to use the SAQ. In addition, each school was directed to establish a school-improvement team composed of administrators, staff, students, parents, and members of the community. The team received ongoing training and support from the external developers and, along with the rest of the staff, used the survey to identify a set of concerns that became the basis for developing a comprehensive planning document.

Thus, in school B the conditions for initiation were more favorable (i.e., the project was part of a school-improvement effort backed by the district with both pressure and support) and the process was collaborative and received assistance. The gains made were broader than in school A, but they were not huge improvements. (Stated more fairly, it was too early to tell whether they would lead to substantial changes.) The study gives some notion of the processes followed, but no insight into the dynamics of change. Unanswered questions include, How did the team develop? What was the relationship between the team and the rest of the constituency? Were there ebbs and flows to the process as it unfolded? Moreover, in the research study as a whole, there is no serious dependent variable such as staff or student commitment, retention rate, attendance, or student achievement.

Matthes (in press)

Matthes (in press) studied four exemplary rural high schools, selected from a subset of 52 rural schools included in the data collected on 571 high schools recognized during the period 1983–1985 by the U.S. Office of Education as part of the Secondary School Recognition Program. As in the previous study, the focus was on rural schools. The four schools ranged in size from 400 to 1,200 and were located all across the country. In gathering data, 1 week was spent in each school during interviews, observations, and collecting documents.

The findings are presented in terms of eight broad characteristics considered to describe effective rural secondary schools:

1. The teachers perceived the school as an integral part of the community.
2. The teachers perceived their efforts as transcending the immediate (sense of broader mission).

3. Expectations for students and teachers were clear.
4. Achievement of teachers and students were recognized.
5. Teachers had a sense of empowerment.
6. Teachers had a sense of self-worth and efficacy.
7. Teachers were committed to professional growth.
8. Teachers demonstrated entrepreneurial skills (vis-à-vis business and community).

Again, most of these themes are recognizable. This small study both confirms some of the findings from the larger effective-schools literature and contributes some special knowledge about *rural* secondary schools. In particular it is likely that closeness to the community (#1) and entrepreneurial activities (#8) are easier to achieve in effective rural secondary schools than in urban ones. Matthes (in press) also suggests that the sense of place in time (#2) and empowerment (#5) are "unique to these rural high schools." In my view, however, these factors may be more a function of size. Indeed, the majority of factors appear to be facilitated by size (three of the four schools had enrollments ranging from 400 to 700).

More central to the point of this review, Matthes' (in press) paper tells us virtually nothing about process, either in terms of how these four schools got to be effective, or even how they function in their present state.

Leithwood (1987)

Leithwood's (1987) review of research on characteristics of exemplary secondary schools provides an important checkpoint, because he analyzed and synthesized the findings from 20 original studies and also compared the findings with those from research on elementary schools. He concluded that there are several categories of characteristics that distinguish effective high schools:

1. Shared goals (clarity and commitment about purpose)
2. Teachers (dedication, expectations, collaboration)
3. School administrators (active leadership, support)
4. School organization and policies (academic achievement, resources, small size, discretion, district support)
5. Program and instruction (rigorous curriculum, focus, instructional time)
6. School culture (positive, orderly, shared)
7. School/community relationship (use of community resources, seeking community support)

In all, Leithwood (1987) identified 34 subcharacteristics within the seven categories. Of the 34, Leithwood found that there was support for 24 in both elementary and secondary studies, which reflects a good deal of commonality. However, there were 10 important differences in emphasis and/or focus between the two; that is, compared with effective elementary schools, effective secondary schools

1. Pursue a broader range of goals
2. Are more concerned about developing a sense of community and affiliation within the school
3. Attribute more importance to the job satisfaction, employment status, verbal skills, and attendance rates of teachers
4. Attribute more importance to such basic beliefs of administrators as a view of teachers as professionals
5. Require administrators to consider a broader array of factors in the school, in order to exercise influence
6. Have to address problems related to size of staff and student body more explicitly
7. Require more school-level decision-making discretion
8. Expend more effort on the design of a program that is useful for all students and provides enough variety to address a more diverse set of needs
9. Have to promote and support more precise, concrete talk among teachers concerning their classroom practices
10. Have less need for close parent involvement

Leithwood did not delve into the question of change processes per se, although his related study (Lawton, Leithwood, Batches, Donaldson, & Stewart, 1988), to which I will refer in the second part of this chapter, raises some important issues.

Stevenson (1987b)

Another synthesis has been developed by Stevenson (1987b) focusing on the relationship between staff development and effective secondary schools. The critical importance of ongoing staff development is one of the most consistent and significant findings in the effective-schools research. Stevenson suggests that there are three major dimensions of staff development: governance (those involved in deciding and planning), the process and conditions of program implementation (how it is done), and purpose (societal, organizational, or instructional). The list of characteristics of effective schools used by Stevenson is adapted from Purkey and Smith (1985).

Stevenson applied this framework to nine studies of staff development and found two major themes and another tentative one. First (and this is not as self-evident as it seems), staff governance and/or collaborative staff-development planning were related to an outcome called "enhancement of collegiality." Second, technical assistance was related to several outcomes, with the source of assistance (peers, district, parties external to the district) being multiple in most cases, although the patterns of internal and external sources were difficult to discern. Third, and more tentative, the leadership role of the principal appeared to vary. When specific instructional improvement was the goal, directive leadership was effective; but when the goal involved broader institutional improvement, a more complex role for principals was evident. The latter role demanded greater attention to developing collaboration and collegiality.

Stevenson's (1987b) review does not go very far in clarifying the three themes identified. He does, however, ask some interesting questions. He observes that collaboration and ongoing interactive assistance, which are essential, "are inhibited by a number of structural features of secondary schools" (p. 243), such as socialization into teaching as an individual activity, subject-based focus, departmentalization, physical isolation, large size, and diversity. In acknowledging the research finding that staff development is most effective in schools where norms of collegiality and experimentation already prevail, he asks the more critical process question: "How were the structural barriers to such interactions overcome in establishing these norms?" (p. 244). He notes that the literature he reviewed did not address this question (also see Stevenson, 1987a).

Firestone and Rosenblum (1988)

Let us now turn to some case examples involving urban high schools. Firestone and Rosenblum (1988) base their paper on a larger study of 10 inner-city comprehensive secondary schools, two each from Baltimore, Newark, Philadelphia, Pittsburg, and Washington, D.C. In each case, "the superintendent was asked to pick two schools with similar student bodies, one of which reflected the most difficult problems" (p. 5). The median size was 1,500. In 7 schools, 75% or more of the students were black; in 8 schools, 40% or more received a free lunch. Interviews—at least 35 in each school—were conducted. Note that the schools were not selected on the basis of effectiveness (half of the schools were identified because they were experiencing problems).

The conceptual framework developed by Firestone and Rosenblum (1988) is reproduced in Figure 8.1. The first observation we can make is that the authors use a more explicit and more comprehensive framework than similar studies do to depict the relationship among variables. This is bound to give us a better sense of how the process works, but not necessarily of how school improvement works, that is, how factors within the model get altered. Also, within this framework the dependent variables or outcomes are made explicit; they are teacher commitment, student commitment, and student behavior. Starting with outcomes, the authors make a clear and convincing case, backed up with data, not only about the importance of teacher and student commitment but also how they feed on each other in either a positive or negative spiral. Commitment is defined multidimensionally: For teachers, commitment is to students, to teaching, and to the school; for students, it is to learning and to the school.

The authors identify five major school context factors that influence teacher and student commitment: relevance, affiliation, support, expectations, and influence. Relevance or sense of purpose, Firestone and Rosenblum claim, is especially difficult to achieve in urban high schools. Some teachers and students acquire a sense of academic purpose, but most do not. The authors suggest that effective schools do a better job of developing relevant (meaningful) programs for low-achieving students, including work/study programs, career-orientation, and counseling.

Affiliation is the sense of connectedness that students and teachers have to their surroundings. Its opposite—isolation—is more the norm in large high schools. These authors found that students were concerned with how adults in the school treated them:

> The teachers who blame students for difficult classroom situations are the most likely to display an "attitude" to students, to be abrupt with them, and not explain things in detail. Students receiving such treatment recognize that they are not respected, which in turn reduces their commitment to the school. [p. 18]

At-risk students are more likely to find themselves in such situations. For teachers, the sense of affiliation or isolation pertains to the relationships with administration and colleagues. The researchers found great variations, ranging from some schools in which there was a high degree of isolation to some in which teachers were thoroughly engaged with each other on instructional matters.

FIGURE 8.1. The Dynamics of Teacher and Student Commitment

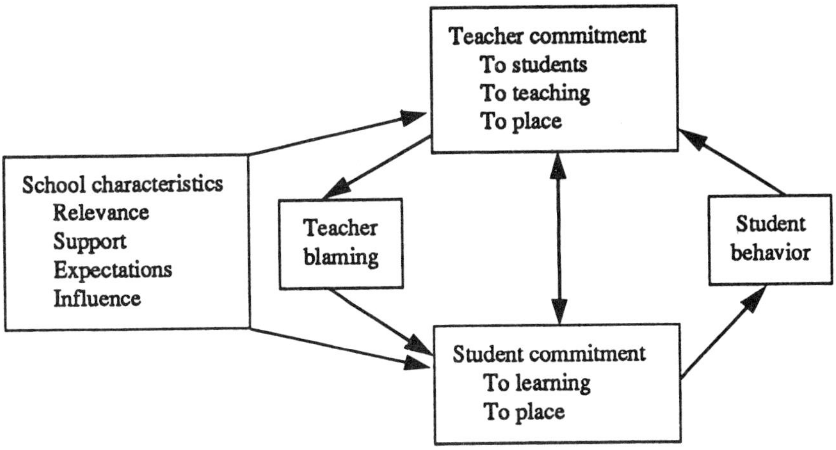

Source: Firestone & Rosenblum (1988), p. 4. Reproduced with permission.

The third factor, support, appears in many other studies as well. Firestone and Rosenblum (1988) stress that *consistency* is the key:"A consistent environment is one where order is maintained, roles are clear, and rules are enforced fairly and rigorously, but not harshly" (p. 21). They also found that various degrees of personalized support between administration and teachers, and between teachers and students, were important.

The fourth factor, expectations, is also a familiar theme in the effective-schools literature. A certain amount of stress in the form of high expectations (combined with the other factors) serves to improve performance. Firestone and Rosenblum found three relatively distinct groups of schools: "In most schools there is little pressure for good teaching and student achievement" (p. 23); however, in a second, smaller group, there is good support for teachers for instruction, but "there is no special training or pressure for them to teach better" (p. 23). The third group (which appears to be one school) "combines strong management and incentives for students with an extensive program of teacher training and inservice" (p. 23).

The fifth factor described is influence. The authors found that teachers had limited interest in major policy decisions. They were concerned more with day-to-day matters pertaining to supplies, instructional leeway, and the like.

The Firestone and Rosenblum (1988) study has a number of strengths and some limitations. Relative to the former, the conceptual framework is clearly spelled out. It is consistent with effective-schools research (e.g., the role of expectations and support), but complements it with new elaborations (e.g., relevance, affiliation, and the focus on teacher and student commitment). With respect to limitations, the paper is as much a conceptual model as an empirical study; that is, the model is not really grounded systematically. The authors do not, for example, supply measures of the degree of commitment by school, or of any of the five school characteristics. The authors indicate that in 2 of the 10 schools, student and teacher commitment were particularly high, which is not bad, in light of the conditions faced and the nature of the sample selected. We do not, however, have any direct notion of how the variables in the model actually worked themselves out in a given school. From the perspective of school improvement we are missing two critical ingredients: (1) assuming that the model is accurate, by what processes did the successful schools get that way; and (2) even if we had the answer to #1, what are the implications for addressing the key factors in new situations? These limitations notwithstanding, Firestone and Rosenblum do propose a rather clear, reasoned, and convincing model for consideration.

Pink (1988)

Pink (1988) provides a useful critical perspective on the problem of reforming secondary schools for at-risk youth. He examined a school-within-a-school (SWAS) alternative program. It originated with a proposal from a local school of education to a superintendent of an urban school district, whose principals were then asked to volunteer their school to pilot a SWAS project. Four of the nine principals volunteered. The SWAS project involved

> (1) identification of low-achieving students entering their first year of high school, (2) the selection of four teachers (English, mathematics, reading and social studies) in each school who would team teach an integrated curriculum that emphasized reading comprehension, to (3) the low achieving students in small classes, in (4) a section of the school building designated for SWAS students only. [p. 6]

An evaluation of the pilot phase was conducted by the district's office of research. Pink summarizes four major problems: (1) the program was conceptualized by university faculty without teacher input, (2) the program enjoyed little real support from the central office, (3) essential support materials (e.g., teaching materials) were not made available to teachers, and (4) the lack of line authority by the university consultants resulted in a confusing and uneasy alliance among the consultants, SWAS site coordinators, and teachers.

Despite these serious problems, and providing some confirmation that reform initiatives are less than rational, at the end of the pilot phase, the district designated the SWAS model as the "major reform of secondary schools in the district" and mandated that every secondary school (nine high schools and seven junior high schools) would have a SWAS program. It is not difficult to predict the results. There was insufficient orientation, staff development, coordination, central office support, and so forth. No provision was made to provide SWAS teachers with feedback about their classroom performance, and no staff development focusing on classroom feedback was provided to school site coordinators.

An external evaluation was carried out by Pink (1988), in which specific instructional strategies were named by SWAS teachers as reflecting implementation. Pink, using observation protocols, nonetheless found that SWAS teachers were making little use of the instructional strategies they themselves had identified. The senior high schools experienced more problems of implementation in all respects than did the junior highs.

Why include such an obvious example of failed implementation in this review? One reason is that such politically generated initiatives, which neglect or underestimate the complexities of coordinating implementation, are not atypical; in fact, this is a common problem. A second and more fundamental insight is offered by Pink (1988). He argues that the wrong lessons are frequently derived from cases like this. The typical conclusions, erroneous in Pink's view, are that (1) given more time, teachers will refine their instructional skills and coordinators will become more efficient; (2) allocating more money is essential; and (3) tightening supervision will improve the program.

Pink (1988) suggests that the whole approach is fundamentally flawed. Striving for a relatively uniform program, controlled from the central office, misreads secondary schools, because

it ignores the fact that a secondary school (1) is a complex organization which generates its own norms and operational ethos, (2) frequently contains too many conflicting programs that fragment the school and make goal consensus problematic, and (3) creates and sustains a working culture for teachers that is characterized by departmentalism and isolation. [p. 37]

Pink proposes an alternative line of thinking, which he bases on the literature. His position, compatible with the ideas presented in the second part of this chapter, is that school reform is best accomplished through "(1) the development of site generated and supported improvement plans, and (2) through a leadership style that emphasizes innovation, establishes values through modelling, and that motivates others via shared decision-making and the actualization of common goals" (p. 38).

Wilson and Corcoran (1988)

A more comprehensive study, by Wilson and Corcoran (1988), takes on the ambitious task of developing a synthesis of those school conditions that promoted school improvement in a national sample of outstanding public secondary schools. The data for these authors' analysis derive from documentation on 571 secondary schools that were recognized by the U.S. Department of Education as unusually successful in the 1983–1985 period. Wilson and Corcoran's book contains detailed discussion of the nature of the sample and the range of performance indicators and other data bases used, which I will not relay here, other than to say that a wide range of data were available. What is interesting is their attempt to move more directly into process issues: "The focus is on the dynamic and human dimensions of school success rather than static lists of variables" (p. 6).

Wilson and Corcoran's (1988) synthesis produced six themes, which they claim represent the set of conditions associated with success:

1. Active leadership (setting the direction)
2. Professional work environments (motivating staff)
3. Positive learning environments (motivating students)
4. Broad community involvement (reaching the community)
5. Continuous school improvement (institutional vitality)
6. Service to all students (equality of educational opportunity)

Each of these will be discussed in turn.

Active leadership.   Wilson and Corcoran identify a number of aspects of active leadership in successful high schools. The main overall finding, consistent with other research, is that school leadership is "credited with providing the vision and the motivation to create and sustain the conditions that led to national recognition" (p. 69). The authors especially stress the role of principals in shaping the educational and professional culture of the school. School leaders do this in concrete ways, such as by helping to create mechanisms for community planning, cooperation, and coordination; by arranging physical space and time for teachers to work together; by attending to policies about class size, grouping, and the like; by generating and making available discretionary resources (money, release time, materials); and by arranging access to knowledge, skills, networking, and other specific forms of assistance.

The role of effective school leaders is illustrated with several examples, such as the following, referring to a high school in Missouri:

> The instructional goals have been addressed and developed through faculty meetings, class meetings, open meetings for parents and teacher advisory meetings. Some of these goals were planned topics at faculty/ Board of Education dialogue breakfasts. In every endeavor, whether it be academic or extracurricular, these goals are explained, discussed, pursued and refined by students, teachers and parents. [pp. 75–76]

Wilson and Corcoran proceed to say that

> The leaders' task is to develop a clear vision of the school's purposes, a vision that gives primacy to instruction, and then to employ it consistently during frequent interactions. The evidence suggests that the recognized schools use bureaucratic linkages to create opportunities for teachers to act on that vision, and, at the same time, use cultural linkages to ensure that the vision becomes part of the teachers' own professional culture. [p. 80]

The authors emphasize two additional matters. First is the great diversity in the leadership style of principals: "In some cases, there are dynamic, powerful principals who seem to be everywhere and orchestrating everything; . . . in other cases, the principals are collegial and low-key, relying on persuasion, delegation, and their ability to select and develop strong faculty members" (pp. 80–81). Second, while identifying the principal as a key player, the authors observe that in successful schools there are a number of people who take leadership roles, including assistant principals, department chairpersons, team leaders, deans, and senior teachers. Good leaders develop other leaders, drawing on the strengths of a diverse set of people.

Professional work environments. Wilson and Corcoran (1988) identified seven aspects of effective working conditions for teachers:

1. shared goals and high expectations of success to create strong communal identity;

2. respectful and dignified treatment as professionals by superiors and by parents and students;
3. participation by teachers in the decisions affecting their work;
4. regular opportunities for interaction and sharing with colleagues that promote a collective identity;
5. recognition and rewards for their effort and achievement;
6. opportunities for professional growth; and
7. decent physical working conditions. [pp. 85–86]

The authors conclude that effective leaders help create and shape these effective working conditions for teachers, which in turn generate and reinforce the continued effort and commitment of teachers.

Positive learning environments. As Wilson and Corcoran (1988) say, "A significant characteristic of unusually successful schools is a deep conviction that all or most students can be motivated to master essential skills and content" (p. 99). They found that the successful secondary schools coupled high expectations for student achievement with rewards. Both teachers and students in these schools were explicitly aware of learning expectations. As one student put it, "Teachers are on you all the time to do better. Even when you think you are working hard, they expect you to keep on improving. They keep adjusting the goals upward" (p. 104).

What was especially noteworthy was that many of the schools in the sample could be classified as "turnaround" schools—moving from poor reputations and negative learning environments to high expectations and improved performance over a 4- to 5-year period.

Broad community involvement. The relationship between community involvement and student achievement has been well established (not to say well practiced) in elementary schools, but it is not at all clear or well researched in secondary schools. Wilson and Corcoran (1988) found that successful high schools had close multidimensional relationships with their communities in at least five areas:

1. Human resources (involvement of community members)
2. Public relations (aggressive marketing)
3. Fiscal resources (additional monies)
4. Community services (involvement of students in the community)
5. Building an identity (symbolic sense of identity)

Continuous school improvement. This dimension, or what the authors also call *institutional vitality*, comes the closest to being a direct process, since it consists of a constant engagement in attempting to get better. In simplistic terms, a capacity for continuous improvement consists of a mental set by which major obstacles are constantly identified and addressed by strategies that result in progress. What was significant about these schools was not that they identified obstacles, but that they did something about them. They did not externalize the blame or the solution; they took action and mobilized ideas and resources.

Service to all students. It is crucial, especially for at-risk students, that the school's efforts extend to all students. Many secondary schools face terrible conditions. The successful secondary schools turned these conditions around in serving at-risk students. Wilson and Corcoran (1988) provide many examples; we quote from only one of these to illustrate the nature of the changes:

> Ribault Senior High School, Jacksonville, Florida. Called a jungle by the news media, and once regarded as the worst teaching assignment in Jacksonville, this large urban high school became a widely publicized lighthouse school in less than five years. Ribault students are a prototypical "at risk" population, predominantly black (99 percent) and largely poor. The steps taken to reverse the situation at Ribault included:
> - appointment of a new principal;
> - changes in the staff, all teachers had to reapply in 1979 and two-thirds were replaced by people who wanted to be at the school;
> - increased parent involvement as a result of parent contacts and intensive public relations;
> - introduction of a strong, clear discipline code, a student dress code; and generally higher standards and expectations;
> - Saturday tutoring in math and language arts for the state test;
> - use of retired teachers as volunteer tutors; and
> - visible activities such as a fine arts festival, a science fair, and a math field day to alter the school's image and raise community and student expectations for success.
>
> The passing rates on the mathematics section of the Florida State test went from 20 percent to 83 percent in four years. The number of students continuing to post-secondary education also increased. [pp. 133–134]

The conclusions drawn by Wilson and Corcoran (1988) are, first, that "quality is the hard won result of dedicated work by competent, committed people" (p. 146). The second is that there are six enabling conditions that make this possible: active, strong leadership; professional working culture; positive learning environments with high expectations; multifaceted public involvement; an orientation to and procedures for engaging in continuous school improvement; and special programs and services for at-risk students.

Using the three process criteria outlined at the beginning of their book, Wilson and Corcoran fare better than the previous studies. On the first criterion they do present a rather comprehensive picture as to how successful schools function, especially in that they are distilling case material from 571 schools. On the second criterion—how successful schools got that way—the analysis is incomplete. They are able to identify the steps taken (appoint a new principal, reassess staffing, focus on new programs, etc.), but there are many unanswered questions about how improvement unfolded. We do know that, in most schools where there was a major turnaround, it took about 5 years of concerted effort. The third criterion—how success is achieved in new situations—is always somewhat speculative. The authors formulate a number of policy recommendations for each of the six themes discussed in this review. While these are helpful as general guidelines for action, they require deeper insights and experience with change processes in order to be specifically useful.

Fullan and Newton (1988)

A colleague and I (Fullan & Newton, 1988) have reported on a major curriculum change undertaken at three schools in a large urban setting. The innovation was the 4MAT system developed by Bernice McCarthy (1982), and its prime movers were the three school principals, along with groups of individual teachers. The decision to change was internal to the school, in that there was no administrative initiative at the district level, although there was some support. We traced the evolution of the change over a 2-year period, with a particular focus on the role of the principal. Our study shows the importance of the role of the principal in large secondary schools, in keeping the innovation going. It also confirms Leithwood's (1987) observations about the broad array of goals and priorities with which high school principals must contend. Given the complexity of the innovation to implement (4MAT requires considerable teacher commitment and instructional development) and the large number of teachers in each school (150, 100, and 50 teachers, respectively), a surprising number of teachers actively worked on the project. However, no direct measures of extent and quality of implementation were available.

We found some of the usual problems of implementation—change-over in leadership (one of the key principals left), lack of time to work out implementation in the classroom, and unclear and uncertain relationships with the district office. We also found a number of themes related to what might be called the microprocesses of change. These themes illustrate the complexities and unknown nature of change processes within secondary schools. For example, one theme we called "change-cycles" because of the dramatic ups and downs that occurred over the 2-year period. Wild enthusiasm gave way to bottoming out, to glimmers of activity, to renewed enthusiasm, to further waning, and so on. Another, "the uphill internal battle," described the complex relationships among principals, vice-principals, department heads, and teachers. Individual departments varied considerably in their interest and activity in implementing 4MAT, which seemed to depend on an amalgam of factors, including the role of the department head and that person's relationship to the principal, the subject matter, and the makeup of the staff in a given department. A third theme was called simply "interest in high schools in curriculum change." We found widespread and diverse interests on the part of individual teachers in attempting instructional changes, but great difficulties in coordinating, orchestrating, and sustaining activities.

We do not analyze these internal themes in any detail, but our report identifies some of the dynamics involved and reminds us of how little we know about the more specific internal subprocesses of change within large secondary schools.

Marsh (1988)

Marsh (1988) conducted 17 case studies of junior (5) and senior high (12) schools and their districts in relation to the implementation of state-wide reform in California, which included 14 major reform components (see also Odden & Marsh, 1988). Schools were selected to represent the geographic and ethnic composition of the state, and because of their reputed progress in implementing the reform. Two of the main research questions were, What were the key local factors associated with successful implementation of the comprehensive state-initiated reform? and, What was the relationship of these implementation factors to the impact of the reform on student achievement and organizational capacity outcomes?

Marsh (1988) uses a causal network of factors organized in the familiar innovation phases of initiation, initial and full implementation, and institutionalization outcomes. There were two outcome measures used. One was based on student achievement gains, comparing 1986 with 1983 in reading and math, using the twelfth-grade California Assessment Program (CAP) for the 12 senior high schools. The other outcome measure—organizational capacity for making further reform—was defined as a combination of improvements in administrative practice (e.g., ability for local administrators to manage complex change processes, ability to develop an educational vision) and in school climate (e.g., shared sense of vision, collegiality, norms of improvement).

There were nine factors that were strongly associated with achievement and capacity outcomes:

1. District and school vision
2. District commitment and leadership
3. Implementation management
4. Initial training
5. Curriculum development
6. Ongoing administrative leadership
7. Program latitude and fidelity
8. Ongoing assistance
9. Teacher effort, mastery of new techniques, and commitment

This is an increasingly familiar list. The authors found that the average gain in CAP scores for all 12 high schools exceeded the statewide average, but there were three clusters: high gains on both reading and math, smaller gains on both, and mixed gains where either reading or math improved but not both. Marsh (1988) describes some of the findings:

> High CAP gain schools were in districts where the district vision of reform was clear and consistent. . . . [They] were much more active . . . in managing implementation [by] using cross role teams and in using implementation plans. Implementation coordination between the school and the district and among the departments in the schools [was] much stronger. . . . Use of initial training was substantially greater, . . . [and] ongoing assistance, both from the district and leaders at the school, also was much greater in high gain schools. . . . Ongoing administrative commitment, . . . pressure and monitoring [were] very high. . . . Two of the four high gain schools had consistently higher ratings for teacher effort, skill mastery and commitment. [pp. 16–17]

Similar findings are reported concerning improvements in organizational capacity and climate. An additional finding of note was that "high gain schools also had more latitude in implementing the reforms with school/district coupling and a direction of change that was consistent" (p. 18). That is, wide latitude and close interaction between the school and district were combined.

There are some question marks in the results. For example, only a limited number of teachers had achieved skill mastery over the more demanding dimensions of the reform. Also, teacher effort and commitment were no greater in schools with higher gains in organizational capacity than in other schools in the sample. Nonetheless, there were above-average gains in virtually all of the 17 schools. Marsh (1988) concludes that "state-initiated, 'top-down, content focused' reform in secondary schools is successful when: (a) the content of the reform fits with the priorities of the district, (b) districts and schools are able to transform the reform into their local agenda and context, and (c) key features of the implementation process . . . are followed" (p. 19).

Miles (1987) and Miles et al. (1988)

Miles and colleagues (Miles, 1987; Miles, Louis, Rosenblum, Cipollone & Farrar, 1988) push the question of school-based processes of change to a deeper level in their case studies of five urban high schools and their related national survey of 170 effective schools. The five schools were involved in a range of school-improvement projects, including business/school collaboration, state-sponsored school improvement efforts, effective-schools programs, drop-out prevention, and school-based planning. Three of the five schools were involved in comprehensive, multiple goal projects, while two had more modest or limited goals (Miles et al., 1988).

Miles (1987) focuses on five key thematic findings, which he labels shared vision, evolutionary development, initiative-taking/empowerment, assistance, and problem coping. In his own words,

1. It seems crucial to develop a clear shared vision a) of the school as it might become; and b) of the nature of the change process that will get us there.
2. Successful change is most likely when the program is evolutionary rather than tightly pre-designed.
3. Supporting initiative-taking by others, relying on empowerment leads to better-quality, committed implementation.
4. Substantial, sustained, relevant, and varied assistance is essential; implementation is not a self-sustained process.

5. Serious change efforts are rife with problems; good problem-coping
   is often needed; important to tailor coping to the problem involved.
   [p. 11]

Miles (1987) presents a causal framework and related findings for 15
factors "leading to successful implementation," ranging from preconditions (e.g., school autonomy, school leadership) to those needed for initial
implementation (e.g., vision, rewards) and for later implementation (e.g.,
power sharing, evolutionary development), to those responsible for outcomes (good implementation, institutionalization).

Two points are especially noteworthy in the research carried out by
Miles and his colleagues. First, they depict rather clearly the basic school-
level dynamics of the change process in successful school-improvement
projects. Second, they explicitly address and attempt to develop ideas for
the much-neglected "third" process question stated in my introduction: To
what extent does the study provide insights and guidelines for how to
achieve success in new situations? In the first paper, Miles (1987) provides
a set of guidelines for how to be successful. He suggests that moving from
knowledge to practice involves acting on the five key themes just listed.
He proposes that such activity is a matter of identifying and doing something, in relation to each theme, about (1) points of relevance, (2) action
images and activity, (3) mustering the will, and (4) developing the skill.
Illustrations and ideas are presented for each of the 20 cells generated by
cross-relating the five themes to the four dimensions of action. Miles et al.
(1988) subsequently formulated 37 "lessons for managing implementation," built on and linked to their major thematic finds.

There are still problems, however. First, we need to know more
about the subprocesses of change within large secondary schools. Second, we are not yet getting at sustained change, as contrasted with
specific improvement innovations. Third, there·is the endless and basically unsolvable problem of "how to implement the how-to guidelines."

We are now in a position to take stock of what these 10 studies tell us
about change processes in secondary schools and to consider the implications of these findings in the light of other literature on the management
of change.

KEY ISSUES IN SECONDARY SCHOOL CHANGE PROCESSES

There are five major areas of conclusion to be addressed. The first
consists of a recognition of the considerable insights and knowledge base

that exist concerning factors and processes associated with school improvement. The second issue is the difference between innovation and institutional targets for improvement, a distinction that I believe refocuses the reform agenda in fundamental ways. The third area takes up the confusing notion of the school as the unit or center of change in the context of centralization and decentralization. Fourth, I will turn to some of the differences between secondary and elementary school reform. Finally, I identify some of the major gaps in our knowledge base and their implications for research.

Insights and Knowledge Base

We know a great deal about the factors associated with successful school-improvement projects, and even about how the process works (Fullan, 1987). In many respects there is strong congruence across the 10 studies reviewed in this chapter. Although there are subtleties and underlying tensions, which I will discuss, there are also several factors that appear in virtually every study. There is also a proposed, but unproven, causal sequence. Without attempting to be definitive, it can be said that successful schools possess characteristics or develop processes that include

- Active and strong school leadership
- Shared goals and vision
- Ongoing assistance and supportive professional working environments
- Demanding and supportive conditions for students
- Community involvement
- A strong focus on relevant curriculum and learning
- An implementation capacity such as evolutionary planning or similar collaborative improvement procedures
- Ongoing monitoring and problem solving

These factors produce or enhance

- Teacher engagement, skill, and effectiveness
- Student engagement and learning

It is not clear, however, whether teacher and student engagement are the outcome or result obtained when individual secondary schools possess or come to possess the eight characteristics just listed, or whether engagement precedes or intermingles temporally with such acquisition. These eight characteristics are mutually supportive (positively or negatively, depending on their direction). They must be considered as a set of interactive factors rather than as an ordered list. For example, active leadership helps shape goals and vision through interaction and input from organizational members; a focus on instruction combined with collaborative planning procedures, monitoring and problem-solving, and professional development support helps move the organization in desired directions, and so on.

In terms of the three process aspects with which I began this chapter, the 10 studies do tell us how successful secondary schools function. Several studies provide insights relative to how those schools became successful, although data are quite incomplete and uneven on this question. And, the question of how to use these findings to influence new situations (i.e., how to effect a transfer of knowledge) is mostly neglected, except for Miles et al. (1988). Indeed, it is an enormously complex question, because we know enough about dissemination to conclude that complex changes, even when well validated in one setting, cannot and should not be "transferred" to other situations. Each setting has its own history, culture, and set of personalities. In any case, if we can make substantial progress on the first two questions—how successful schools function and how they got that way—we will be in a better position to decide on the do's and don'ts of using this knowledge. Several other recent major studies corroborate the foregoing conclusions (Lawton et al., 1988; Louis, 1989; Mortimore, Sammons, Stoll, Lewis, & Ecob, 1988; Newmann, Rutter, & Smith, 1988; and Rosenholtz, 1989).

In the rest of this chapter, I want to go beyond the findings per se. At one level there are a number of insights about the dynamics of change that have been hitherto unappreciated. They involve a combination of factors that have traditionally been seen as separate or mutually exclusive. Here are three examples: Active (aggressive) initiation followed by or coupled with progressive and widening collaboration and empowerment seem to be a powerful combination; both pressure and support are essential for success; and the constellation of ownership, skill, mastery, and commitment is more accurately portrayed as a phenomenon that builds throughout the change process, rather than something that exists or is settled at the early stages (see Fullan, 1987).

These observations are helpful, but only at a somewhat general level because they fail to address some of the deeper distinctions that it will be necessary to unravel. (For one thing, most of the factors operate differently at high schools compared to elementary schools.) It is necessary to identify more basic issues if we are to progress to a more fundamental reform agenda.

Innovation Versus Institutional Improvement

The first important distinction involves clarifying the primary focus of improvement, in order to identify and classify the main variables and clarify their relationships. Variables fall into four categories:

- Background—e.g., type of community, level of school
- Organizational ambience and structure—e.g., collaboration, strong leadership
- Implementation strategy—e.g., evolutionary planning, staff development
- Desired outcomes—e.g., student learning, staff commitment

Background variables or "givens," as Mortimore et al. (1988) call them, are those characteristics of the school and community that are impossible or unlikely to change, at least in the short run. An example is the socioeconomic status of the community. Such factors affect the chances of success because they represent a set of conditions for (or against) change. Organizational variables are what Berman and Gjelten (1984) refer to as "foreground factors," while Mortimore et al. (1988) call them "policy variables." They are relatively fixed at a given point in time, but are potentially amenable to alteration. Examples include the presence of strong leadership and the level of teachers' sense of efficacy. Some of the best research in this area is not on the role of organizational variables in the change or improvement process, but rather their impact on how schools function (Little, 1987; Mortimore et al., 1988; Rosenholtz, 1989).

The category of implementation strategies is a tricky one. I use it (as do Berman & Gjelten, 1984) to refer to the implementation strategies being used in *specific* improvement projects. A good example is staff development. It is true that these factors could become organizational variables if they became institutionalized, that is, if they became part and parcel of how the school approached all school-improvement efforts, not just the particular one being studied. Finally, the desired outcomes, of course, are the result of the previous variables. Teacher commitment is one example. Again, depending on the time and situation being examined, the particular factors may already be in place; for example, staff commitment could be an organizational factor if it were already in place, or an outcome if it resulted from improvements in the organization.

These variables, as already noted, can be identified only when the focus of improvement has been clearly stated. In my view, improvement efforts fall into three categories:

- Type 1(a): Classroom innovation
- Type 1(b): Schoolwide innovation
- Type 2: Institutional change

Let us see what happens when the four categories of main variables interact with these three types of improvements. Research on type 1(a) efforts concerns single innovations such as a new reading or social studies curriculum, microcomputers, and the like. In these cases, organizational factors are treated as causes of implementation, as in the assumption that active support from the principal increases the likelihood of implementation. I would say that these types of studies have pretty much run their course. We do know what makes for success, if we study one innovation at a time. The problem is that schools do not face one innovation at a time, so knowing how one innovation has been implemented tells us nothing about how other innovations are faring in the same school. At the very least we need to study the reality of how schools actually cope with multiple innovations (see Anderson, 1989).

Type 1(b) studies, which focus on schoolwide innovation, at first glance look like they are complete or comprehensive because they take such a broad perspective. They represent significant advances in the study of change, but they are still limited because they focus on *single* (albeit more comprehensive) improvement projects. All effective-schools researchers (e.g., Berman & Gjelten, 1984; Marsh, 1988; Miles, 1987) examine school-improvement plans, schoolwide curriculum efforts, and the like in the context of specific projects or initiatives. These approaches may employ some organizational variables (e.g., collaboration) in their implementation strategy, but they do not focus on these factors as the *primary targets* of long-term change. These initiatives are thus schoolwide but not necessarily "school-deep."

In some cases the schoolwide studies may even assess the impact of schoolwide reforms on organizational capacity. Recall that Marsh (1988) and his colleagues found that, under certain conditions, California's statewide reform increased the school's organizational capacity for further change. This conclusion, however, is rather questionable, both on grounds of causal direction and in terms of durability of the outcome. In principle, specific schoolwide projects can contribute to longer-term institutional changes, but a longer-term effort is required for type 2 changes to occur.

Type 2 changes involve a concerted, direct, and sustained attempt to alter organizational or institutional factors themselves. Without a direct and primary focus on changes in organizational factors, it is unlikely that types 1(a) and 1(b) approaches will have much of a reform impact, and whatever impact there is will be short lived. Berman and Gjelten (1984) draw the same conclusion, namely that school-improvement efforts that ignore these deeper, organizational conditions are "doomed to tinkering." Hargreaves (1989) comes to a similar assessment: "Practical curriculum change at the classroom level could not be effected without substantial changes in the culture and work of teaching" (p. 159).

To sum up this complex issue in somewhat different words, type 1(a) strategies will not have much of an impact because they do not address powerful organizational factors except as explanatory forces. If we are to continue with such strategies, they should have an explicit dual focus: to influence achievement of the innovation-related objectives and to alter organizational factors. Put this way, specific innovations can be seen as strategies for organizational change and assessed in terms of their effectiveness in so doing. They probably are not very effective in this regard, because more powerful strategies are required for this purpose.

Type 1(b) strategies are more potent, but still may not be enough. They give the appearance of addressing organizational factors, but they are project bound (even though the projects may have multiple major reform components) and tend to influence organizational conditions relatively superficially. These strategies may enhance certain organizational strengths that are already in existence, but they do not overcome organizational weaknesses (Berman & Gjelten, 1984). Again, if these strategies are to be used, they should be strengthened to incorporate fundamental and lasting organizational change.

More powerful, multipronged strategies are thus needed that directly address the culture of the organization in the present, in the near future, and for the long term. Examples are the integrative strategies suggested by Anderson and Cox (1987) and Hargreaves (1989). Hargreaves, for example, recommends

> decentralization of curriculum development; administrative support for collaborative teacher culture; mandatory guidelines requiring a broad and balanced curriculum and reinforced through the power of inspection; and a revamped assessment system designed to provide teachers with improved feedback about their pupils and their progress as a basis for curriculum renewal. [p. 170]

Whatever the particulars, powerful strategies for powerful change are required, which restructure and integrate teacher development, principal and school development, student development, and accountability and assessment development, and which cross institutional boundaries (also see Hargreaves, 1989).

Finally, it is no accident that long-term institutional-improvement strategies end up integrating organizational research (e.g., Rosenholtz, 1989) and school-improvement research (e.g., Marsh, 1988; Miles, 1987). Without such integration, the focus in types 1(a) and 1(b) approaches tends to be on the solutions themselves, rather than the underlying conditions.

The School as the Center of Change

The statement that "the school is the unit of change" has always been confusing. In decentralized models, school-based change seems to flounder or is short lived when it occurs. Centralized approaches work superficially at best because they do not get at the significant organizational factors at the school level. Sirotnik (1987) provides one of the clearest and most convincing rationales for the critical role of the school, when he claims that the school should be conceptualized as the *center* of change. As he states, "To say that something is at the center implies a good deal around it" (p. 2). Using epistemological, organizational, and experiential bases, he further argues that

> we are led to the organization, e.g., the school as the center of change. We are not led naively to see the school as isolated from its sociopolitical context, able to engage in miraculous self-renewing activities without district, community, state, and federal support. But we are led to where the day-to-day action is, to where with the proper motivation and support, the prevailing conditions and circumstances of schools can be challenged constructively within the context of competing values and human interest. . . . In short, . . . people who live and work in complex organizations like schools need to be thoroughly involved in their own improvement efforts, assuming significant and enduring organizational change is the purpose we have in mind. [pp. 25–26]

There are two conclusions to be drawn about the central role of the school. First, it follows from the previous section that institutional reform should be the primary focus and will not be achieved unless we conceive of the school as the center of change. Most current educational reform initiatives fail to grasp the essence of this point, as they direct their attention to curriculum reform, testing of students and teachers, school-improvement plans, career ladders, principal training, and the like. Second, and more subtle, the school will never become the center of change if left to its own devices. I said at the outset that it was beyond the scope of this chapter to map out the context of secondary school reform at the district and state levels. More attention is being paid to the *relationship* of the school to the district and other agencies. More research needs to be done, but the gist of the findings is that the district is essential for school reform, and that effective relationships are characterized by frequent two-way interaction rather than laissez-faire or heavy regulation. Both pressure and support are necessary (Cuban, 1988; Firestone, 1988; Fuhrman, Clune, & Elmore, 1988; LaRocque & Coleman, 1989; Louis, 1989; Marsh, 1988; Oakes, 1987; Purkey & Smith, 1985). In short, the main agenda—institutional development in a societal context—is clear.

Differences Between Secondary and Elementary Schools

Secondary schools are more complex and address a wider range of goals and agendas than do elementary schools. They contain many more structural and normative barriers to organizational change, such as departmentalization, individual teacher autonomy, physical isolation, and size. On the other hand, they are more loosely coupled and more impervious to simple (and incorrect) solutions than are elementary schools.

One of the interesting by-products of comparing elementary and secondary schools is the realization that the elementary school's comparatively simpler goal and organizational structure has made it more vulnerable to type 1(a) and 1(b) strategies. Classroom and schoolwide innovation plans appear to make more sense at the elementary level, but this is deceptive in that it diverts primary attention away from fundamental institutional improvement and toward more superficial changes. This has obscured the importance of institutional development at the elementary level as well as at the secondary level, as findings on elementary school innovations have been extrapolated to high schools.

The weaknesses of these strategies are more likely to be noticed at the secondary level, because there are several more factors at work. Among the additional—or at least redefined—factors arising from the 10 studies reviewed in the first section of this chapter are goal and program diversity, teacher commitment (alienation), student commitment (alienation), broad community and business involvement, a more complex institutional-improvement role for school leaders, and a more difficult task of developing collaboration among teachers.

It is worth emphasizing that increased attention to these issues is resulting in more comprehensive institutional-improvement strategies. Wilson and Corcoran's (1988) case material reflects this trend. Lawton and Leithwood (1988) found that the same factors that explain institutional improvement also explain student retention. They suggest that greater coherence and comprehensiveness could be brought to school-improvement efforts, without treating dropping out as a separate problem. Firestone and Rosenblum's (1988) analysis of teacher and student commitment also supports this conclusion.

Effective-schools research and strategies have been criticized for being too narrow and simplistic (Fullan, 1985). The recent work reviewed in this chapter clearly demonstrates that a broader and more fundamental set of strategies is needed. I have also argued that a wider definition of effectiveness is needed at the elementary level, a claim that is strongly corroborated in the research by Mortimore et al. (1988) and Rosenholtz (1989). In the final analysis, elementary and secondary school improvement have something basic in common.

Gaps in Knowledge and Their Implications for Research

Before turning to implications for research, I would like to comment on policy and practice implications. It is beyond the scope of this chapter to map out a broad-based strategy for reform. Sustained efforts focusing on both short-term and long-term strategies are required. These efforts must provide some tangible early success, as well as concentrate on achieving permanent changes in the fundamental organizational factors identified in this review (e.g., active leadership, vision, and collaborative professional work environments). Most reform attempts are superficial and/or short lived. Major alterations are required in structural and normative work conditions of teachers and students. We need powerful strategies for powerful change. Powerful strategies mean working directly on institutional changes over a period of years in the same settings. Two examples of such strategies being employed are contained in Anderson and Cox (1987) and in the work of the Learning Consortium (Fullan, Rolheiser-Bennett, & Bennett, 1989; Watson, Rolheiser-Bennett, Bennett, & Thiessen, 1989).

We also need to continue expanding the kind of sophisticated theoretical and research frameworks we are beginning to see in recent studies (e.g., Mortimore et al., 1988). More particularly, we need research on the short- and long-term processes of institutional or organizational development. The types of factors listed at the beginning of this section should be investigated at the secondary level in their own right, in light of the greater complexity of high schools. For example, what is the meaning of shared goals and vision at the high school compared to the elementary school? How do schoolwide collaborative cultures evolve and become sustained?

Second, what are the subprocesses of institutional improvement within high schools? Research should focus on the relationship of principals and vice-principals to department heads, the ins and outs of developing collaborative cultures of teachers within different subject areas and across subject areas, the process by which implementation capacity develops, and the like. These microprocesses of change are probably the most neglected aspects of research on high schools.

Third, what is the nature and impact of some of the powerful strategies for high school reform that attempt cross-institutional restructuring, such as school district reorganization and partnerships between schools or districts and universities or businesses? Particular interest should be shown where these plans include radical restructuring of the school as an organization.

Fourth, how can we monitor and influence the cumulative long-term development of the significant organizational factors identified in this chapter, including the development of the teaching profession (Carnegie Forum, 1987; Fullan & Connelly, 1988)?

After years of research on elementary school change, one of the ironies of the burgeoning research on secondary schools is that, while a late starter, it could end up making a more fundamental contribution to the educational reform agenda than has research on elementary schools.

REFERENCES

Anderson, B., & Cox, P. (1987). *Configuring the education system for a shared future: Collaborative vision, action, reflection.* Unpublished manuscript.

Anderson, S. (1989). *The management and implementation of multiple changes in curriculum and instruction.* Unpublished doctoral dissertation, University of Toronto.

Bamburg, J., & Andrews, R. (1988, April). *Implementing change in secondary schools using effective schools research.* Paper presented at the annual meeting of the American Educational Research Association, New Orleans.

Berman, P., & Gjelten, T. (1984). *Improving school improvement: An independent evaluation of the California school improvement program.* Berkeley, CA: Berman, Weiler.

Carnegie Forum on Education and the Economy. (1987). *A nation prepared: Teachers for the 21st century.* New York: Carnegie Corporation.

Cuban, L. (1988). *The managerial imperative and the practice of leadership in schools.* Albany: State University of New York Press.

Firestone, W. (1988). *Using reform: A conceptual introduction.* New Brunswick, NJ: Rutgers University, Center for Policy Research.

Firestone, W., & Rosenblum, S. (1988). *The alienation and commitment of students and teachers in urban high schools.* New Brunswick, NJ: Rutgers University, Center for Policy Research.

Fuhrman, S., Clune, W., & Elmore, R. (1988). *Research on education reform: Lessons on the implementation of policy.* Unpublished manuscript, Center for Policy Research Consortium, Rutgers, Michigan State, Stanford, University of Wisconsin-Madison.

Fullan, M. (1985). Change processes and strategies at the local level. *Elementary School Journal, 85,* 391–421.

Fullan, M. (1987). *Implementing education change: What we know.* Washington, DC: World Bank.

Fullan, M., & Connelly, M. (1988). *Teacher education in Ontario: Current practice and options for the future.* Toronto: Ministry of Education.

Fullan, M., & Newton, E. (1988). School principals and change processes in the secondary school. *The Canadian Journal of Education, 13,* 404–422.

Fullan, M., Rolheiser-Bennett, C., & Bennett, B. (1989, March). *Linking classroom and school improvement.* Paper presented at the annual meeting of the American Educational Research Association, San Francisco.

Hargreaves, A. (1989). *Curriculum and assessment reform.* Milton Keynes, England: Open University Press.

LaRocque, L., & Coleman, P. (1989). Quality control: School accountability and district ethos. In M. Holmes, K. Leithwood, & D. Musella (Eds.), *Educational policy for effective schools* (pp. 168–191). Toronto: OISE Press.

Lawton, S., Leithwood, K., Batches, E., Donaldson, E., & Stewart, R. (1988). *Student retention and transition.* Toronto: Ministry of Education.

Leithwood, K. (1987). *A review of research concerning characteristics of exemplary secondary schools.* Unpublished manuscript, The Ontario Institute for Studies in Education.

Little, J. (1987). Teachers as colleagues. In V. Koehler (Ed.), *The educator's handbook* (pp. 491–518). New York: Longman.

Louis, K. (1989). The role of school districts in school innovation. In M. Holmes, K. Leithwood, & D. Musella (Eds.), *Educational policy for effective schools* (pp. 145–167). Toronto: OISE Press.

Louis, K., & Smith, B. (1989, March). *Teacher engagement and student engagement.* Paper presented at the annual meeting of the American Educational Research Association, San Francisco.

Marsh, D. (1988, April). *Key factors associated with the effective implementation and impact of California's educational reform.* Paper presented at the annual meeting of the American Educational Research Association, New Orleans.

Matthes, W. (in press). Conditions for professional practice in exemplary high schools. *Journal of Rural and Small Schools.*

McCarthy, B. (1982). Improving staff development through CBAM and 4Mat. *Educational Leadership, 40*(3), 20–25.

Miles, M. (1987, April). *Practical guidelines for school administrators: How to get there.* Paper presented at the annual meeting of the American Educational Research Association, Washington, DC.

Miles, M., Louis, K., Rosenblum, S., Cipollone, A., & Farrar, E. (1988). *Lessons for managing implementation.* Unpublished manuscript.

Mortimore, P., Sammons, P., Stoll, L., Lewis, D., & Ecob, R. (1988). *School matters: The junior years.* Somerset, England: Open Books.

Newmann, F., Rutter, R., & Smith, M. (1988). *Organizational factors affecting school sense of efficacy, community and expectations.* Madison: University of Wisconsin-Madison, National Center on Effective Secondary Schools.

Oakes, J. (1987). *Improving inner-city schools: Current directions in urban district reform.* Santa Monica, CA: Rand Corporation, Center for Policy Research in Education.

Odden, A., & Marsh, D. (1988). How comprehensive reform legislation can improve secondary schools. *Phi Delta Kappan* April: 593–598.

Pink, W. (1988, April). *Implementing an alternative program for at risk youth: A school within a school model for school reform.* Paper presented at the annual meeting of the American Educational Research Association, New Orleans.

Purkey, S., & Smith, M. (1985). School reform: The district policy implications of the effective schools literature. *Elementary School Journal, 85,* 353–390.

Rosenholtz, S. (1989). *Teachers' workplace: The social organization of schools.* New York: Longman.

Sirotnik, K. V. (1987). The school as the center for change [Occasional Paper No. 5]. Seattle: University of Washington, Institute for the Study of Educational Policy.

Stevenson, R. (1987a). Autonomy and support: The dual needs of urban high schools. *Urban Education, 22,* 366–386.

Stevenson, R. (1987b). Staff development for effective secondary schools: A synthesis of research. *Teaching and Teacher Education, 3,* 233–248.

Watson, N., Rolheiser-Bennett, C., Bennett, B., & Thiessen, D. (1989, June). *The Learning Consortium: Year one of a school-university partnership.* Paper presented at the annual meeting of the Canadian Society for Studies in Education, Quebec.

Wilson, B., & Corcoran, T. (1988). *Successful secondary schools: Visions of excellence in American public schools.* East Sussex, England: Falmer Press.

9

Three Views of Curriculum Policy in the School Context: The School as Policy Mediator, Policy Critic, and Policy Constructor

WILLIAM H. CLUNE

    This chapter is an overview of findings about curriculum policy and schools, based on data from a large research project conducted by the Center for Policy Research in Education (CPRE). CPRE studied the background, implementation, and effects of curriculum policies, including graduation requirements, student testing, curriculum controls, and indicators (see Clune, White, & Patterson, 1989, on graduation requirements and related policies). In addition to the 188 interviews conducted at the state level with government officials and policy makers in six states, CPRE also conducted 524 interviews in 59 local schools within those states. I was asked to write a paper bridging the gap between the policy-centered focus of CPRE and the school- and teaching-centered perspective of the Center for Research on the Context of Secondary School Teaching (CRCSST). The main question to be addressed was, What did we learn from our research about curriculum policy in the school context?

    This chapter, which is the result of those efforts, concentrates on curriculum policy in high schools, because that is the area of my own research. It tends also to emphasize effects at the level of school planning and organization (e.g., types of courses offered), rather than classroom teaching. CPRE interviewed many teachers, but did not do classroom observations; hence there is not much data on the interaction of curricu-

The writing of this chapter was supported by funds from the U.S. Department of Education, Office of Educational Research and Improvement (Grant No. G0087C0235). The research was also supported by the Center for Policy Research in Education and the Wisconsin Center for Education Research, School of Education, University of Wisconsin-Madison. The opinions expressed in this publication are those of the author and do not necessarily reflect the views of the above-mentioned organizations.

lum policy and instructional practice. (See Richards & Shujaa, 1988, on interviews with teachers.)

The chapter begins with an introduction to the three perspectives from which policy can be analyzed. This is followed by a methodological (or, perhaps better, an epistemological) discussion on how to analyze curriculum policy in the school context, especially on how to handle the shifting normative perspectives created by looking at the topic from different viewpoints. Next comes a related discussion of general reasons why the perspectives of policy and school context are likely to be different. This is followed by three sections that comprise the heart of the chapter, describing the three roles the school can play in influencing policy, as policy mediator, policy critic, and policy constructor. After a short section on what probably would be learned from a deeper look at classrooms and instruction, the conclusion draws some general lessons for curriculum policy.

THREE PERSPECTIVES

The ultimate question about policy in the school context is how the perspective of school context changes our views of policy. In the case of curriculum policy, this transformation of perspective can be grasped conveniently by looking at policy from three different viewpoints, each deeper in the school context and less tightly or necessarily linked with policy as a reference point. While each viewpoint is, therefore, successively less "top-down" and more "bottom-up," even the most policy-oriented of the three is far more sensitive to field-level action than the regulatory perspective that provoked the original bottom-up critique (Elmore, 1979).

The first and most policy-oriented question is how the school context mediates policy outcomes. Regardless of how curriculum policy is formulated, schools and teachers exercise an extraordinary amount of discretion about how the policy will be implemented (e.g., what kinds of courses will be offered to which kinds of students by which teachers through what pedagogy). Research on school-level decisions relevant to policy may suggest ways to make those decisions more consistent with policy goals.

The second question is how the school acts as policy critic. The usefulness and effectiveness of recent curriculum reforms rest on a variety of empirically testable assumptions about, for example, the value of academic courses, extra classes, a uniform curriculum across schools, and the relative incapacity (or comparative institutional disadvantage) of schools and teachers as curriculum innovators (Clune, 1987). Research in schools can provide many insights about the validity and limits of such assumptions. The school as policy critic is an extension of the school as policy mediator. In both cases the goals of policy are the reference point, and research examines how school-level decisions affect those goals. But the school as policy critic allows for the possibility that the policy goals cannot be achieved at the school level, or that policies have adverse effects that outweigh the benefits of any goals achieved.

The least policy-oriented (and thus the most "contextualized") question is how the school acts as policy constructor. Here, the assumption is that schools are engaged in the same kind of activity as policy makers— the construction of ideal curriculum content and pedagogy—at a level that responds to a different set of needs and priorities. Schools, under this view, are not simply or even primarily the implementors of exogenous policy commands; rather, they have their own complex, shifting, and contradictory agendas. On the one hand, these field-level agendas for curriculum resemble the full range of plausible policy options more than they resemble the particular policy direction in force at a particular time (e.g., including aspirations toward high-quality vocational, humanistic/ elective, and child-oriented education, as well as a movement toward more rigorous academics). On the other hand, school curriculum policies presumably operate with a different set of dynamics because they respond to different needs and political pressures (e.g., on the idealistic side, the educational needs of complete, individual children; on the less idealistic side, powerful pressures toward routinization of instruction).

The view of policy as an initiative that must crowd in and compete with existing agendas has many important implications. To be effective, policy must overcome a much more complex set of obstacles and figure out how to enter the ongoing school-level "conversation" about curriculum policy. Conversely, the view of schools as policy makers obviously has the potential for turning normal assumptions about hierarchy upside down. A close inspection of schools may demonstrate how schools need to change, but it may also demonstrate that policy should change. Policy may learn from schools as well as schools from policy, not simply about the weakness of a particular policy (as under the critical role), but also about entirely new possibilities.

The focus on school as context also introduces the possibility of benign subversion. What appears as sabotage from a policy perspective may look quite constructive and adaptive at the ground level. Much of the instability of policy, the constant adjustments and refinements, probably comes from its relationship with the school context. From this point of view, policy is an endless, recursive dialogue, rather than a series of self-sealing implemented commands.

An interesting feature of each of these three perspectives is that they seem to require different theoretical frameworks and methodologies. The school as policy mediator requires a model of organizational dynamics oriented around the particular policy outcome (e.g., academic course taking). The school as policy critic requires a more analytical model of hypothesis testing (e.g., looking at what must be true at the school level to support the assumptions of policy). The school as policy constructor requires a model of schools and teachers as involved in the social construction of reality (both knowledge and action) and a methodology that is correspondingly more anthropological and ethnographic.

POLICY AND SCHOOL CONTEXT AS MUTUAL PERSPECTIVES

The notion of the school as offering three different "views" or "perspectives" raises an important methodological or epistemological issue: How do we conduct research on social locations that differ in both factual context and normative perspective? Policy context and school context are not simply places where different things happen; they also are places with different normative standards (looking at things through different lenses, as it were). Because the fundamental issue is much broader than the topic of this chapter, the discussion here cannot do it full justice.[1] Instead, I will try to clarify some basic points of and sketch in areas of likely consensus.

First, to raise the issue at all, we must be dealing with a situation where both perspectives actually exist. This is not necessarily or always the case. If curriculum policy were completely irrelevant to the school, we would no longer have a topic of "policy in the school context," but only "school context" (or "policies that never make it into the school context in the first place"). Many policies do not affect schools at all. But curriculum policies, like graduation requirements, standardized tests, curriculum guides, and textbook selection, seem to have strong (if not always positive) impacts. In other words, the topic of "curriculum in the school context" is an important one partly because neither partner overwhelms the other; both have significant impacts.

Second, though sensitive to school context, this chapter adopts a systematic policy perspective. Each of the categories (mediator, critic, constructor) can be considered to be "policy centric," because the common thread is what policy can learn from the school context. On the other hand, each perspective also can be characterized as "bottom-up" or field sensitive, because the school context is actually observed and taken seriously.

Third, though sharing a common policy perspective, the categories become less policy centric in the order presented; that is, the school as policy critic is less supportive of policy than the school as policy mediator; and the school as policy constructor begins to recognize the school as an appropriate source of alternative policy perspectives. The normative perspective can shift even within categories. Within the mediator category, for example, one might take a strong policy perspective, such as agency theory (McDonnell, 1988), and characterize all divergence from policy as "shirking" by the schools. Or, one might take the more traditional view of implementation research and think about building on variations in local goals and capacities (Berman, 1984).

Fourth, the importance of the common policy perspective becomes apparent when we realize that some commentators take the opposite approach, becoming "school centric," and evaluating policy from the perspective of its impact on the desirable goals of the school (Cuban, 1984; David, 1987).

I am convinced that there is no objective criterion capable of specifying which perspective is "correct," which kind of centricity really is central. Good reasons exist for taking either perspective. On the side of policy, one might rely on the force of law, the political consensus of democracy, the need for action, the undesirable state of local practice, the healthy prospects for progressive change, or the intrinsic wisdom of the policies. On the side of a school perspective, one might rely on the wisdom of those closest to the children, the lack of wisdom of the policies, suspicion of politics, or skepticism about the feasibility of change, especially with regard to the feasibility of the policy itself (Cuban, 1984; David, 1987). In one sense, the choice comes down to the personal world view and political stance of the researcher, as well as the job that one has been asked to do. A governmental agency, for example, might want to know how its program is faring.

In another sense, the discrepancies become less sharp and polarized in a genuine dialogue. If the analysis is open to the interplay of policy and school context, most essential facts will surface, and different normative perspectives will emerge more clearly when coupled with specific facts. The only important general point is that the shift from policy to school context involves not simply a different factual foundation but often a difference of normative perspective as well. Part of the challenge and subtlety of policy analysis is the often implicit choice of normative perspectives. An example of this is taking the "purposes" of policy, themselves often ambiguous, as a given, while remaining free to criticize policy results against some independent standard, such as a broad definition of quality education (see Kennedy, 1987).

GENERAL DIFFERENCES BETWEEN POLICY AND SCHOOL CONTEXTS

The previous section discussed how to manage research on differing factual and normative contexts. This section discusses some general differences between the policy and school contexts which make that kind of discussion necessary. What explains the distinct perspective of the school? How are policy and school different?

The easiest place to begin is with the most basic lesson of implementation research, namely, that policies are shaped and changed during implementation because of the discretion exercised by the field-level agents who actually deliver services. Despite the fundamental and by now obvious nature of the general proposition, actual research on implementation never fails to reveal important and interesting insights about the interaction of policies and local, variable circumstances and discretion (McLaughlin, 1987).

In the case of schools, or any other policy target, these general categories of discretion and variable local circumstances can be usefully refined and specified. First, the political and educational goals of the school may be different from those of policy. Schools and teachers may favor policy goals, or they may have alternative goals (e.g., vocational education, electives rather than a required core curriculum, rote learning rather than higher-order thinking). Schools are more likely to be responsive to the demands of their clients, such as for less homework or more extracurriculars. Above all, schools and teachers have views regarding student capacities. The belief that students of different abilities are capable of learning different things goes a long way to explain pervasive stratification of learning opportunities. Some of the more sophisticated research on policy focuses on the indigenous cultures of schools, embedded conceptions of knowledge, and the like (Cohen, 1987; Cusick, 1983; Powell, Farrar, & Cohen, 1985; Sarason, 1971).

Consistent with the idea of diverse educational goals, one of the basic experiences of research in the school context is the encounter with a range of opinion and perspective about curriculum that is much broader than the approach of new policies. Policies can be justifiably criticized as fragmented and "irrational," but a set of policies enacted at any given time is likely to be more coherent than policies over the long run. Because the school as an organization has developed over the long run and contains people of different ages and backgrounds, perspectives at the school site are likely to resemble the diversity of historical opinion more than the coherence of a specific historical moment. Consequently, the researcher is likely to observe a variety of curricular philosophies distinct from current policies and from each other.

A second area of variable local circumstance and discretion relates to the fact that schools inevitably will experience a broader array of considerations bearing on the policy objectives than will policy makers concerned with specific policy instruments. A primary consideration confirmed by CPRE's research is the need to keep students in school and engaged in learning (see McDonnell, 1988). Schools often will bend over backward to keep students in school, a goal that is one reason for stratification of learning opportunities. Schools also are sensitive to the need for engaged teachers (partially explaining concessions made to teachers' preferences for subject matter), as well as other preconditions of effective instruction (a safe and orderly environment, a school culture supporting academic achievement).

A third consideration is the "bottleneck" phenomenon: Schools are collective enterprises that must integrate a variety of policies with a variety of local goals. In one sense, schools are the end of the line for policy fragmentation (Cohen, 1983), the agencies that must pick up all the loose change and somehow create effective, integrated programs. For example, schools must implement new subject-matter requirements with their own inventory of subject-matter specialists (teachers) and subject-matter goals (things the students should learn). Some schools in our study implemented new social studies requirements in light of the existing social studies programs and faculties. In one district,a school decided to teach American rather than ancient world history to immigrant students in need of basic socialization into American society.

A fourth discretionary function of schools is the allocation of resources, and schools have different amounts of resources to allocate. Increased graduation requirements presented schools with the problem of how to allocate experienced math and science teachers. Most schools seemed to have responded by sending the more experienced teachers to the upper track, teaching college-bound students (McDonnell, 1988). In addition, schools varied in the number of experienced teachers they had to allocate. Urban schools with high turnover tended to have fewer experienced teachers and were more often presented with the problem of teachers teaching out of field (e.g., shop teachers moved to basic-level mathematics).

THE SCHOOL AS POLICY MEDIATOR

The school as policy mediator is the first, least critical perspective on policy provided by the school context. The essential insight is that schools make decisions relevant to policy, so, from a propolicy standpoint, the objective is to encourage decisions that are most favorable to policy goals.

In the recent wave of educational reforms, the most important kind of discretion exercised by schools was the quality of courses offered to different groups of students. The combination of graduation requirements (which entailed regulating selection of courses by students) and curriculum control (which entailed regulating the content of courses) was not tight enough to prevent wide variations in the level and quality of courses. Consistent with a very general policy requirement, such as "three mathematics courses," schools offered drastically different levels of math (remedial, basic, general, college prep, and so on). In other words, the existing system of stratified learning opportunities (Gamoran, 1987) was largely reproduced in response to the new policies.

In addition to variations in the level of courses were variations in quality and, in particular, some evidence of repetition and watering down of course content. Some districts allowed watering down in both time and content; for example, one district responded to reform by offering seven 50-minute periods as a substitute for six 60-minute periods (a decline of 10 instructional minutes but an increase in number of courses and credits). Some respondents in this same district claimed that an additional math course was fashioned by stretching the content of first-level general math into two courses. Watering down of content also may occur through the substitution of vocational equivalents (increasingly authorized by state law), such as baking math, nursing math, and cosmetic math.

A second important kind of discretionary response is remediation and alternate routes. One impact of high standards on low-achieving students who have trouble meeting the standards is a proliferation of alternative routes (e.g., summer school, night school, adult education, GEDs, and schools with special missions and types of students). Such alternate routes may contribute to the goal of academic rigor by, for example, getting the student up to speed; on the other hand, they may detract by providing a tempting safety valve through lower standards or by serving as a dumping ground.

A third school-level response that is important to the goal of increased academic rigor is the assignment and recruitment of teachers. Schools and districts do not have complete discretion about these decisions, but they do exert significant influence. For whatever reason, some schools are better able than others to stock new required courses with qualified teachers (e.g., math courses taught by teachers certified in math, versus courses taught by coaches displaced by declines in physical education enrollments).

These examples are sufficient to show the large amount of discretion that exists beneath the level of formal compliance (offering courses with the required labels). Evaluating the substance beneath the form actually is quite tricky, because, quite apart from the difficulty of gathering all the necessary data, one cannot automatically assume that "more rigorous is better." Some lower-level and remedial courses may do a better job at getting students up to speed and preventing academic failure than standard college prep courses offered to the same students. The ideal compromise, which may be relatively rare up to this point, is an effort to convey the essence of higher-order content at a somewhat slower pace. Hence, even the top-down analysis called for in this section demands an extraordinary understanding of what is going on in the school context.

Correcting stratification of learning opportunities and variations in course quality—in other words, drastically upgrading the course content for lower-track students—is the great unfinished task of curricular reform. In an effort to control school-level discretion, policy makers might be tempted to approach the task with a much tighter set of policies. An understanding of the school as policy mediator should cast serious doubt on such a top-down approach. Even if state law required "algebra," "geometry," and "advanced algebra" for all students (instead of "three mathematics courses") and specified the content of each course, many important decisions would be left at the school level. Teachers would not necessarily cover all the material (Freeman & Porter, 1988). If teachers were forced to cover the material by "pacing guides," students of different abilities might not learn the material well. If standardized tests controlled the award of course credit, many students might fail and drop out of school.

Ultimately, there is no substitute for teaching a quality course with high expectations appropriate for the particular group of students in a school. The teachers must know how to teach the material, be comfortable with the conception of knowledge, and believe that the students can learn what is taught. The school must be involved in planning a curriculum with high expectations, in a logical, coherent fashion. An example would be to permit movement from one level and sequence of courses to another. Remedial courses must "accelerate, not remediate" (Levin, 1988).

In other words, one of the critical unfulfilled tasks of curriculum policy is involvement of the school as policy mediator. The curriculum policy of the future should not be conceptualized as a set of mandates exhausting the task of policy and leaving only the mechanical exercise of school compliance. Rather, the delivery of high-quality curriculum materials to the school should be viewed as only the first step, to be followed by subsequent phases of schoolwide planning, teacher training, and measurement of student performance. The appropriate conceptual model for such policy is something more like structured school-by-school instructional improvement than uniform state regulation (Fennema, Carpenter, & Peterson, in press; Slavin & Madden, 1989).

THE SCHOOL AS POLICY CRITIC

When the school context is viewed as a policy critic, the basic point is that existing policies have failed to achieve their intended goals; they cannot achieve them, given the realities of the school context; and, consequently, they should be abandoned or fundamentally restructured. Such findings are all too common in policy research, examples including mastery learning and pull-out programs (Slavin, 1987; Slavin & Madden, 1989; Turnbull, Smith, & Ginsburg, 1981). In such a situation, the school still might be considered a policy mediator, but, because of perverse incentives, the mediation inevitably produces effects that are contrary to policy goals.

As far as is known, the curriculum policies of the 1980s were not of this kind, because they achieved modest progress toward the goal of a more rigorous uniform education for all students. There is, however, a school of criticism of curriculum policies that claims systematic policy failure in the school context. Curriculum controls are said to drag down the best practice of teaching; encourage the wrong kind of content for lower-track students (rote memorization, drill, and practice, rather than higher-order thinking); increase stratification between levels of courses, as a response to more rigid requirements (see Shepard & Smith, 1988); and drive the best teachers away from education (Darling-Hammond & Wise, 1985; McNeil, 1987a, 1987b).

Such claims to this point seem mostly speculative and unsubstantiated. Even more problematic, advocates usually do not specify the kind of curriculum controls being discussed, allowing each side of the debate to condemn the worst possible practices of the other (e.g., advocates of curriculum control citing the worst examples of unregulated teaching, and advocates of unregulated teaching citing the worst examples of curriculum control). CPRE does have some work in progress designed as an empirical test of some of the claims. The important point for this chapter is a reminder of the possibility that research in the school context can demonstrate that a policy is unworkable, rather than in need of further refinement.

THE SCHOOL AS POLICY CONSTRUCTOR

The view of school context as policy constructor allows for the possibility that schools can be sources of alternative policies rather than simply mediators or critics of the policies currently in force. There is the potential for criticism here—not of the failure of existing policies to achieve their own goals, but of the narrowness of existing policies and the suppression of desirable alternatives at the school site.

In our research, we found school-level representation of all of the great rivals of the current philosophy of a rigorous academic education. Advocates of vocational education claimed that vocational courses were necessary to keep students in school, far better for the employment prospects of the noncollege bound, and often superior in content to the weaker academic courses. Champions of electives argued the merits of diversity and variations in individual student preferences, the cosmopolitan character of a diverse curriculum, the advantages of letting teachers teach in their favorite subject matters, and, again, the positive motivational impact of courses selected by students themselves.

As indicated by these examples, a common emphasis at the school site was keeping students in school and engaged in learning. Another application of this "student-centered" perspective was tolerance for alternative educational experiences, such as extracurricular activities, alternative schools, night schools, special schools, schools within schools, and GED certificates.

The lessons for policy of school-site normative dissension are not clear and place the researcher in the potentially difficult political position of researching the attainment of policy goals while becoming sympathetic to other goals at the school site. Perhaps the best that can be done under these circumstances is to call attention to some of the alternative policy goals that seem to deserve special recognition. In my own research (Clune et al., 1989), I recommended a "second look" at high-quality vocational courses and streamlined requirements that did not interfere so greatly with electives and extracurricular activities.

TEACHER AND CLASSROOM PERSPECTIVES

As mentioned earlier, the CPRE data base did not include classroom observations, but the interviews did include some questions on the impact of curriculum policy on teaching practice, summarized in Richards and Shujaa (1988). Another source of insights about the interplay of policy and teaching, which is based on classroom observation, is emerging research on the elements of effective teaching practice (Fennema et al., in press; Peterson & Comeaux, 1989; Slavin & Madden, 1989; Smith & O'Day, 1988). At the risk of oversimplification, one general conclusion that might be drawn from this research is that there is a lack of one-to-one correspondence between policy instruments and effective teaching.

Policy can deliver a high-quality curriculum to the school doorstep, but the instructional practices most effective for teaching those materials are unlikely to be adequately described by the policy. For example, innovative mathematics curricula may truly aim at higher-order thinking and active learning and, in that sense, encourage a particular kind of pedagogy (Romberg, 1988). But the actual pedagogy appropriate to achieving the curriculum goals requires special attention. To get students engaged in higher-order thinking, problem solving, and active learning, teachers may rely on learning in groups, peer tutoring, new forms of teacher/student dialogue, creative exercises, and new kinds of examinations (Archbald & Newmann, 1988).

In other words, the realities of teaching may well argue against the kind of "scripting" of curriculum content that is popular in some curriculum policies. Scripting has a number of apparent advantages that explain its popularity. It is clear about its objectives, it looks easy to follow in practice, and it provides the weak teacher with a clear blueprint for instructional success. Unfortunately, the technique of breaking knowledge down into small, easily digested packets may be inconsistent with the kind of open-ended, complex problem solving intended by the next generation of curriculum policy.

In that case, the commendable goals of clear objectives, easy implementation, and "value added" for the weak teacher must be achieved in some way other than the scripted curriculum. The policy package that seems to be emerging combines very sophisticated but also clear learning objectives, powerful pedagogical exercises, careful training of teachers, and much more sophisticated examinations.

CONCLUSION

The lessons learned from looking at the roles of the school as policy mediator, policy critic, and policy constructor actually all point in a similar direction. From my own and others' research, it seems clear that schools and teachers must be actively engaged in the exercise of constructing a high-quality curriculum for their students; that some types of curriculum policy have the potential for increasing stratification and thus lowering the overall quality of instruction; that schools and teachers have their own perspectives on curriculum policy, some of which should be encouraged by policy; and that the "scripted" curriculum popular in some districts and schools may not provide the best means of translating sophisticated curriculum goals into teaching practice.

These conclusions have in common a recognition of the impact and importance of the decisions, knowledge, and values operating in schools and classrooms. Curriculum policy probably should not abandon its efforts to push curriculum content and teaching in new directions. The emerging goals of sophisticated content, problem solving, and active learning seem especially worthwhile (Raizen, 1987; Romberg, 1988). But any set of curriculum goals, and especially those aiming for active learning, are likely to require a new and different blend of policy instruments.

In general, the new policy instruments appropriate to a second generation of curriculum policy should have a core set of higher-learning (or content) objectives; interfere less with school, student, and teacher discretion (in that sense, be more "streamlined"); do a better job of enlisting the active cooperation of school decision makers and classroom teachers; and be expressed in accountability measures (e.g., examinations and demonstrations) that are more compatible with the new learning objectives.

Earlier, I made the comment that the new policies will resemble structured school improvement more than uniform regulation. The notion of "content restructuring" captures the goal of school restructuring built around ambitious goals of curriculum content. This type of policy would be much more ambitious in its goals than existing policy (perhaps especially for low-achieving students), but also would be much more sensitive to the school context.

NOTE

1. The broader context would include not simply all research on implementation, with its inevitable clash between policy and field-level perspectives, but all research on differentiated social structures, such as race, class, and gender. One of the disorienting (but also invigorating) features of contemporary social science is the description of the same social events told from different perspectives. This is a problem with direct significance for the curriculum, as in the debates over the efforts of Hirsch, Bloom, Bennett, and others to define a standard canonical curriculum.

REFERENCES

Archbald, D. A., & Newmann, F. M. (1988). *Beyond standardized testing: Assessing authentic academic achievement in the secondary school.* Reston, VA: National Association of Secondary School Principals.

Berman, P. (1984, January). *Improving school improvement: A policy evaluation of the California School Improvement Program: Vol. 1. Executive summary and recommendations.* Berkeley, CA: Berman, Weiler.

Clune, W. H. (1987). Institutional choice as a theoretical framework for research on educational policy. *Educational Evaluation and Policy Analysis, 9*(2), 117–132.

Clune, W. H., with P. White & J. Patterson. (1989). *The implementation and effects of high school graduation requirements: First steps toward curricular reform.* New Brunswick, NJ: Rutgers University, Center for Policy Research in Education.

Cohen, D. K. (1987). Educational technology, policy, and practice. *Educational Evaluation and Policy Analysis, 9*(2), 153–170.

Cohen, M. (1983). Instructional, management, and social conditions in effective schools. In A. Odden & L. D. Webb (Eds.), *School finance and school improvement: Linkages in the 1980's: Fourth annual yearbook of the American Educational Finance Association* (pp. 17–50). Cambridge, MA: Ballinger.

Cuban, L. (1984). School reform by remote control: SB813 in California. *Phi Delta Kappan, 66,* 213–215.

Cusick, P. A. (1983). *The egalitarian ideal and the American high school: Studies of three schools* [Research on Teaching Monograph Series]. New York: Longman.

Darling-Hammond, L., & Wise, A. (1985). Beyond standardization: State standards and school improvement. *The Elementary School Journal, 85,* 315–336.

David, J. L. (1987). *Improving education with locally developed indicators.* New Brunswick, NJ: Rutgers University, Center for Policy Research in Education.

Elmore, R. F. (1979). Backward mapping: Implementation research and policy questions. *Political Science Quarterly, 94,* 601–616.

Fennema, E., Carpenter, T. P., & Peterson, P. L. (in press). Teachers' decision making and cognitively guided instruction: A new paradigm for curriculum development. In K. Clements & N. F. Ellerton (Eds.), *Facilitating change in mathematics education.* Geelong, Victoria, Australia: Deakin University Press.

Freeman, D. J., & Porter, A. C. (1988). *Do textbooks dictate the content of mathematics instruction in elementary schools?* Paper prepared for the Institute for Research on Teaching, College of Education, Michigan State University.

Gamoran, A. (1987). The stratification of high school learning opportunities. *Sociology of Education, 60,* 135–155.

Kennedy, D. (1987). Critical theory, structuralism, and contemporary legal scholarship. *The New England Law Review, 21,* 209–289.

Levin, H. M. (1988, September). *Accelerated schools for at-risk students* (CPRE Research Report Series RR-010). New Brunswick, NJ: Rutgers University, Center for Policy Research in Education.

McDonnell, L. M. (1988). *Coursework policy in five states and its implications for indicator development.* Working paper prepared for the Rand Corporation, Santa Monica, CA.

McLaughlin, M. (1987, Summer). Learning from experience: Lessons from policy implementation. *Educational Evaluation and Policy Analysis, 9*(2), 171–178.

McNeil, L. M. (1987a, April). *The cooptation of the curriculum.* Paper presented at the annual meeting of the American Educational Research Association, Washington, DC.

McNeil, L. M. (1987b). The politics of Texas school reform. *Journal of Education Policy, 2,* 199–216.

Peterson, P. L., & Comeaux, M. A. (1989). Assessing the teacher as a reflective professional: New perspectives on teacher evaluation. In A. E. Woolfolk (Ed.), *Research perspectives on the graduate preparation of teachers* (pp. 132–152). Englewood Cliffs, NJ: Prentice-Hall.

Powell, A. G., Farrar, E., & Cohen, D. K. (1985). *The shopping mall high school: Winners and losers in the educational marketplace.* Boston: Houghton Mifflin.

Raizen, S. A. (1987). *Increasing education productivity through improving the science curriculum.* Paper prepared for the Center for Policy Research in Education, Rutgers University, New Brunswick, NJ.

Richards, C. E., & Shujaa, M. (1988). *The state education accountability movement: Impact on the schools?* Paper prepared for the Center for Policy Research in Education, Rutgers University, New Brunswick, NJ.

Romberg, T. A. (1988). *Changes in school mathematics: Curricular changes, instructional changes, and indicators of changes* (CPRE Research Report RRO-007). New Brunswick, NJ: Rutgers University, Center for Policy Research in Education.

Sarason, S. B. (1971). *The culture of school and the problem of change.* Boston: Allyn & Bacon.

Shepard, L., & Smith, M. L. (1988). *Flunking grades.* Philadelphia: Falmer Press.

Slavin, R. E. (1987). Taking the mystery out of mastery: A response to Guskey, Anderson, and Burns. *Review of Educational Research, 57,* 231–235.

Slavin, R. E., & Madden, N. A. (1989). What works for students at risk: A research synthesis. *Educational Leadership, 46*(5), 4–13.

Smith, M. S., & O'Day, J. (1988). *Teaching policy and research on teaching.* Paper prepared for Center for Policy Research in Education, Rutgers University, New Brunswick, NJ.

Turnbull, B., Smith, M., & Ginsburg, A. (1981). Issues for a new administration: The federal role in education. *American Journal of Education, 396,* 407–409.

About the Editors and Contributors

NINA BASCIA is a doctoral student in Stanford University's educational administration and policy analysis program and a research assistant at the Center for Research on the Context of Secondary School Teaching. Her research concerns issues of teachers' professional identities, and she is currently engaged in several studies of teachers' unions.

WILLIAM H. CLUNE is Voss-Bascom Professor of Law at the University of Wisconsin Law School, director of the Wisconsin branch of the Center for Policy Research in Education (CPRE), and a member of the executive board and faculty of the LaFollette Institute of Public Affairs at Wisconsin. His past research on education policy has included school finance, school law, implementation, special education, and public employee interest arbitration. His present research with CPRE concerns the effects of graduation requirements and other student standards, school site autonomy, and regulation of the curriculum. He co-directed a conference on educational decentralization and choice at the LaFollette Institute.

THOMAS B. CORCORAN is a consultant affiliated with Organizational Analysis and Practice, Inc., in Ithaca, NY, and the Institute for Educational Leadership in Washington, DC. His clients include public school districts, state education agencies, education associations, research organizations, and state and national foundations. His primary research interest is the development of more effective policies and programs for youth in urban communities. He has published numerous articles and is co-author of two books on working conditions in schools, including a recently released report on New Jersey's public schools, and two books on the characteristics of the schools selected for national recognition by the U.S. Department of Education. He is currently working on a book on education reform.

MICHAEL FULLAN is a professor in sociology and education and Dean of the Faculty of Education at the University of Toronto. His current research links teacher development to climate and school change. He has just completed the second edition of *The Meaning of Educational Change* for Teachers College Press.

271

SUSAN MOORE JOHNSON is an associate professor of administration, planning, and social policy at the Harvard Graduate School of Education, where she is also a member of the research staff of the National Center for Educational Leadership. She is the author of *Teacher Unions in Schools* (Temple University Press, 1984), which examines the impact of collective bargaining on day-to-day school operations, and *Teachers at Work* (Basic Books, 1990), which considers the school as a workplace from the perspectives of exemplary teachers. Currently, she is studying the leadership styles of new superintendents.

JUDITH WARREN LITTLE is an assistant professor of education at the University of California, Berkeley. Her research interests center on school as a workplace, teachers' conceptions of work and career, and policies and practices of professional development.

KAREN SEASHORE LOUIS is an associate professor of educational policy and administration at the University of Minnesota. Recent publications include "Knowledge Use and School Improvement" (*Curriculum Inquiry*, 1988), *Supporting School Improvement: A Comparative Analysis* (Acco, 1989), and (with Matthew B. Miles) *Improving the Urban High School: What Works and Why* (Teachers College Press, 1990).

MILBREY W. MCLAUGHLIN is a professor of education at Stanford University, where she is also Director of the Center for Research on the Context of Secondary School Teaching. Her research interests focus on planned change in education, intergovernmental relations, the organizational context of teaching, and evaluation. Prior to joining the Stanford faculty, she was a policy analyst with the Rand Corporation, where her research centered on federal and state efforts to promote educational change and improvement. She is the co-author (with Richard S. Pfeifer) of *Teacher Evaluation: Improvement, Accountability, and Effective Learning* (Teachers College Press, 1988).

MARY HAYWOOD METZ is a professor of educational policy studies at the University of Wisconsin—Madison. She has written two books based on ethnographic studies of classrooms, schools, and school systems: *Classrooms and Corridors: The Crisis of Authority in Desegregated Secondary Schools* (University of California Press, 1978) and *Different by Design: The Context and Character of Three Magnet Schools* (Methuen, 1986). She is currently at work on a book based on the study reported here.

ARTHUR G. POWELL is a senior research associate at the National Association of Independent Schools in Boston, where he is writing a book on independent schools since World War I. He is the author of *The Uncertain Profession: Harvard and the Search for Educational Authority* (Harvard University Press, 1980) and (with Eleanor Farrar and David K.

Cohen) *The Shopping Mall High School: Winners and Losers in the Educational Marketplace* (Houghton Mifflin, 1985).

JOAN E. TALBERT is a senior research associate and Associate Director of the Center for Research on the Context of Secondary School Teaching at Stanford University. Her research and teaching over the past decade have concerned social and organizational conditions that shape individuals' work lives. She has published articles on teachers' careers and public-private school organization.

Index

Index